History from the Sources
General Editor: John Morris

ARTHURIAN PERIOD SOURCES
VOL. 6

ARTHURIAN SOURCES

Vol. 6
Studies in Dark-Age History

ARTHURIAN PERIOD SOURCES

1 **Arthurian Sources, Vol. 1**, by John Morris
   Introduction, Notes and Index
       How to use *Arthurian Sources*; Introduction and Notes;
       Index to *The Age of Arthur*

2 **Arthurian Sources, Vol. 2**, by John Morris
   *Annals (**A**) and Charters (**C**)*

3 **Arthurian Sources, Vol. 3**, by John Morris
   Persons
       Ecclesiastics (**E**) (alphabetically listed)
       Laypeople (**L**) (alphabetically listed)

4 **Arthurian Sources, Vol. 4**, by John Morris
   *Places and Peoples (**P**), and Saxon Archaeology (**S**)*
       Places and Peoples (alphabetically listed)
       Saxon Archaeology:
           The Chronology of Early Anglo-Saxon Archaeology;
           Anglo-Saxon Surrey; The Anglo-Saxons in Bedfordshire

5 **Arthurian Sources, Vol. 5**, by John Morris
   *Genealogies (**G**) and Texts (**T**)*
       Genealogies
           Editions by Egerton Phillimore (1856-1937): *The Annales Cambriae*
           and Old-Welsh Genealogies from B.L. MS. Harley 3859; Pedigrees
           from Jesus College (Oxford) MS. 20; Bonedd y Saint from N.L.W.
           MS. Peniarth 12
       Texts discussed
           Gospel-books; Honorius's Letter; Laws; Martyrologies; Muirchú's
           Life of St.Patrick; *Notitia Dignitatum*; *Periplus*; Ptolemy; The 'Tribal
           Hidage'; Welsh Poems

6 **Arthurian Sources, Vol. 6**, by John Morris
   Studies in Dark-Age History
       Celtic Saints—a Note; Pelagian Literature; Dark Age Dates; The Dates
       of the Celtic Saints; The Date of Saint Alban; Christianity in Britain,
       300-700—the Literary Evidence; Studies in the Early British Church—a
       Review; Gildas

7 **Gildas**, edited and translated by Michael Winterbottom
       The Ruin of Britain; Fragments of Lost Letters; Penitential or Monastic
       Rule

8 **Nennius**, edited and translated by John Morris
       'Select Documents on British History'; The Welsh Annals

9 **St. Patrick**, edited and translated by A.B.E. Hood
       Declaration; Letter to Coroticus; Sayings; Muirchú's Life of St. Patrick

ARTHURIAN SOURCES

Vol. 6
Studies in Dark-Age History

JOHN MORRIS

PHILLIMORE

1995

Published by
PHILLIMORE & CO. LTD.
Shopwyke Manor Barn, Chichester, Sussex

© Mrs. Susan Morris, 1995

ISBN 0 85033 765 8

Printed and bound in Great Britain by
HARTNOLLS LTD.
Bodmin, Cornwall

CONTENTS

	page
Celtic Saints: a Note	1
Pelagian Literature	17
Dark Age Dates	53
The Dates of the Celtic Saints	95
The Date of Saint Alban	145
Christianity in Britain, 300-700: the Literary Evidence	155
Studies in the Early British Church: a Review	175
Gildas	179

CELTIC SAINTS

A NOTE*

IN THE FIRST THREE-QUARTERS OF THE SIXTH CENTURY A.D. SOME hundreds of earnest evangelical reformers preached to the peoples of western and northern Britain, of Ireland, Brittany and northern Gaul. Their words were welcomed, and engendered a mass movement. A new conception and a new organization of church and state was fashioned; large numbers of people migrated to new homes, and in their new homes shaped a new economy. The pattern of life which their descendants elaborated has preserved significant peculiarities even to our own day. Yet the age of the saints is romantic and misty, half legend and half history, a little more real than the tales of their contemporary Arthur, far more shadowy than the deeds of their contemporary Justinian. The purpose of this note is to try to recover an outline of what these men did, and why and when; and to assess their effect upon the history of Europe.

The saints lived in a generation that was no longer Roman, and not yet medieval. Its rapid and discordant changes are hard enough to grasp when they are well recorded, as they are in Europe; there, administrative institutions and literacy survived, transformed by the impact of Teutonic settlers; events were recorded by men trained in the factual logic of the Roman tradition, and were recorded by different men in different places whose accounts confirm and correct each other. In Britain, the old institutions died; literacy all but perished; what was recorded was set down in an imaginative idiom that had little in common with the rational traditions of Rome, traditions which the modern historian and the dark age chronicler alike inherit. The material is unscientific; and scientific history is not rich in techniques for handling unscientific material. The quantity of ancient manuscripts dealing with sixth-century Britain is very large; most of them are in Latin, and for most of them a more or less adequate text has been published in print. But until our own day they have received very little serious historical study.

The most important single document is the tract of Gildas, *De Excidio Britanniae*,[1] written somewhere between 530 and 550. It is a bitter and moving indictment of the sins of the early sixth-century rulers and bishops, in western and south-western Britain, prefaced by a short historical explanation of how these ills came to be.

---

* Reprinted from *Past and Present* 11 (1957) 2–16, by kind permission of Mrs Susan Morris.

The preface has provoked the irritated condemnation of many students who have sought to wring from it information on fifth-century Britain; the main body of the work has received almost no comment, though in the course of his invective Gildas illuminates the society of western Britain in the sixth century, its political, ecclesiastical and social institutions, with a vivid detail not again matched until the end of the Saxon period.

Britain was ruled by a number of independent chiefs, called indifferently "kings", "princes", "chiefs", "judges" (*reges, tyranni, principes, duces patriae, judices*). They wage war; they catch thieves; they maintain prisons; they dispense justice and give alms in coin to the poor; they succeed each other by hereditary succession and make dynastic marriages. The areas which these rulers control are, in the five instances that Gildas names, of about the size of one or two Roman *civitates*, rather larger than modern counties, and may or may not be continuations of such *civitates*. Society was graded according to *qualitas*, with the greedy retainers of the kings at the top. In these little states are church buildings, equipped with revenues, serviced by priests and bishops. The clergy are simoniac; they buy their sees and benefices from the tyrants for money; they travel abroad and are in touch with continental churchmen. The authorities with whom Gildas had to deal were developed states, in which a certain minimum of monetary economy still lingered, with a church hierarchy thoroughly dependent on the lay rulers. Nothing is said of their education, but Gildas wrote in good Latin, cited Virgil and the Fathers, and evidently expected his readers both to understand his words and appreciate his quotations. Gildas says little about the economy by which state and church maintained themselves; but the Saints' Lives and charters abound with references to annual payments in kind, normally beer, meat, bread and honey, extracted by both laymen and ecclesiastics from a reluctant peasantry. In later centuries these payments were fixed by royal ordinance; how far they were fixed in the early sixth century is a matter for speculation.

A number of documents record the succession of lay rulers, their achievements and chronology. Many thousands of lines of heroic verse are preserved in the manuscripts known as the *Four Ancient Books of Wales*;[2] much of this verse has a literary merit not inferior to the heroic literatures of Germany, Iceland or the Balkans, though unlike them, it has not yet been translated into intelligible English. Recently, the work of Sir Ivor Williams and others has established that some of the major poems were certainly written in the early seventh century. The majority have not yet received a thorough philological study. A single set of Annals,[3] of rather uncertain chronological basis, provides some dates for the sixth and seventh centuries. More important are the Genealogies or King Lists, extant in three main collections, with numerous subsidiary adjuncts.[4] The purpose of two of these collections is to demonstrate the descent of newly established paramount kings of the high middle ages from all the separate dynasties of the Dark Ages; they end in the tenth and twelfth centuries respectively. The third provides ancestors among the same dynasties for the saints, and closes in the late sixth or seventh centuries. The manuscripts are late, and their content must be judged on the internal evidence, save for the general consideration that the aim of such documents is to relate living persons to ancient rulers who are known or believed to have existed, and not to concoct imaginary heroes of the past, unknown to contemporaries.

It is somewhat meaningless to ask whether these genealogies are "reliable" or "unreliable". What matters is to discover how they came into being, and upon what basis they rest. The most instructive among them are those which give the remote ancestry of the late fourth- and fifth-century chiefs. There are two main versions. One goes back in two versions through a list of Roman emperors to Augustus. The earlier version (*vita Cadoci* 45) begins *Augustus Caesar, in cuius tempore natus est Christus, genuit Octavianum; Octavianus genuit Tiberium; Tiberius genuit Gaium; Gaius genuit Claudium; Claudius genuit Vespasianum* and continues through successive emperors to Constantius II (337-361) and Maximianus (383-388). It is, with some errors, a correct list of Roman emperors; it is not correct that each was son to his predecessor; Augustus and Octavian are the same person, and Nero is omitted in his proper place and conflated with Nerva; a pleasing textual corruption gives the emperor between Valerian and Aurelian as "Cleopatra". The proper reading should be either Gallienus or Claudius; the probability is that in the original "Cl . . . " alone survived and that the compiler made the best prosopographical guess he could. The second version (Harleian MS. 3859, genealogy xvi) carries the emendation further; the compiler evidently had antiquarian learning; the emperor Decius becomes Decius Mus, a hero of early Rome, and Cleopatra is supplied with her consort Antony, Antun Du (the black). Antonius Niger, king of the Greeks, subsequently plays a role in medieval Welsh fancy, sometimes as king of the underworld.

It is easy to write off the whole of these documents as a waste of time. Cleopatra did not rule third-century Rome, and was not married to the king of the underworld. The Roman emperors were not normally father and son, and were not lineal ancestors of St Cadoc or his father Gundleius, king of eastern Glamorganshire in the early sixth century. But the nonsense is built on fact. The list is an accurate list of Roman emperors, barring a few bizarre textual corruptions; and it is an accurate list of the sovereigns of eastern Glamorganshire for the five centuries from Claudius to Gundleius. Fact and fancy are interwoven, and require a critical apparatus to disentangle them.

The alternative ancient genealogy,[5] extant in half a dozen versions, traces various dark age heroes back to Belin the Great and his mother Anna, cousin of the Virgin Mary, by way of dubious names, often paired in doublets (Doli, Guordoli, Dumn, Guordumn and the like). Belin who ruled in London before the Romans came, is Orosius' name, based on a corrupt reading of Suetonius, for Cunobelinus, who ruled south-eastern England in the time of Christ. His mother was not the cousin of the Virgin Mary, but she was an exact contemporary; and Belin (*circa* 10-40 A.D.) is separated by some twelve or thirteen generations (360-390 years at thirty years to a generation) from Coel Hen, Padarn Pesrut and other heroes of the Dark Ages who lived in the decades about 400. The genealogies on this model provide a rough and ready time scale.

The genealogies provide lists of persons who exercised sovereign authority in the same areas, and an approximate indication of their date. For the fifth and sixth centuries, they cover the multiple dynasties of most of Celtic Britain; they name most, and perhaps all, of the five kings named by Gildas; they make them contemporary with each other, and with the saints and other rulers of the same generation who figure in the saints' lives, and they locate them in the same areas as Gildas; in several instances later generations are given a date in the Annals, and normally that date approximately equates with a 30-year generation interval from the ancestors recorded in the early sixth century, as these in turn are separated by a proper interval from their fourth- and fifth-century predecessors. The whole structure is a complex interlocking compilation of several hundred names, which makes reasonable sense, both within itself, and in comparison with the other evidence. If it were the work of a forger, then dark age or medieval Wales possessed a genius without parallel among the known forgers of ancient records. The genealogies certainly derive from a tradition of real persons; though they require an elaborate monograph before details can be accepted with confidence.

Some forty charters preserved in the *Book of Llandaff*[6] and the life of Cadoc present somewhat analogous problems. They cover a period of about 200 years, from the late sixth to the late eighth centuries, with one or two that are possibly earlier. There are a few palpable concoctions, such as a right of sanctuary granted by Arthur and witnessed by Cai and Bedwyr. Those in a regular form have elaborate witnesses, abbots of the three principal monasteries of Glamorganshire, the bishop, and the king, as well as a considerable number of attendant lay and clerical notables, the laymen succeeding each other as father and son. No two charters have the same witnesses; between one and another, someone among the many persons involved has died, to be replaced by a successor, while the other signatories remain. The whole forms a connected series, based on over a hundred names, in which each charter is definitely dated before and after another, with no chronological discrepancies. Again, it would be quite unrealistic to suppose that such precision was an invention of a later age; the evidence of the recognizable forgeries is enough to put such an assumption out of court; it does not of course follow that the content of a charter placed between a genuine superscription and genuine witnesses is itself genuine. But the sucession of kings and abbots and notables stands; and the body of the charters, many of them granted in expiation of crimes of violence, bear witness to the efforts of the clergy to maintain their independence of the lay rulers, and to curb the turbulence of the nobility.

These documents receive a little contemporary comment from the large number of fifth- to seventh-century inscriptions; recently, Professor Kenneth Jackson and the late Dr Nash-Williams[7] have provided a reasonably close chronology of the development of their orthography; and a few of them mention persons who appear in Gildas, in the Saints' Lives, and in the genealogies. Even more impressive is the evidence of place names.[8] During the fifth and sixth centuries, well over three-quarters of the villages and hamlets of Wales, Cornwall, and Brittany received new names, which they still for the most part retain; and these names incorporate the names of persons, a high proportion of whom are recorded in the Saints' Lives or other documents. Most of these persons were saints, Llanbardarn or Llansadyrnin, Davidstow or St Ives, Samson, St Malo or St Pol-de-Leon; but many were lay chieftains, Ceredig son of Cunedda who named Ceredigiaun, Cardigan or Fracanus the father of Winwaloe, remembered at Plou-Fragan in Brittany. Nowhere, save in a few border areas lost to the English or Normans and subsequently recovered, is there any sign of dedications later than the early Dark Ages; the churches of Paternus or Saturninus, Paul of Leon or Samson, were established and named either by these saints or by their immediate disciples. The study of the distribution of these names locates the saints and laymen recorded in the documents, and supplies a route for the travels of many who are not elsewhere recorded.

The core of all these documents is provided by the corpus of Saints' Lives.[9] Most of the manuscripts are of the late middle ages, and are filled with improbable miracles. Their sense of time and place is vague in the extreme. As in the other documents, fact and fancy are blended, and need to be distinguished. To do so, it is necessary to enquire how the later editors worked. For whereas the clerk who copied a scriptural text or a classical manuscript strove to copy the original as accurately as he might, he was faced with a different problem when a worn Saint's Life needed replacement. The life was essentially a homily, to be read on the Saint's day. It was meant to edify, and conceptions of what was edifying changed from generation to generation. Attempts to guess at the importations of succeeding ages are apt to mislead; the only secure way is to look at such lives as are preserved in separate manuscripts of different dates, and note how they in fact evolved. The key life is that of St Samson; it is extant in three versions, of the seventh, the tenth and the twelfth centuries,[10] from Pentale on the Seine, from Anjou, and from Llandaff near Cardiff, all foundations connected with Samson. Moreover, Samson was the greatest and most influential of the saints who travelled abroad, and he alone is securely dated by external evidence. At the close of his life he was involved with various notables of Brittany in conflicts dated to 550-560 by the contemporary Frankish historian Gregory of Tours; the biographer records his visit to King Childebert at Paris and his name appears among the signatories at the Council of Paris in 555.[11] He was then an old man, and had behind him a long and vigorous career. His birth can hardly be set much later than 480 or 490.

In the seventh-century life, he was born of noble parents in Demetia (Pembrokeshire-Carmarthenshire) and sent at the age of five to the monastery of Eltutus (Llanilltud Fawr, or Llantwit Major, in Glamorgan), who in his youth had been ordained by St Germanus. St Germanus of Auxerre visited Britain in 429 and *circa* 445, approximately half a century before Samson came to Llantwit. Eltutus was the most learned teacher of the scriptures and of the branches of philosophy, geometry, rhetoric, grammar and arithmetic.

The monastery was Eltutus' "earthly inheritance" (*terrenum hereditarium*); after some fifteen years Samson quarrelled with Eltutus' nephews (*nepotes*) and moved to the monastery at Caldey Island, where the aged Piro had long taught. There he learnt that his father was ill, but refused to visit him, since he had renounced the things of the world. Piro, reinforcing a warning against the arrogance of excessive asceticism which Iltud had once made, rebuked him and sent him home. As he drove through the woods, he was startled by the appearance of a wild woman, who had lived alone and demented since her husband and children had been killed. Samson cursed her for a witch and killed her. When he got home, his father recovered, and all his family were converted, save a sister "given over to worldly pleasures" (*ad mundanas voluptates data*), whom Samson wrathfully rejected. The converts gave three-quarters of their property to the poor and entered monastic life. Soon after Samson's return to Caldey, the aged Piro, who had drunk somewhat heavily at dinner, got up in the night, and in the darkness fell down a well. He made a *magna ululatio*, and was rescued, but died of the shock. None the less, says the biographer, he was *vir sanctus et egregius*, a saint and a gentleman. Samson was elected his successor, but after eighteen months he left Caldey to found a monastery in Ireland, and on his return lived for some time in a cave near the Severn. Later, a synod constrained him to become abbot of a monastery "said to have been founded by St Germanus", where he was ordained priest by three bishops according to the ancient British custom. Some time later he left this monastery, and crossed the Severn to the monastery of Docco (Docheu or Docwin) still so-named in the fourteenth century, at St Kew, near Padstow. He suggested to Juniavus, the head of the monastery that he should settle there, but Juniavus, with forethought (*praevidens*) suggested that it would be unwise, since Samson's asceticism was *melior* than that in force at St Kew. Samson was *stupefactus* at this doctrine, harnessed his carriage (*currus*), put his *spiritualia utensilia* and his *volumina* on a waggon (*plaustra*) and made for the sea which leads to Europe. In the meantime, *in pago Tricurio* (St Kew lies in the district of Cornwall named Trigg), he dispersed an assembly worshipping a standing stone, on which he carved the sign of the cross, and cured a sick boy. In Brittany, he founded Dol, and intervened on behalf of a local chief named Judualus in a conflict with a wicked count Conomorus. Conomorus had backed Childebert's rebellious son, and Samson went to Paris in the interest of Judualus. It is this rebellion which Gregory of Tours relates and dates. There Samson had a protracted quarrel with the queen and an evil count, in which he destroyed a wild horse and a lion and a serpent by the sign of the cross, and founded a monastery on the Seine at Pentale. Judualus was eventually reinstated, Samson returned to Dol, was granted the Channel Islands, where he distributed gold coins (*numismiuncelli auri*) to the poor, and helped his patron to kill Conomor and make himself king. Samson then died.

In the later versions of the life much of the picturesque detail is omitted or abbreviated; the unpleasant touches, Eltutus' and Piro's rebukes of his arrogance, are omitted and the incident with the witch is toned down. The Llandaff version omits the whole incident at St Kew, while the Pentale life makes Juniavus invite Samson to settle permanently instead of politely refusing the honour: Llandaff omits the whole of the Paris incidents, while the Pentale life expands them with a great many miracles, a dinner with St Germanus of Paris, and a long speech citing Isidore of Seville and Gregory the Great, who was a boy when Samson died. Llandaff, the twelfth century life, is flat and dull, expanded with stock miracles plundered from the lives of other saints, and full of anachronisms; *papa* Dubricius, the bishop, becomes *archiepiscopus*, *pistor* becomes *cellararius*, and the like. The later lives add nothing but standard and traditional miracles; they omit the names of people and of places and add no new ones; they twist the rugged incidents of the early life to pious and edifying proprieties.

A comparison of the several versions of the life of St Paul Aurelian, and of a few others where more than one version exists, leads to the same conclusion. Unusual and ungainly incidents, the names of persons and places, are likely to belong to the original version from which a late life is derived. St Alban[12] suffered under Severus and Caracalla, nicknamed from the kind of overcoat he affected. By the sixth century, Severus' name was omitted, and *caracalla* has become again an overcoat, worn by a cleric whom St Alban impersonated. In the eighth century, the nameless emperor has become Diocletian; later, *caracalla* is rendered by a synonym, *amphibalon*, and emerges in the full middle ages as a person, St Amphibalus, teacher of St Alban. But the fictitious St Overcoat does not threaten the reality of St Alban.

The evidence is plentiful; but is is very difficult to handle, and easy to dismiss *en bloc*, as "unreliable". Unreliable it is; but it is capable of critical discussion. The elementary outline of events which underlies its fancy is stirring enough. The monastic reform movement was in the direct line of development of European monasticism, and it hit Britain at a formative point in British history.

Despite all the obscurities of dark age history, the main trend of events is clear enough. When the imperial government could no longer help the defence of Britain, the civilized province was exposed to attacks from Picts and Scots; its authorities called in Saxons to help, and the Saxons rebelled. At first, the Saxon victory was as complete as the Gothic and Burgundian and Vandal conquests abroad. But the British provincials, unlike the continental Romans, managed to drive back and conquer the Saxons, in a long war that ended somewhere about 500. Thirty or forty years later Gildas rebuked readers who had enjoyed perfect peace for more than a generation, since the Saxons had been defeated. There was no fear of a comeback. In fact, the Saxon attacks were renewed in the years after 550, and completed the conquest of England in half a century or so. But in the first half of the sixth century that conquest still lay in the future and was not foreseen. It was in that age that the saints lived.

Throughout the Lives, the debt of the British reformers to the Egyptian desert forces itself upon the reader; the desert fathers are held up as an example, by name and by description; the literature is full of Greek technical terms, not commonly found in Gaul. There is, however, little sign of direct contact with Egypt. The immediate connections point to southern Gaul. Here the monastic movement had a different emphasis; whereas the Egyptian fathers were essentially ascetics who withdrew from the world to outdo each other in ever more exuberant rigours, the earlier monks of Gaul withdrew to houses of learning, often on their own property, and remained in active contact with the bishops and congregations of the world without. They were not missionaries; there is no expanding chain of settlements which derive their origin from Lérins or Marmoutiers (St Martin's foundation near Tours). The influence of Lérins was achieved when its members were chosen as bishops by the great churches of southern Gaul. Such was the ideal which long ago had attracted the young British Pelagian nobleman, whose letters, dateable to *circa* 411-418, Caspari edited under the title *Briefe, Abhandlungen und Predigten*. The author moved in Italy in the same circles and the same years as Germanus and the founders of Lérins. If he lived to a normal age, he could have known Illtud, who must in any case have been familiar with the major British Pelagian writings, these included. The earliest foundations of Wales were Llantwit and Caldey, the schools of Illtud and Piro. There the sons of noblemen learnt Latin, as polished as any still written in Italy or Gaul, and they may have learnt Greek; they studied the scriptures and the fathers, and the humanities. There was manual labour, but it was subordinate to learning; the abbots at least kept a carriage and pair, and a gentleman's larder and cellar. A number of the pupils of these schools initiated the reform movement; but there is nothing to show that a majority of their fellow students took part in it or that such a movement was an original purpose of these foundations.

The distinctive feature of the Celtic monks was their missionary zeal. Like Samson, they established a community in a deserted spot, attended by a fair number of followers. Paul Aurelian took to Brittany some two dozen noble relatives together with humbler attendants and slaves, and in a matter of months, either the leader or one of the followers was off to found a fresh lonely monastery. Sometimes the holy man set up as a hermit in a cave or shack, and many of the greater saints had periods of retirement as solitaries between their abbacies. What made the movement was the response of the people; to each new monastery and to each new hermit came large numbers of the local people, eager to renounce their land and calling, and enter a community of devout farmers. Like Samson, very many of the saints established communities overseas, in Ireland, Cornwall and Brittany. Within little more than half a century of the first foundations, these communities were numbered by the hundred, and the greater part of the little towns and villages which today carry the name *Llan* or *Saint* in their name were in being.

In the course of this rapid growth, the corrupt episcopate that Gildas denounced disappeared. The bishops depended on the kings, and the movement swept the kings along with it. King Mark of Cornwall — better known in the Tristram legend — persuaded Paul Aurelian to leave his community and serve as a reluctant bishop[13]; but Paul left him after a year or two. Royal bishops are no more recorded and the vitality of the church henceforth rested on the *Lans*. In the early days, *papa* Dubricius, Bishop, presumably of Ariconium or Caerleon, made regular inspections of Llanilltud. In the seventh century, there seems to have been for a period a multitude of small local bishops in Glamorganshire, but the chief bishop was a monastic bishop, much as Aidan of Lindisfarne was Bishop of the Northumbrians. In Ireland, the movement took on the social colouring of Irish society, and the bishop became a peripatetic subordinate of the abbot; this feature however is peculiarly Irish and is not repeated in Wales or Brittany. In Brittany, to maintain the independence of the British against the Franks, Samson's successors assumed or acquired the title of bishop or archbishop in opposition to the see of Tours, a claim that neither

Tours nor the Frankish court ever permanently recognized. But the essence of the church organization was the rural monastery rather than the urban parish. In Wales and Cornwall the ultimate episcopal organization took shape under English and Anglo-Norman influences long after the age of the saints was past.

The migration of the saints was a mass movement; in Brittany, and perhaps in most of northern Gaul, they found small communities of Britons, mostly laymen, already in being. Paul Aurelian landed, passed a deserted city tenanted by wild beasts,[14] and settled in the ruins of a Roman villa, where he had trouble with a wild bull. The practical problem was water; the saint tapped in the ruins with his stick, and, as with Moses, water miraculously flowed from a stone in the ground. The saint had discovered the villa's well. He met a swineherd, who told him that the nearest neighbouring chief was named Wittur (Victor). "He is my cousin" exclaimed Paul, and made an amicable arrangement with him. Somewhat earlier Fracan, the father of Winwaloe, landed and immediately chanced upon a deserted Roman clearing, just the right size for his party.[15] It is still named Plou-Fragan. He made contact with the nearest British chief, Riwal of Dumnonia, and challenged him to a novel contest; each chose their fastest horses and set upon them their lightest boys (*levissimi pueri*) to see who could race fastest across country. One of the noble youths fell, and was killed by striking his head on a stone. The bystanders murmured at the risks of the new sport, until someone remembered that Fracan's son was a saint. Winwaloe stepped forward and restored the boy to life.[16] The tale has interest, for it seems to be the first recorded horse race in the modern sense, where light jockeys race from point to point with no car or chariot behind them. Such stories of contact with earlier settlers occur in many lives, so do the accounts of forest clearance. One of St Malo's problems was to dipose of the large number of tree trunks his men had felled in establishing one of their inland sites; the little stream would not take them away. By a miracle, the saint's prayers produced a phenomenal thunderstorm that swelled the river and washed the tree trunks away.[17]

The missionary energy and the migration produced a split within the reformers. Samson was *melior* and was *stupefactus* at Juniavus' comfortable life at St Kew. Juniavus feared Samson's strictness. The greatest figure among the ascetics was David "the water-drinker", whose emphasis lay upon manual labour, a frugal diet, walking rather than riding in a carriage. Professor Bowen[18] has pointed out that the foundations of David and his disciples concentrate in the poorer upland country above the 500-foot contour line, and in country where Irish settlement was thick, while the more gentlemanly houses in the tradition of Illtud and Piro tend to flourish in the vale of Glamorgan, where educated Roman life had taken deeper root.

From the middle and later sixth century the most prominent foundation in this tradition was the chair of Cadoc at Nantcarban. Cadoc's medieval biographer preserved a record, which he glosses over somewhat awkwardly, that once when Cadoc was absent on a pilgrimage, David called a synod over his head. Cadoc was furious at the affront, but forgave David. In the life of David this synod is one of the central stories, told with a lively description of the fiery little Welshman, too short to be seen in the crowd, who had to be lifted on a dais to make himself heard, but whose burning words moved the synod to repentance. The contemporary record is even more telling. Some isolated fragments are preserved of Gildas' writings on monasticism, set down in his old age, long after the monastic movement had set right the abuses he lamented in his tract. The language is sharp:

> "The better people (*Meliores*) are those who fast without ostentation, and do not immoderately scorn what God has created, not those who refuse to eat meat or ride in carriages or on horseback, and think themselves thereby superior. For death comes upon them by the windows of pride".
>
> " 'Many shall perish', says the Apostle, 'who have a zeal for God but not according to knowledge'. They eat bread by measure, but boast of it beyond measure. They drink water, and they drink the cup of hatred. They sup of dry dishes and slander . . . they put slaves before their masters, the rabble before kings, lead before gold . . . the hermit's cell to the church, severity to humility, in a word they prefer man to God. They obey not the Gospel and the apostles, but their own will and pride".
>
> We ought to approve "holy abbots, against whom there is no complaint but that they own beasts and carriages, either because it is the custom of the country or because they are infirm. For these things are less harmful, if they are used with humility and patience, than dragging ploughs and digging ditches with pride and arrogance" (*aratra trahentes et suffosoria figentes cum praesumptione et superbia*).[19]

Gildas names no names. But the tradition that he attacks is the tradition of David the water-drinker. In his own day Gildas was a sage, adviser to monasteries in Ireland and Britain, and Columban cites him to Gregory the Great as an authority whom Gregory knew and respected.[20] What survived in the main was the precept of David, though in later ages the practice was one that Gildas and David alike would have deplored.

In Wales and Cornwall the monastic reform set the pattern of life for the middle ages. But its vigour was spent well before the end of the sixth century and its impact is but a brilliant local episode.

Abroad, its influence was more far reaching. The Irish monastic movement derives from three main centres, Aran, Clonmacnoise and Clonard. Almost all the later houses derive from their disciples. In the Irish Saints' Lives, there is no claim that any of these foundations had anything to do with the earlier mission of Patrick to the north and centre.[21] Nor do the biographers of Patrick make any such claim. The traditions of the earliest Irish monks held that they derived their inspiration from Wales, from visits to or from Illtud, David, Samson, Cadoc and others. The Welsh lives also record the visits of Irish students to Wales and Welsh teachers to Ireland, though the stories are minor incidents, with no conception of their import. As far as our evidence goes, the monastic movement of Ireland like that of Cornwall and Brittany, owes its origin to the schools of South Wales, and not to the established episcopalian church of Roman Britain or of Patrician Ireland.

The Irish movement was also missionary, and also sent its teachers overseas, to Iona, and to Lindisfarne. The Anglo-Irish monasteries of Northumbria in their turn were responsible for the conversion of the greater part of England in the seventh century, for the double monasteries, the itinerant preachers, and the humility of Chad, in contrast to the episcopal glory of Wilfred. Though at Whitby the majority of the Anglo-Irish monks chose communion with Rome, and conformity in the externals of the tonsure and the date of Easter, they kept the content of their learning, their piety, and their preaching, under the tolerant patronage of Theodore of Tarsus. In the next century, it was these Anglo-Irish missionaries who established the bulk of the monasteries of the Rhineland, of Austria, of Italy, and reached as far as Kiev and Iceland. In each region, the initial vigour of the first generation was succeeded by the abuse of the irresponsible wandering monk; one by one, the monasteries accepted the rule of Benedict, or were reinforced by new Benedictine foundations, like Jarrow and Wearmouth, that could give the stability which the age of conversion could not supply. But their first foundation came from England.

It is in the light of these foundations that the age of the saints in Wales acquires its historical importance. They are not a romantic local phenomenon, but a stage in the main chain of development of European monasticism, a chain that runs from Egypt by way of Gaul to Llantwit and Caldey, and returns in a circle through Ireland, Iona, and Northumbria to lowland England, and then to the great monastic houses of medieval Europe.

NOTES

[1] ed. Th. Mommsen, *Monumenta Germaniae Historica, Auctores Antiquissimi*, XIII, 25 ff; ed. Hugh Williams (with translation), *Cymmrodorion Record Series* 3 (University of Wales Press, Cardiff).

[2] W. F. Skene, *The Four Ancient Books of Wales* (Edinburgh, 1868). Sir Ifor Williams' fundamental edition of the *Canu Aneirin* (in Welsh) (Cardiff, 1938) is extensively reviewed in *Antiquity*, xiii, 25, cf. xvi, 237.

[3] *Annales Cambriae* (Harleian MSS. 3859); printed in *Y Cymmrodor*, ix, 152 (1888), and in E. Faral, *La Légende Arthurienne*, I, iii, 44 (Bibliothèque de l'Ecole des Hautes Etudes, Sciences historiques et philologiques 257, Paris, 1929).

[4] The main collections are *Bonedd y Saint* (63 entries to the mid seventh century) printed in Wade-Evans, *Vitae Sanctorum Britanniae et Genealogiae* (Board of Celtic Studies, History and Law Series, 9, 1944, University of Wales Press, Cardiff), from numerous MSS.; Harleian MSS. 3859 (32 entries to the 10th century) printed in *Y Cymmrodor*, ix, 169 (1888), and E. Faral, *Légende Arthurienne*, I, iii, 50; Jesus College, Oxford, MSS. 20 (51 entries to the twelfth century) printed in *Y Cymmrodor*, viii, 83 (1887). Twelve northern genealogies are also contained in MSS. Hengert 536 (to the early seventh century) and are printed in Skene, *Four Ancient Books*, 2, 454, under the title *Bonedd Gwyr y Gogled*.

[5] *Vita Cadoci*, 46, 47; *vita Dewi* (Welsh text, Rees, *Cambro-British Saints*, 102); *vita David* (Rhygyfarch) 68; *vita Beuno*, 23; Harleian MSS. 3859, genealogies i and x; Jesus College MSS. 20, genealogies iv and v.

[6] Ed. J. Gwenogvryn Evans (Oxford, 1893); also ed. W. J. Rees (Welsh MSS. Society, Llandovery, 1840). Breton cartularies are preserved from Landevennec, ed. de la Borderie (Rennes, 1888), from Quimper (*Bulletin de la Commission diocesaine*, Quimper, 1901), and from Quimperlé, ed. Léon Maître and Paul de Berthou (Paris, 1896).

[7] V. E. Nash-Williams, *Early Christian Monuments of Wales* (Cardiff, 1951), reviewed in *Antiquities Journal*, 32, 90, etc.; K. Jackson, *Language and History in Early Britain* (Edinburgh, 1953), 149; C. A. Ralegh Radford, *Early Christian Monuments of Scotland* (1941), reviewed in *Antiquity*, 16 (1942), cf. *Proc. Soc. Ant. Scotland*, 74 (1941); see also *Proc. Cambridge Antiquarian Soc.*, 24 (1923) (Isle of Man); and R. A. MacAlister, *Corpus Inscriptionum Insularum Celticarum*, vol. I (1945), vol. II (1950), (Stationery Office, Dublin), reviewed in *Antiquity*, 19, 207, and *Antiquities Journal*, 26, 200.

[8] cf. E. G. Bowen, *The Settlement of the Celtic Saints in Wales* (Cardiff, 1954).

[9] The *Acta Sanctorum* of the Bollandists prints the lives of Saints under the day on which their festival falls due, usually the reputed day of the Saint's death. The monumental Corpus, in progress, in calendar order, for 300 years, has now reached the middle of November. From 1882 onwards the ephemeral *Analecta Bollandiana* has published numerous texts discovered since the appropriate volume of the *Acta*. Wade-Evans, *Vitae Sanctorum Britanniae*, is a useful collection of the more important lives. S. Baring-Gould and J. Fisher, *Lives of the British Saints* (Hon. Soc. Cymmrodorion, London, 1906-1913), in four volumes, is a comprehensive digest of the MSS., in alphabetical order, with full references, though its use requires considerable caution.

[10] *Acta Sanctorum*, July VI, p. 573; *Analecta Bollandiana*, vi, 79 (1887); *Liber Llan Dav*, 6, transl. T. Taylor (S.P.C.K., 1925).

[11] *Historia Francorum*, 4, 4, and 4, 20. Mansi, Coll. Concil. 9, 747.

[12] W. Meyer, Die Legende des heiligen Albanus (22 June), *Abh. der Königl. Gesellschaft zu Göttingen, Phil-Hist. Klasse, Neue Folge*, 8, 1, (1904).

[13] Paul as Bishop to "Rex Marcus Quonomorus", (*vita* 22, Anal. Boll. 1, 226). A double ringed earthwork a mile or two above Fowey Harbour, called Castle

Dore, is traditionally the stronghold of King Mark. Half a mile to the south is a sixth-century memorial stone, commemorating Drustagnus or Drustaus, son of Conomorius (for the reading see *Journal of the Royal Institution of Cornwall*, new series, 1, app. 117-9 (1951). In the twelfth century Tristram romance of Béroul (lines 1155, 2359, 2438, 2453) "la ville . . . du roi Marc" is at Lancien (cf. also Gerbert de Monteuil's continuation of Perceval, "la grant chité Lancien", lines 3642, 3880), hard by the chapel of St. Samson (lines 2792-2796). Castle Dore is situated in the parish of St. Samson, a mile from the ancient parish church, and in the Domesday manor of Lantyen. The recent excavations of Mr Ralegh Radford recovered imported imitation Samian pottery of the sixth century A.D. from Castle Dore, whose original construction dates back to the Iron Age. The four separate strands of evidence — the pottery, the inscription, the names of the parish and manor, the passage in the *vita* (written in the ninth century but employing archaic orthography of the sixth-seventh century, and describing Mark's stronghold by a still older name, Caer Banhed) — are here sufficient to establish what lies behind the legend. Tristram, son (not nephew) of King Mark, lived at Castle Dore, Lantyen, and was young when Arthur was old. Iseult is not as yet attested. The example is typical of the relation between legend and fact.

[14] *Vita*, 43-44.
[15] *Vita Winwaloe*, 1, 2. "Fundum quendum . . . non perparvum sed quasi unius plebis modulum".
[16] *Vita Winwaloe*, 1, 18.
[17] *Vita Maclovius.* cf. *Vita Brioc*, 47, cf. 44, etc.
[18] cf. note 8.
[19] ed. Williams, pp. 258 ff.; Haddan and Stubbs, *Councils*, 1, 108; MGH, pp. 86-7.
[20] MGH. Epp. iii, pp. 158-9.
[21] The Irish tradition is formalised in the *Catalogus Sanctorum Hiberniae*, dividing the saints into three periods, *ordines*. "Primus ordo (432-544) . . . erat in tempore Patricii. Et tunc erant episcopi omnes clari et sancti . . . Secundus ordo (544-598) . . . pauci erant episcopi et multi presbyteri . . . A Davide episcopo et Gilla et a Doco Britonibus missam acceperunt . . ." Columban, writing to Gregory the Great c. 595, quotes rulings recently given by Gildas to St. Finian (of Clonard?). MGH. Epp. iii, 159.

PELAGIAN LITERATURE*

SOME seventy separate Pelagian writings survive, printed in Migne, comprehensively catalogued in 1958 in the first Supplement.[1] The fact is remarkable. Most heretical literature is known from the passages which the orthodox quote in the process of refutation, often in misleading isolation from their context. Moreover, Pelagianism had an exceptionally brief legal life, attacked, defined, condemned, and repressed within a decade, cut off *nequitiae adolescentia*.[2] Yet medieval

---

[1] Cols. 1101–9 (Pelagius); 1571–2 (Iulianus); 1679–83 (Coelestius, Anianus, Rufinus, and *alia scripta Pelagiana*), with full references to the texts in Migne and elsewhere, and the principal discussions on their authorship. The references for the main texts discussed below are:

Expositiones in Epistolas S. Pauli   P.L. Sup. i. 1110–1374 where Souter's pagination is reproduced.
Epistola ad Demetriadem   Hieron. *Ep.* 1 = P.L. 30.3 = 33.1099.
De Vita Christiana   P.L. 40, 1031.
De Virginitate   Hieron. *Ep.* 13 = P.L. 30.162 = 18.77 = 20.227 = 103.671.
De Divina Lege   Hieron. *Ep.* 7 = P.L. 30.104.

C. P. Caspari, *Briefe, Abhandlungen und Predigten* (Christiana, 1890).
Letter I (*Honorificentiae tuae*)   = P.L. Sup. i. 1687. Caspari, p. 3
Letter II (*Humanae referunt litterae*) =   ,,   1375   ,,   14
De Divitiis   =   ,,   1380   ,,   25
De Operibus   =   ,,   1418   ,,   67
De Possibilitate non peccandi   =   ,,   1457   ,,   114
De Castitate   =   ,,   1464   ,,   122

The Migne Supplement prints Caspari's pagination. The Caspari documents are also reprinted, together with the *de Vita Christiana*, with an English translation, by R. S. T. Haslehurst, under the title *The Works of Fastidius* (Society of SS. Peter and Paul, Ltd., Westminster, 1927).

The modern works referred to in this article by abbreviation are:

G. de Plinval (1934), 'Recherches sur l'œuvre littéraire de Pélage', *Revue de Philologie*, lx (3,8) (1934), pp. 9–42.
—(1939), 'Le problème de Pélage sur son dernier état', *Revue d'Histoire ecclésiastique*, xxxv (1939), pp. 5–21.
—(1943), *Pélage, ses écrits, sa vie et sa réforme* (Lausanne, 1943).
—(1947), *Essai sur le style et la langue de Pélage* (Fribourg en Suisse, 1947).
T. Bohlin, *Die Theologie des Pelagius und ihre Genesis* (Uppsala Universitets Årsskrift, 1957, 9).
R. F. Evans, 'Pelagius, Fastidius, and the Pseudo-Augustinian de Vita Christiana', *J.T.S.* N.S. xiii (1962), pp. 72–98.

I have not been able to consult Ivo Kirmer, *Das Eigentum des Fastidius in pelagianischen Schrifttum* (Missionsdruckerei, St. Ottilien, 1938), whose views are summarized in de Plinval (1939, pp. 7 ff.).

[2] Rescript of Honorius, 30 April 418, *ad conturbandam*, P.L. 56.490, &c., cf. p. 42, n. 2, below. *Adolescentia* is the reading of the Vienna MS.; it is tempting to read, with Orielensis 42 and Paris. lat. 3842 A, *adolescentis* (for *adolescentes*), cf. p. 43 below.

---

* Reprinted from the *Journal of Theological Studies*, N.S., 16 (1965) 26–60, by kind permission of the publisher.

libraries elected to preserve a great part of its literature, equivalent to something over 1,000 columns of Migne, most of it disguised under the respectable names of Augustine, Hieronymus, or various popes. Manuscripts are normally copied and recopied so long as their content is considered edifying. It is evident that much of Pelagius's views retained a wide appeal for centuries, when the literature of other heresies once formidable in the West was allowed to perish. It is therefore important to observe closely the rich variety of Pelagian thought, for the fundamental concept of man's free will to choose between good and evil opens many doors to widely diverging social and religious philosophies. That is why the problems of authorship of these documents are more important than usual; they are not merely scholars' problems, of distinguishing between the work of a master and his pupils, of attaching a name to a document. For the majority of these tracts were written within a year or two of Alaric's sack of Rome in 410. The disaster was rationally predictable, emotionally inconceivable; and when it came it destroyed for ever the comforting illusion of eternal Rome. Men looked to an uncertain future with hope or fear, effort or resignation, as their different ages, temperaments, circumstances impelled them. The principal philosophical controversy of these years was the clash between Augustine and the Pelagians, and its literature is our best witness to the various ways in which thinking men reacted to the fall of Rome. The problem of authorship is therefore not so much a matter of finding names, as of grouping together works by the same writer, or by groups of closely related writers, and distinguishing them from others of different tendencies. If unlike works are lumped together on insufficient evidence, their meaning is obscured; if the works of one writer are artificially separated, his thought is likely to be ill understood.

A few works were certainly written by Pelagius himself. According to Augustine,[1] he wrote to Pope Innocent in the spring of 417, enclosing a *Libellus Fidei Suae* and naming his works; Augustine quotes the letter at length, including references to four works.[2] Two of these are lost; one, *pro Libero Arbitrio*, is known only from Augustine's quotations, but the fourth, the *Letter to Demetrias*, is extant in full. It is certainly the same letter, since Augustine cites from it five longish passages which occur in the surviving text. The *Commentaries on the Pauline Epistles* are also extant. Augustine's extract from Pelagius's letter does not mention them, but he and Mercator[3] both quote from a *Commentary on*

[1] *scribens ad Innocentium, quem defunctum esse nesciebat.* Innocent died in the middle of March 417; his letters to the African bishops endorsing their sentence on Coelestius are dated 27 January 417.
[2] *de Gratia Christi* i. 37-40, 45.
[3] See *de Gestis Pelagii* 39; *de Gratia Christi* ii. 24; Mercator, *Commonitorium* 2

Romans ascribed to Pelagius. These quotations correspond to the appropriate passages on Romans in the Commentaries on XIII Pauline Epistles whose text and attribution Souter has established to the satisfaction of most scholars. The Demetrias letter is therefore quite certainly Pelagius's work, claimed by him and identified by Augustine's quotations; Augustine and Mercator confidently credited him with the *Commentary on Romans*, and there is no evident reason in style or content to separate it from the author of the Demetrias letter. Thus far ancient authority; modern scholarship has argued plausibly for the addition of the Commentary on the rest of the Epistles and for the identification of the *Libellus Fidei*, and, somewhat less decisively, for a letter addressed to Celantia. Augustine also quotes extensively from lost works; but where such quotations can be checked against their originals, in the Demetrias letter and *Romans* commentary, they are often loose paraphrases, a fallible guide to style, an uncertain index of argument and meaning. Furthermore, such quotations, however accurate, are a doubtful illustration of the argument their author intended, for, by definition, they are the weak points that the critic selects to justify his counter-argument. For an unequivocal exposition of Pelagius's own views it is wise to restrict attention to the Demetrias Letter and the Commentary.

The most important of the other Pelagian writings, and the most frequently discussed in modern times, are the *de Vita Christiana* and a group of six tracts published by Caspari in 1890, together with two others properly belonging to the same group, called *de Virginitate*, and *de Lege Divina*. For the past century scholars have disputed the authorship of the *de Vita Christiana*, assigning it usually either to Pelagius or to the British Bishop Fastidius, though Caspari claimed it for the author of his tracts. Thirty years ago, however, de Plinval divided Caspari's collection, claiming for Pelagius himself five of the pieces, together with the *de Vita Christiana*, the *de Virginitate*, and a dozen Pelagian works preserved under the name of Hieronymus. His argument has been accepted by some, doubted, rejected, or ignored by others.[1]

(*P.L.* 48, 83 ff.). In *de Gestis Pelagii* 39 Augustine cites as from 'quaedam expositiones epistolae Pauli quae scribitur ad Romanos, quae ipsius Pelagii esse dicitur'. Mercator is more certain: 'Pelagius . . . ausus est memoratus ante vastationem urbis Romae in apostolum Paulum commentarios condere. . . . In epistola igitur quae est ad Romanos . . . ita loquitur.' Mercator's citations are close to the extant text; Augustine's are recognizably drawn therefrom.

[1] Accepted, with little criticism, by J. Ferguson, *Pelagius* (1956); with some reserve (p. 30) by Hugo Koch, *Religio*, xi. 1 (1935), pp. 21–30. Koch promises a fuller study to 'confirm and complete' de Plinval's argument; I have not been able to discover whether he was able to fulfil this promise. His article supplements de Plinval's parallels with a number of others, which (p. 27) 'sono manifestamente

But it permeates the classification adopted by Hamman in the recent Migne Supplement. His *Operum Recensio* of Pelagius is divided into A, *Opera Pelagio iam diu adscripta*, the Demetrias Letter, the Commentaries, the *Libellus Fidei*, and the Celantia Letter; B, *Plurimos enim libros Pelagio nuper adscripserunt eruditi*, comprising fifteen of the eighteen additional writings claimed for Pelagius by de Plinval, and no others; C, *Scripta dubiae fidei*, three works over which de Plinval hesitates; and D, *Opera deperdita et fragmenta*, those listed as such by de Plinval, with a few additions. The works rejected by de Plinval are relegated to a separate heading elsewhere in the volume, *alia scripta Pelagiana*. Despite the cautious wording of the short notes attached to each entry, this arrangement, which now becomes the standard survey and catalogue of Pelagian literature, gives a tacit approval and an air of finality to de Plinval's attributions.

I do not think that these attributions can stand. The argument rests upon the citation of parallel passages and similarities of style, with little analysis of the selection and use of scriptural quotations and slight attention to the content and ideas. It is assumed without argument that if two works contain a number of passages that are word for word identical, or closely echo the same thought or use similar language, then the works should be by the same author. The assumption is dubious; there are, for example, remarkable similarities between the *Octavius* of Minucius Felix and Tertullian's *Apology*. It would be absurd to pretend that the two men are identical; both were brought up in African towns and both studied in Rome; they were approximate, perhaps exact contemporaries, and had much in common, as well as important differences of outlook. The possible explanations, much discussed, are either that one copied from the other, or that both were inspired by a common source.

Ancient habits of quotation are not always easy to detect. Modern printed editions help their readers by setting up quotations in italic type or between inverted commas when the quotation is easily recognizable or acknowledged by the writer, but these conventions are foreign to the manuscripts. Christian writers, particularly since Origen and Eusebius, quoted documents in full with adequate references more commonly than traditional Greek and Roman writers, but the unacknowledged quotation was still common, and remains a source of confusion. The polemical Pelagian literature is rich in examples. For instance, *de Virginitate* [7]

---

parafrasi abbondanti e un po' troppo verbose delle osservazioni brevi del commento', and, in fact, are further proof that Caspari's author was thoroughly familiar with the Commentaries. The attributions are doubted by Evans, rejected by Kirmer, ignored by Bohlin.

adduces 1 Corinthians vii. 34 and follows straight on with Pelagius's commentary on the verse ('nuptam viro placere adserit . . . innuptam vero Deo', &c.). To de Plinval (1943, p. 35 = 1934, p. 26) this is 'une preuve véritablement cruciale' that Pelagius wrote the *de Virginitate* as well as the Commentaries, and was quoting himself ('de voir l'auteur . . . emprunter . . . à son propre Commentaire'). Yet the argument of the *de Virginitate* suggests a simpler explanation. The author quotes from the Pauline Epistles thirteen times. His text usually differs from that which Pelagius used in the Commentary; though he here quotes from the Commentary, his text is not the version that Pelagius used there; but it is the text that Pelagius used in the Demetrias letter. Yet this text is the only one of the thirteen which is followed by an extract from the Commentaries. The reason is plain; it is the only one of these texts in which the Commentary concerns the author's theme, virginity. The author cites Scripture and Commentary as his argument requires; scriptural quotations are normally prefixed with a 'dicit Dominus', 'dicit Apostolus', or the like. Such vague rubrics do not serve the modern purpose of enabling the reader to find and verify the text. Their purpose is to lend authority to the argument; a 'dicit Pelagius' inserted before the extract from the Commentary imparts no authority, and is not employed, so that there is no signal in the manuscript to warn the reader where Paul's words end and Pelagius's begin. He is supposed to know. This is straightforward quotation, indicating nothing of the source quoted, whether it be another work of the same author or the work of a different writer.

It is not easy to decide when a fifth-century ecclesiastical writer is quoting, and when he is repeating himself. Decision must needs be based on the whole of the works concerned, on the form and frequency of the similarities, and must also take account of the differences; placing a number of isolated passages side by side proves nothing by itself. There can be no certainty in such argument; but there can be strong probability. It is perhaps a common sense rule of thumb to expect that the nearer a passage is to a verbatim transcript of its fellow, the more likely it is to be a quotation; while an idea rephrased is a more open question, and two works that are full of rephrased echoes of each other may quite well be the work of the same author, provided that the differences do not outweigh the similarities.

I do not think that parallel passages can be held to show common authorship; but if they did, they would very strongly argue that Caspari's six documents were not written by Pelagius. These documents consist of two letters, both preserved in two south German manuscripts, there attributed to Hieronymus; and four tracts, three of them in letter form, prepared for publication, preserved in a Vatican manuscript, and known as *de Divitiis*, *de malis Doctoribus et Operibus fidei* (or, more shortly, *de Operibus*), *de Possibilitate non peccandi*, and *de Castitate*. Caspari devotes 166 pages (pp. 223–389) to the comparison of their differences and similarities, tabulating ten passages closely similar in each of the two letters (pp. 279–82) and a further thirty-five parallels drawn between the letters of the German manuscripts and the tracts of the Vatican manuscript (pp. 304–16), twenty of which are taken from the first letter; and handling many other passages in this discussion. He concludes that all six documents are the work of a single author,[1] and if parallels be accepted as a valid test, his conclusion is well founded.

De Plinval separates the documents, accepting the second letter and the four tracts as the work of a single author, in his view Pelagius, but rejecting the first letter because it 'comporte des détails autobiographiques qui ne sauraient convenir à Pélage' (1943, p. 30). These details, discussed below (p. 28, cf. p. 29), certainly do not fit Pelagius; if Caspari is right, that both letters and the tracts belong to a single author, then that author is certainly not Pelagius. If the other five documents are Pelagius's work, it must be shown that Caspari is wrong, and that the first letter is by a different writer. The proof is not convincing. De Plinval (1943, pp. 32–33) takes two of the twenty passages which Caspari compared with the first letter, and compares them instead with similar passages in the *de Virginitate*, leaving out the similar passages in the letter. On grounds of style, the first letter is characterized (1939, pp. 10–11) as an 'agglomération incohérente de phrases détachées', to be separated from the other tracts by 'l'examen des clausules métriques', none of which are instanced, and by 'la proportion anormale et pour ainsi dire monstrueuse de la conjonction *nam*'. It is true that in eleven pages fourteen sentences begin with *nam*, which is less frequent in the other documents; but it is not uncommon in them, and when it is used, it is used repetitively, for example, three times in two pages of the second letter (pp. 15–16), four times in three pages (pp. 36–39) of the *de Divitiis*. Moreover, the style of a private and intimate letter to a relative, shot through with personal emotions, may be expected to differ from the style of works prepared for the general public. Elsewhere I have found one other discussion of the first letter, where it

---

[1] Caspari (pp. 387–8, cf. 347) oddly suggests as author 'Agricola Pelagianus, Severiani Pelagiani episcopi filius' (Prosper, *Chron.* 429), and is driven to some ingenuity in discussing whether or not the wealthy 'parens', to whom letter 1 is addressed, is to be converted to Pelagianism and consecrated bishop in the 420's. Caspari's sole reason for this identification is that Agricola is the only other British Pelagian whose name we know. There were many whose names are unknown, and the author of the tracts must be numbered among them.

is dismissed (1934, p. 37) as 'une enfilade de pensées et de phrases qui sont détachées tour à tour du traité de la Virginité, du de Divitiis, du de Vita Christiana'; the accompanying footnote refers to one of Caspari's twenty parallels. Yet these parallels stand on all fours with one another and with those whereby de Plinval links the various works claimed for Pelagius. It is not enough to assert without argument that those which contradict the thesis of Pelagius's authorship are quotations ('phrases détachées'), while those which support it are self-repetition. Caspari's heavily buttressed argument requires thorough discussion; colourful words like 'incohérente', 'enfilade', &c., are no substitute for such discussion; nor does this letter really justify this description (cf. pp. 29–30 and 37 below).

The stylistic argument (1939, pp. 5 ff., 1947, pp. 10 ff.), based on Kirmer, is more impressive, but double-edged. Kirmer interpreted his results as confirmation of Caspari, and assigned to his author the *de Vita Christiana, de Virginitate, de Lege Divina*, and several other works as well. De Plinval interprets the same evidence as proof of Pelagius's authorship of all the tracts, save the first letter, but refrains from any analysis of that letter's style. The minute examination of word and clause is nowadays a labour more fitting for a computer than for the slow pace of the human eye and hand; the scholar's discretion is required in estimating the various possible interpretations of the mechanical results, in avoiding hair-raising over-simplifications, in programming the questions. For comparison must be made with other contemporary writers; differences must be investigated no less than similarities; allowance must be made for the development of one man's thoughts and style, for the impact of new ideas; and for those common idioms which derive from the influences and writings in which a group of like-minded writers have soaked themselves. Some groups of nineteenth-century nonconformists share an idiom derived from the writings and orations that inspired them, and so do many twentieth-century Marxists. Stylistic analysis must inquire how far Pelagians shared a common Pelagian idiom before it can determine whether one man or a dozen men wrote the works that use that idiom; and that inquiry requires a more elaborate analysis than has yet been possible.

Parallel passages and stylistic analysis are a part of the evidence, by themselves inconclusive. Content is as important. Some of the works concerned show at least some negative evidence of who did not write them. The tract *de Vita Christiana* is in most manuscripts attributed to Augustine; one assigns it to Pelagius, one to Bishop Fastidius. It is a Pelagian document, certainly not by Augustine, and opinion has fairly evenly divided between the two other attributions. Gennadius (*de Viris*

Inlustribus 57) knew of a Fastidius; 'Britannorum episcopus scripsit ad Fatalem quendam *de Vita Christiana* librum et alium *de Viduitate Servanda*, sana et Deo digna doctrina.' Gennadius's inventory is arranged in roughly chronological order, and the place of this entry should lie in the 420's. It is tempting to identify the text that the manuscripts call *de Vita Christiana*, ascribed by one Monte Cassino manuscript to Bishop Fastidius, with that which Gennadius names; yet our text is addressed to a woman, Gennadius's to a man; perhaps Gennadius, or a copyist, made a mistake, writing 'quendam' for 'quandam'. Gennadius ought not to have called a Pelagian text 'sana doctrina'; perhaps he read it hastily, perhaps he wished to smuggle it into the accepted reading of late fifth-century Gaul. In such an argument one may really choose either side, but can hardly claim finality.

There are, however, two passages in the work, one much discussed, the other very little, which bear upon its date and authorship. The book is a consolation to a wealthy young woman, who has recently lost her husband, and is urged to live retired from the world, devoting her time to charity to the poor, to meditation and prayer. The author (ch. 11) recommends a remarkable prayer which horrified both Hieronymus and Augustine. Hieronymus (*Dialogus* 3. 14) is certainly citing from our text, since he quotes not only the prayer, but also the sentence with which the author introduces it: 'Ille autem ad Deum merito extollit manus, ille preces bona conscientia fundit, qui potest dicere . . . .' Pelagius was accused at Diospolis of having written this work, and of having addressed unseemly flattery to the same lady, in whom resided a piety and truthfulness found nowhere else on earth. He and his followers denied authorship, but Hieronymus refused to believe the denial, on grounds of style; the brilliance and Ciceronian diction were characteristic of Pelagius. Hieronymus's stylistic argument may be given neither more nor less weight than modern stylistic arguments. Augustine, translating the Council's proceedings (*de Gestis Pelagii* 6 (16)), sets down the same two passages, but adds that they come from different works addressed to the same widow. He records an open verdict on Pelagius's authorship, content to say that the Council was quite right to accept his denial in default of evidence. Some modern misunderstanding has been caused by Augustine's statement that the prayer came 'post orationem Domini et Salvatoris Nostri', which Evans (p. 83) and others have understood to mean that 'the celebrated prayer stood after a quotation or discussion of the Lord's Prayer', which seems unnecessary, since chapter 11 of the *de Vita Christiana* is devoted to a discussion of the futile indecency of 'preces ad Dominum' offered up by unrepentant evil-doers. Augustine's words may mean 'a prayer to the Lord' rather than 'the Lord's Prayer'.

Augustine, however, pursued the matter (6 (19)), and found that 'quidam sancti fratres' had regarded these works addressed to the 'unnamed' widow as written by Pelagius since they had come to know them 'ante quattuor ferme annos'; but they had never heard Pelagius admit authorship, and he therefore admitted that Pelagius might be telling the truth. The works were known in 413; they were written by 412 at latest, but perhaps not much earlier, since the brethren knew Pelagius personally and were presumably reasonably up to date in Pelagian literature.

This much discussed passage gives a date to the composition of our *de Vita Christiana* some ten or fifteen years earlier than the approximate date at which Gennadius enters the name of Fastidius. But bishops may live and write for twenty years or more, and the passage leaves the problem of authorship as undecided as it was in 415. But another passage, less remarked, offers strong pointers to the place and time of composition. Chapter 3 consoles the widow for the apparent injustice that her virtuous husband has been taken while so many wicked men are left alive. But, says the author, 'we see before us plenty of examples ... of wicked men, the sum of their sins complete, who are at this present moment being judged, and denied this present life no less than the life to come. One can easily understand it if, through changing times, one has been waiting for the end of successive magistrates (*iudicum*) who have lived criminally; for the greater their power, the bolder their sins ... and since, while they judged over others, they were unafraid of the judgement of any other man, they were prompt to sin. Thus it is fitting that those who had no man to fear when they gave vicious judgement should feel God as a judge and avenger.... Those who freely shed the blood of others are now forced to spill their own. Some ... lie unburied, food for the beasts and the birds of the air. Others who unjustly killed vast numbers of people have individually been torn limb from limb.... Their judgements killed many husbands, widowed many women, orphaned many children. They made them beggars and left them bare ... for they plundered the children of the men they killed. Now it is their wives who are widows, their sons who are orphans, begging their daily bread.'

This is a vivid description of the violent overthrow of a government, just before the book was written. The magistrates of the party in power had executed their enemies, declared their estates forfeit; when they were overthrown, the victorious party did the same to them. Both sides were men of property. The author approved the new régime, and a good deal of the rest of the argument is devoted to setting forth the principles upon which good government should be based; men of wealth and power should be charitable and kind to their inferiors, not cruel oppressors. It is in part a political pamphlet, issued to and in support of the victorious rebels. The rebellion is an actual political event of the early fifth century; but an odd one, for there were a good many risings in the late fourth and early fifth century, and a great deal was written in praise of the victors. Without exception, the defeated enemy is abused as a 'nefandus tyrannus' or the like, his associates branded as 'satellites'; for government was personal, its head an emperor, a single individual, and the first act of any rebels was to proclaim their leader emperor; even when, in 408, Stilicho fell from power, abuse concentrated on his person and his satellites. The government here overthrown, and its successor, are unique in that they are not headed by emperors, but consist of a number of magistrates, *iudices*. The author is well aware of its exceptional structure; the words 'dum alterius iudicium non timent qui alios iudicant, ad peccandum precipites sunt. Ita fit, ut qui hominis non timent in delinquendo iudicium, Deum iudicem sentiant et ultorem' argue that what makes this government so exceptionally bad is that it, unlike others, had no superior, no 'alter' or 'homo' to fear. No emperor, prefect, or vicar stood above it.

There is one recorded set of circumstances which fits this abnormal situation. From 407 the British obeyed the rival emperor Constantine III; in 410, when he was plainly defeated, besieged in Vienne but not yet taken, Honorius wrote to the cities of Britain telling them to look to their own defence. It is universally and rightly assumed that Honorius answered a letter from the council of the *civitates* of Britain, who had renounced the failing Constantine, returned to their legitimate obedience, and asked for governors and generals, troops and money, which Honorius was unable to supply at the time of the fall of Rome. The government which renounced Constantine and opened negotiations with Honorius acknowledged no superior prefect or emperor; its immediate predecessor obeyed Constantine in name, though from the end of 409 onward his authority can have been no more than nominal; and it is quite possible that Honorius's refusal to help may have led to the overthrow of the party which came to power in order to procure that help. Whatever the detail of these possibilities, the change of government described in the *de Vita Christiana* fits the events in Britain in 410–11, the approximate date at which the treatise was written, and does not seem to fit any other known rebellion. It is therefore likely that the tract was written in Britain; if so, it cannot therefore have been written by Pelagius, who, though himself a Briton, had lived for at least ten years in Rome. The author might or might not have been called Fastidius; but he was probably a colleague, compatriot, and contemporary of Fastidius; and since no other works of Fastidius are known, it may be convenient to call him 'Fastidius', in inverted commas, without venturing to decide whether or not the pamphlet is identical with either or both of the tracts named by Gennadius.

Two of the other separated works offer some evidence of authorship. Writing about 540 Gildas (*de Excidio Britanniae* 38) quotes 'ut bene quidam nostrum ait, "non agitur de qualitate peccati, sed de transgressione mandati"'. The quotation is from *de Virginitate* 6. The paragraph, discussing the nature of Adam's sin, is found in much the same general form in the first Caspari letter (p. 6) and in the *de Operibus* (13, p. 90), and may be an extension of Pelagius's comment on Romans v. 14, 'eos qui praeceptum, sicut Adam, transgressi sunt', cf. 19 'sicut exemplo inoboedientiae Adae' (pp. 46–47), but the sentence does not occur in the first letter, and the *de Operibus* reads 'enim actum est' in place of 'agitur'. It is therefore certain that the *de Virginitate* was also written by a Briton, or at least that it was so thought in Britain a century later. Pelagius was British; but, though the opinion can only be subjective and personal, it seems scarcely likely that Gildas would describe Pelagius as 'quidam nostrum'. It is doubtful if he knew that Pelagius, a long-dead heretic once active in Italy, had been British by birth; and the natural interpretation of his words is that he meant a work written in Britain and preserved in Britain. Similarly, the author might be identical with Caspari's author, who was also British. But the passages are so close that they tend to suggest quotation by one writer from the other, rather than repetition, between the *de Virginitate* and the *de Operibus*, whereas the differences in the order of thought and sentence between the *de Operibus* and the first letter seem more fitted to the work of a single author expressing the same idea on two different occasions. Such opinions cannot be pressed; the *de Virginitate* might be the work of Pelagius or of Caspari's author, but seems on the whole more likely to be the product of a third, separate author familiar with the writings of both.

The *de Divina Lege* comes from a senatorial milieu; expressions that occur naturally to the author include, for example (ch. 6), 'In nostra classe viri fortes opprobria sciunt portare, non munera'; 'retrahit quidem verecundia senatorem, ne sequatur pauperem Christum'; 'Turpe est inter parentes senatores atque grammaticos scholasticum pro Christo voluntaria humilitate deiectum verbis simplicibus esse contentum.' The author shares Pelagius's reaction that the fall of Rome presages the end of the world and the Second Coming; the words (ch. 9) 'vindictae dies et retributionis... qui imminens ac vicinus esse et saeculi ruinis undique concurrentibus et Scripturarum contestatione probatur' are not far removed from Pelagius's comparison (*Demetrias* 30) between the 'Gothorum clamor' and the 'adventus Christi... quae consummationem saeculi quasi certum praemii tui tempus exspectas'. This reaction differs widely from that of the author of Caspari's first letter, who replies to the 'vulgi sententiam' that 'totus mundus perit' with the optimistic reminder that 'temporibus Noe totum periisse mundum', but that if God then saved the human race, he can do so again (p. 7).

But the *de Divina Lege* expresses forthright views on monasticism: 'Ego te Christianum volo esse, non monachum dici, et virtutem propriae laudis possidere magis quam nomen alienum; quod frustra a Latinis in turba commorantibus imponitur, cum a Graecis solitarie viventibus legitime deputetur' (ch. 9). The viewpoint here is closer to Hieronymus than to Pelagius, himself a monk 'in turba commorans'. The writer is neither Pelagius nor Caspari's author; nor is he easily equated with the British author of the *de Virginitate*, for he seems to be at home in the city of Rome.

Caspari's six documents are, however, linked to one another by more than parallel passages and style. The first letter is a reply by a young man, father of a young daughter, to an elder relative, rich and powerful, who bids him return home. His home is Britain, for he equates 'in Francia et in Saxonia' with 'in omni Barbaria', an outlook natural to northern Gaul and Britain; and he twice explains that his journey involved a difficult and dangerous sea voyage, indicating travel from Britain rather than Gaul. He writes from Sicily, where a senatorial lady has shown him the way of truth, and dissuaded him from his previous intention 'ad orientem ire'. His reference to the 'common saying "The whole world is dying"' suggests a date not far from 410; the senatorial lady in Sicily is quite likely to be one of those who left the city after the sack, in which case the date would be about 411–12.

Apart from his personal problem, the letter has a single theme, the text (Matt. xix. 21, &c.) 'Si vis perfectus esse, vade, vende omnia tua'; which he urges as a simple literal precept applicable to all Christians, castigating, with the youthful enthusiasm inspired of a new-found truth, the sluggards who shelter from its plain meaning behind other texts, such as 'Melius est dare quam accipere' (Acts xx. 35) (ch. 4, p. 10). This simple concept, as eagerly urged, but much more fully developed, is the theme of the third document, *de Divitiis*, whose chief and repeated conclusion is that rich men cannot enter heaven.

In 414 Augustine (*Ep.* 156)[1] received a plea for help from a supporter in Sicily named Hilarius, troubled by a recent publication in the island of a work whose theme was 'Divitem manentem in divitiis suis in regnum Dei non posse ingredi, nisi omnia sua vendiderit, nec prodesse eidem

---

[1] To which *Ep.* 157 is the reply. Cf. 186.9.32. Hieron. *Dial.* iii. 19 (415); Orosius, *Lib. Apol. contra Pel.* (415), called the letter 'recent'.

posse, si forte ex ipsis divitiis fecerit mandata'. Additional detail comes from the proceedings at Diospolis; Pelagius was confronted (*de Gestis Pelagii* 23) with the 'capitula ... quae mihi de Sicilia missa fuerant ... quibus per librum ad Hilarium scriptum ... respondi. Ista sunt autem "Posse hominem sine peccato, si velit, esse. Infantes, etsi non baptizentur, habere vitam aeternam. Divites baptizatos nisi omnibus abrenuntiant, si quid boni visi fuerint facere, non reputari illis, neque regnum Dei posse eos habere".' The first sentence is an exact summary of the surviving portion of the *de Possibilitate non peccandi*; the greater part of this work is lost, but might very well have continued with the argument summarized in the second sentence. The third sentence is an exact summary of the *de Divitiis*, a work certainly Pelagian and certainly written at about this time. The views expressed are not found in any other writer. Caspari (p. 266) therefore makes the *de Divitiis* 'wesentlich identisch' with the work Hilarius sent to Augustine from Sicily. The first letter was written in Sicily some two to three years earlier; its theme is the same unique idea, as yet undeveloped, but expressed in very similar language and with the same uninhibited approach; it is on these grounds, as well as on the strength of nine parallel passages, that Caspari identified the author of the first letter and the author of the *de Divitiis*. It would be perverse, almost meaningless, to dissent from these conclusions. It is theoretically possible that two men wrote two works expressing identical views in the same place at the same time and in the same idiom. Two men actively committed to the same movement, knowing each other intimately and expressing themselves in a similar way might do so; but if the authors were distinct on this level, the distinction is so slight as to be historically unimportant.

Hilarius's letter links the first Caspari letter, the *de Divitiis* and the *de Possibilitate non peccandi*; another of his complaints, that his disturbing Pelagians maintain that Christians 'non iurare debere omnino' joins with them the *de Operibus*, the *de Castitate*, and the *de Virginitate*. The prescript 'ut non maledicas, non mentiaris ... ut omnino non iures' (*de Virginitate* 6); 'Christianus est qui nunquam mentitur, nunquam maledicit, qui in toto non iurat' (first letter, i. 1, p. 5); 'iubemur enim non mentiri, non maledicere ... sed nec iuste quidem iurare' (*de Divitiis* 19. 2); 'praecipitur nobis non mentiri, non maledicere ... non iurare quidem vel iuste' (*de Castitate* 10. 8 cf. 12. 3); 'qualis transgresio (*sic*) est aut frustra irasci, aut mentiri ... aut iurare' (*de Operibus* 14. 1 cf. 22 (p. 110) 'neque per aliud quodcumque genus se iurare debere') opens what amounts almost to a private commandment of the Sicilian Pelagians. Its origin is to be found in Pelagius's advice to Demetrias (19) 'Mentiri autem, maledicere atque iurare lingua tua nesciat'; but there it is an incidental detail in a long passage on the language proper to a virgin, and it is not developed by other Pelagian writers. This small distinctive detail both links the documents and adds a further pointer to their authorship; of the five tracts that list these commandments, three are ascribed to the same author in the Vatican manuscript; two, the *de Divitiis* and the first letter, were written in Sicily; two, the first letter and the *de Virginitate*, were written by a Briton. They are evidence that the author of the *de Virginitate* was at least acquainted with the work of his compatriot in Sicily; if the author of the first letter made good his promise to his relative to come home eventually to Britain, he might also be the author of the *de Virginitate*; but, on balance, the tract is more probably the work of a fellow countryman and friend (cf. p. 26 above).

Hilarius's letter joins all four of the Caspari tracts with the first letter; a copyist's error connects one of them with the second letter. In the Vatican manuscript there is an evident lacuna, printed as such by Caspari (p. 119, cf. pp. 325 ff.) at the end of chapter four of the *de Possibilitate non peccandi*; the remaining three chapters are a word for word transcript of the second letter. The original manuscript clearly contained the rest of the *de Possibilitate*, now lost, and the beginning of the second letter; we do not know how many leaves are wanting, and they may have included the first letter. The copy that survives ascribed the whole of its contents to a single author, and it is probable that its original did the same. The second letter also contains hints that it was addressed to the same recipient as the first letter, and addressed to Britain. Both letters twice greet the recipient by the title 'Honorificentia tua', all but unique in Latin literature; and the second letter closes with the greeting 'Opto te semper Deo vivere et perpetui consulatus honore gaudere'. The consulate is a precise and terrestrial term, and the sentence means that the addressee was a consul. The date of the letter is uncertain; it was written after Pelagian views had hardened and begun to develop, but shows no sign that they had yet become the object of acute and dangerous attack, as they were from 416 onward; moreover, its thought seems more developed than that of the first letter, though this is a matter of opinion hardly to be proven. The probable limits are therefore between 411 and 415, the reasonably likely limits between 409 and 415. In these years all but one of the western consulates were held by the emperor; the sole private consul was Heraclian, the murderer of Stilicho, who rebelled and was killed in Africa in the year of his consulate, 413. It is difficult to suppose that the letter was written to Heraclian, and the consul was therefore one not officially recognized in the *Fasti*. He might have been one of the consuls nominated by the usurper Constantine in Gaul or Britain; but there is a further oddity in the adjective 'perpetui'. It is hardly sensible to emend the word to the adverb 'perpetue', for the honour of a consulate was held for a year only, the dignity of an ex-consul lifelong. The title 'perpetual consul' is twice recorded; Augustus declined it, and the short-lived emperor Vitellius accepted it in A.D. 69. It then had aristocratic overtones, compromising between the 'libertas' of the senate and the fact of monarchy. We do not know what titles were used by the independent government which the British set up on the receipt of Honorius's letter; it is not impossible that one of the expedients used to solve their embarrassing and novel constitutional problem was the revival of an ancient dignity appropriate to the president of an aristocracy. It is easy but insufficient to shrug off this unparalleled but precise phrase and leave it unexplained; but it is not easy to suggest an explanation save in the novel circumstances of Britain after 410.

Caspari's six documents are therefore to be assigned to one author, not only on grounds of style and of parallel passages, but by external evidence, by manuscript tradition, and by the indications, tenuous in the second letter but clear in the first, of the author's nationality. They have a number of ideas in common that are peculiar to themselves, not found even in other Pelagian writings. The author's name is not to be recovered; he was a Briton who wrote in Sicily, and is therefore most fitly described as the 'Sicilian Briton'. Augustine is, however, positive on the views that shaped him. He attacks the *de Divitiis* a fourth time (*de Gestis Pelagii* 33 (57)), accepting Pelagius's denial that the work was his, but 'taking it ill' that in his 'chartula' he had not anathematized those who shared its viewpoint. He reproaches him with maintaining some sort of defence of the opinions of Coelestius, 'quae (sententiae) istae sunt', (1) that Adam was created mortal, his sin harming himself alone, (2) that unbaptized infants inherit eternal life, (3) that the rich, though baptized, cannot inhabit the kingdom of heaven. The first two of these propositions are those for which Coelestius had been arraigned at Carthage in 412 (*de Peccato Originali* 2); Pelagius's own view differed, for on Romans v. 12 (p. 44) he commented 'cum non esset peccatum, per Adam advenit, ita enim, cum paene apud nullum iustitia remansisset, per Christum est revocata'. But at Diospolis Augustine charged Pelagius with these views 'quae in doctrina Coelestii discipuli eius referuntur inventa' (*de Gestis Pelagii* 11 (23)); the master was held responsible for his pupil's development of his views. So here, the attacks on the rich, nowhere else alleged against Coelestius, are credited to the teacher, asserted to be the opinion of Coelestius, raised against Pelagius. Coelestius was not in Sicily in 414 (Augustine, *Ep.* 157; *de Perfectione Iustitiae Hominis* 1), though he had been there at some time (Prosper, *de Ingratis*

2. 38, placed immediately before his visit to Africa, in 412) probably in 411, after the sack of the city. His influence was widespread in Sicily, where there were 'multi talia garrientes', and where the 'brethren heard what he taught and wrote'.

It is possible that Coelestius also came from the British Isles. Just enough is known about him to encourage interesting questions about his early life and temperament, but not enough to warrant a confident decision. In an obscure invective (*Praef. Lib. 3 in Jeremiam*) Hieronymus asserts that one of the major Pelagian leaders 'habet enim progeniem Scoticae gentis, de Britannorum vicinia'. Whom he means is, of course, a matter of argument; Pelagius is a possibility; he was British, not Irish, and Hieronymus knew it, and knew the difference between Britain and Ireland. It remains possible that he was abusing Pelagius as having an Irish grandmother; but such an interpretation seems a little far-fetched, for Pelagius is so well known as British, so frequently described as such, that Hieronymus would have made his point more effectively with a phrase like 'British with Irish blood'. In fourth-century literary convention Britain still evoked the familiar descriptions of Caesar and Tacitus, a land remote and barbarous enough to serve as an insult; Hieronymus wrote for readers who knew the man as a Scot, but needed to be told that the Scots lived near Britain. The same readers knew Pelagius as British, and would not identify the unnamed Scot with him unless they were told. It is much more natural to understand the passage as referring to someone the world knew to be Irish, not someone it knew to be British. Of the other Pelagian leaders, Anianus was Italian, and so was Julian, not yet in the forefront, and Rufinus was a Syrian. The unknown was clearly a leading Pelagian, unlikely to be someone whose name has not come down to us; by elimination he is most likely to be Coelestius, the best-known follower of Pelagius, the only well-known follower whose national origin is not otherwise attested. But this is an inference that cannot be asserted with finality.

Gennadius (ch. 44) adds that 'adhuc adulescens scripsit ad parentes suos de monasterio epistolas', before he met Pelagius. Mercator calls him 'nobilis natu' (*Liber Subnotationum* 4). The phrase is much stretched by ecclesiastical writers, but usually in honour of their heroes rather than their villains, and it must have meant something in application to a living, or very recently dead, contemporary. It is possible, but unlikely, that Mercator would so describe a chieftain's son from the non-Roman island; if Coelestius were Irish, he is more likely to have applied nobility to one of the leading families of the numerous Irish settlements that had been established for a century on the west coast of Britain, whose power and status the imperial government had acknowledged for half a century.[1] Such an origin would better fit Hieronymus's unknown, described not as a Scot, but as a man with Scot ancestry.

No one else calls Coelestius a monk; but Gennadius is not lightly accused of so large a factual error, and Augustine complained that the Pelagian heresy originated 'a quibusdam monachis' (*de Gestis Pelagii* 61). The plural may well include Coelestius, for he is the only other leader Augustine names. Augustine never calls him monk, and several times speaks of 'Pelagius monachus'; but he also names Pelagius many times without the epithet, and Pelagius is named more often. Coelestius was not only a monk; at first he lived in a *monasterium*, and *monasteria* were not as yet numerous in the west. Lérins and Marseilles were not yet founded; there is no evidence that the monastic discipline of the cathedral clergy of Vercellae or Milan included young laymen. Tours is possible, but if Coelestius were born and brought up in western Britain, it is more probable that the *monasterium* whence a young man wrote home to his parents was also in Britain. In 396 Victricius of Rouen, Martin's enthusiastic disciple, had visited Britain, advocating his overriding concerns, the worship of relics, the foundation of monasteries, and the conversion of country-folk and border barbarians. His visit[2] is the most probable occasion for the foundation of Whithorn, St. Albans, and doubtless other houses that perished without record. There is no certainty, but it is quite possible that Coelestius's monastic residence was in one of these British foundations. He did not, however, stay long in his *monasterium*, wherever it was. He is hardly likely to have renounced his vows, or we should have heard of it from his enemies; but some years before 410 he was in Rome, 'in turba commorans', like Pelagius, frequenting the circle of Pammachius (Aug., *de Peccato Originali* 3), whose vows were expressed by flaunting his monastic habit among his fellow senators (Hieronymus, *Ep.* 66. 6) rather than by secluded retreat. Coelestius himself earned his living in the law courts ('illius temporis auditorialis scholasticus'), according to Mercator, like Tertullian and other Christians before him. What little is known of him argues a mind cautious and accustomed to court procedure. Augustine preserves the transcript of his examination by the African bishops at Carthage in 412

---

[1] The best evidence for the status of these coastal peoples in the fifth century is Patrick's letter to Coroticus of Altclyde 'militibus mittenda Corotici, non dico civibus meis atque civibus sanctorum Romanorum, sed civibus demoniorum'. This seems to mean that the Clydesiders, far beyond the then Roman frontier, were accepted as Roman citizens. The peoples long settled in the western Roman provinces will have enjoyed a still better title to citizenship, their leading citizens acceptable as 'nobiles' rather than 'plebeii' or 'peregrini'.

[2] See below, pp. 145-53.

(*de Peccato Originali* 2-4); it reveals a man laconic in his answers to a board that he regarded as hostile prosecutors rather than as an open-minded committee of inquiry, a man unwilling to affront or submit to an authority that insisted upon answers to questions upon which he was undecided, and unwilling to name names to their possible detriment. If these several small strands of evidence each bear what seems their natural interpretation, then Coelestius will have been a slightly older compatriot and social equal whose acquaintance the Sicilian Briton is likely to have made in Rome about 408 or 409, a man whose outlook is likely to have attracted, inspired, and guided his own.

Pelagians differed. Pelagius's own views were scarcely crystallized when he wrote the Commentaries, before controversy sharpened the issues; they are clearly and concisely set forth in the Demetrias letter, especially in chapter 3, written in the early stages of the dispute, and are illustrated by the passages selected by Augustine from the *de Libero Arbitrio*. The assertions and denials cited by Augustine in and about 415 are the statements of a man already old, anxious at all costs to avoid controversy, unwilling to engage his persuasive dialectic with the alien unilinear logic of Augustine. Coelestius, of whose authentic pronouncements much less is known, seems to have been more willing to argue on Augustine's ground, and to have developed ideas latent in Pelagius; a younger man, he travelled and organized, with a sharper understanding of the realities of ecclesiastical politics. Julianus, defending a declared heresy in the 420's, was the most energetic controversialist, most extreme in his formulations, 'in disputatione loquacissimus, in contentione calumniosissimus' (Augustine, *Operis imperfecti*, 4. 50), attacking the 'Punic Manichee' with a tongue as sharp as Hieronymus's.

Augustine concentrated his attack upon the nature of the sin of Adam, and forced his opponents to stand and fight upon the ground he chose. He thereby assailed the fundamental basis of all Pelagian philosophy, the inherent goodness of human nature. Pelagius took it for granted in his early writing, an assumption scarcely needing argument; and it is doubtful if anyone else in A.D. 400 required argument, before Augustine demonstrated the dangerous implications. Coelestius was in doubt in 412 about the answer to Augustine's questions on the transference of sin and of infant baptism, for the questions were foreign to his thinking and largely irrelevant thereto. The Sicilian Briton thought on lines independent of either; Adam's sin was disobedience, and man, free to obey or disobey the plain commandments of the Law, sinned when he disobeyed, as most men often did, and all men sometimes.

Augustine did not discuss this view; he attacks the Sicilian Briton for his singular argument on poverty and riches. It is his central thesis, the theme of his longest and most vigorous work, the *de Divitiis*, whose doctrine is repeated and summarized in all his other works except in the surviving fragment of the *de Possibilitate non peccandi* (cf. Letter 1. 4; Letter 2. 5; *de Operibus* 18. 3; *de Castitate* 17). His argument is unique in his own time, and he pushes it to a dialectical conclusion to which I know no parallel in the social thinking of Greece and Rome. But it is the emphasis and application, not the sentiment itself, which is unique. His text, Matthew xix. 16–24, is clear, and the Fathers of the second century had no doubt that the terms *Christianus* and *Dives* were incompatible; Barnabas (i. 10) warned Christians not to 'associate with men who do not earn their bread by their own toil and sweat, but live by the unrighteous exploitation of other men's labour'; Hermas (*Sim.* 2) is aware that he is an innovator on the defensive when he argues that after all the rich man, though admittedly useless in himself, supports the virtuous poor, just as the barren elm supports the fruitful vine; Irenaeus (iv. 30. 1, ii. 248 Harvey) asked 'Unde possessio?' and replied 'Ex Mammona iniquitatis' and illustrates his thesis with a curious argument that a slave, wrongfully enslaved, whose labour has much increased his master's substance, may justifiably steal a 'small part' of 'that great accumulation which his own labour has created'. The qualifications are evidence that Irenaeus was apprehensive of the dangers to which his argument led, but even in the early third century Clement of Alexandria, echoing the 'amazement' of the disciples, still found it necessary to write *Quis dives salvetur?*

Two centuries had passed since Clement wrote, and Christians had learnt to live with the realities of the society into which they were born. The counsel of Matthew xix was expressly stated to be a counsel of perfection, and few men were perfect. Hieronymus cited it when he wrote to Demetrias (*Ep.* 130. 14), using language that he would perhaps not have employed a year or two later, when the significance of the views of Pelagius and of the Sicilian Briton had become clear to him: 'Apostolici fastigii est, perfectaeque virtutis, vendere omnia et pauperibus distribuere. . . . Nobis, imo tibi diligens credita est dispensatio, quamquam in hoc, omni aetati, omnique personae, libertas arbitrii relicta sit. "Si vis" inquit "esse perfectus". Non cogo, non impero; sed propono palmam; tuum est eligere, si volueris in agone atque certamine coronari. . . . Non partem bonorum tuorum vende, sed "omnia" . . . "et da pauperibus", non divitibus, non propinquis.' Her riches have now begun to be Christ's, but, 'avia vivente vel matre, ipsarum arbitrio dispensanda sunt'.

In this advice, verses 23 and 24, concerning the rich man's difficulty in entering heaven, play no part. But they are even less prominent in Pelagius, much less important than, for example, to John Chrysostom. Pelagius draws Demetrias's attention (22) to a different text in Matthew (v. 7), 'Blessed are the merciful', and advises her to leave charity to her mother and her grandmother, 'sed quaeso hanc curam vice tua avia materque suscipiant'. She should devote her wealth to a different project, that (14) can outshine the unchristian consular glories of her masculine relatives; 'Ad consulatum eorum diversae totius orbis provinciae, ad quas domus vestrae potentia extenditur, peregrinas feras et ignota animalia transmiserunt, quae crudelis arenae solum vel suo, vel hominum, sanguine cruentarent. Ad te electae quaeque virgines mittuntur; quas tu ... offeras Deo ... non tibi, sed tecum Deo, servituras.' She has chosen to spend her fortune on a convent for girls, many, if not all, chosen from the estates of the Anicii throughout the provinces, a project that, had it matured, might have made her convent the mother house of an empire-wide order. There is no word here, or elsewhere in the letter, of giving away her property, let alone of the hindrance that riches constitute to those who seek the kingdom of God.

Nevertheless, the germ of the Sicilian Briton's concept is latent in Pelagius. Discussing baptism, the *Commentary* on 1 Corinthians xii. 13 (p. 197) reads 'Ut unum corpus efficeremur in Christo; quorum ergo spiritalia et caelestia communia sunt, hi debent terrena et carnalia communiter possidere, secundum sententiam prophetae (cf. Mal. ii. 10) "Nonne pater unus est omnium?".' The phrase is clear enough, its context somewhat less so; for it harks back to the comment on xi. 21 (p. 190) 'dominica cena omnibus debet esse communis', and the reader is given no hint as to how far beyond the sacrament the 'terrena et carnalia' reach into everyday life. Pelagius did not extend them to include the estates of the Anicii, not even in the limited sense that Hieronymus advocated; no other Pelagian is known to have developed the theme, and the Sicilian Briton shows no more than indebtedness to the passage. Yet the sentence is there, implicit in Pelagian thought, a passing observation not followed up, but filled with explosive potential if any were to pursue its logical implications. That is what the Sicilian Briton did.

The Sicilian Briton's thesis is already conceived in the first letter (4); meeting the arguments of his relative who told him to come home, he replies

When you tell me that I ought to be afraid of poverty in foreign parts, and lay it down that in any case we ought to give to others rather than receive from them, [I wonder whether you learnt] that from infidels or from Christians, who know that the poorer they are the better they are. It is not your view alone, but is common to all who excuse their avarice and disobedience....

And because it is difficult and hard for them to despise all their property for perfection's sake, as the Lord commanded, they generally make use of the quotation 'It is more blessed to give than to receive' (Acts xx. 35). But if you ask for the reference or context of this statement, that the Apostle attributes to the Lord, they will be quite unable to answer; and yet they dare to cite in defence of their pleasures a piece of evidence of whose origin and context they are ignorant. But, briefly, to show that it does not bear this interpretation, if it were better to give than to receive, [how is it that] we read elsewhere that the Lord said 'If thou wouldst be perfect, go sell all that thou hast'? The man who is bidden to sell all his property, who is not permitted to own anything, now or in the future, must of course receive from others.

Even by itself this is a startling passage, bold and fresh. The exegesis that challenges a statement of St. Paul on the grounds that he failed to give a reference to the extant gospels is not easy to parallel. It reads like the enthusiasm of a young man, rash and inexperienced in theological controversy; scarcely 'incoherent', or 'une enfilade de phrases détachées' (cf. p. 23 above).

But this is no more than the beginning of the argument. It is a little matured in the second letter. In the first, he takes it for granted that all Christians ought to be perfect, or at least aim at perfection. In the second letter (5), addressed to the 'perpetual consul', he writes

It is not lawful to be avaricious, to own too much, to vaunt earthly honours and resources ... In the Gospel the Lord said 'It is easier for a camel to enter through the eye of a needle than for a rich man to enter into the kingdom of Heaven' (Matt. xix. 24; Mark x. 25; Luke xviii. 25). Know that he who keeps these [commandments] is a great Christian, understand that he who thoroughly despises them is not one, and is vainly so called.

The commandment 'nec superflua possidere' now permits the retention of small property, and the phrase 'magnum Christianum' implies the category of less-perfect Christians.

These are personal letters, expressing a thought as it occurred to the writer at the time of writing. The long tract *de Divitiis* is a thought-out full-length presentation of the argument, whose conclusion is summarized and referred to in the later works, in the *de Operibus* (18. 3), written in or after 418, when the Pelagians already 'haeresis etiam perfunduntur infamia' (17. 2, p. 101) and 'liberum ... sermonem proferre vix tutum sit' (1. 1, p. 67), and in the *de Castitate* (17).

The tract opens with the thesis that the three deadly sins, gluttony, avarice, and lust ('tria enim sunt ... gula scilicet et avaritia et libido'), are inseparably intertwined, but that avarice is the most dangerous, for it alone is insatiable. The argument is built up with uncompromising logic, shot through with fierce moral indignation, but relieved by stern dry humour, and culminates in a causal analysis quite alien to its age. The work is so different from any other hortatory work, Pelagian or Catholic, or indeed from any other propagandist work of antiquity, that its individuality cannot be made plain without extensive quotation.

Indignation colours the whole work, but is concentrated in a number of striking passages, for example (8. 2–3):

> One man owns many large mansions adorned with costly marbles, another has not so much as a small hut to keep out the cold and heat. One man has vast territories and unlimited possessions, another has but a little stretch of turf to sit upon and call his own. ... Are these riches from God? ... If God had willed universal inequality, he would have distributed all creation unequally, would not have permitted ... equal shares ... in the sky, the earth, the elements. ... Does the rich man enjoy the blessings of fresh air more than the poor man? Does he feel the sun's heat more keenly or less? When earth receives the gift of rain, do larger drops fall upon the rich man's field than upon the poor man's? ... What God himself distributes ... is shared equally; what we own in unjust inequality is everything whose distribution was entrusted to human control. ... Is there one law for the rich, another for the poor? ... Are the rich reborn from one Baptism, the poor from another? ... If God distributes the gifts of flesh and spirit with fully equal affection towards all mankind, it begins to be clear that inequality of wealth is not to be blamed upon the graciousness of God, but upon the iniquity of men.

The cadences are as 'Ciceronian' as Pelagius's own, and the opening words of the last sentence, 'Quod si tam in carnalibus quam in spiritualibus dispensatoris Dei erga humanum genus aequalissima indulgentia invenitur', following upon the equality of baptism, are evidence enough that the Sicilian Briton knew the *Commentary on Corinthians*. But there is a world of difference between this impassioned rhetoric and the half-dozen words left buried in the *Commentary*.

He is angered not only by economic inequality, but also at social inequality, in the relations of man to man.

> When does your prosperous man remember the frailty of his condition? ... From his proud and lofty eminence, he disdains acquaintance with the fellow men who share his nature. ..., the lord of many riches, slave to sins as many. ... Listen to your rich man calling your poor man 'wretch', 'beggar', 'rabble', because he dares to open his mouth in 'our' presence, because in his rags he reproaches 'our' morality and behaviour, because he disturbs 'our' comfortable conscience by his reasoned argument and his recognition of the truth. As if the rich alone had a right to speak, as if the understanding of truth were a function of wealth, not of thought (17.2).

It sounds as though the Sicilian Briton was actually acquainted with plebeian preachers who denounced the rich as such; at all events, his justification of a Thersites is unusual in polite letters, striking at the basis of the social assumptions, not only of the pagan past, but of the society which Christianity had inherited. But when he turns to attack the excuses which the apologists of wealth bring forward, his scorn is mixed with humour. He continues with another citation of the passage 'It is easier for a camel to pass through the eye of a needle than for a rich man to enter into the kingdom of Heaven' and comments (18.1):

What need to argue about so clear a statement? except to warn the rich that ... they will not possess the glory of heaven until they find a needle big enough for a camel to go through its eye, or a camel small enough to pass through the tiny eye of a needle. But if this is quite impossible, how can the rich man achieve what has been defined as impossible? Only if he distributes his wealth rightly, makes himself a poor man, or a man with enough, and then tries to enter where the rich man cannot. 'But', you say, 'it does not mean a camel, which cannot possibly pass through a needle's eye, but a *camelus*, which is a kind of ship's hawser.' What intolerable sublety when human greed ... grasps at the names of ropes to keep its earthly wealth! ... It is a rotten argument that will do the rich no good. As if it were any easier for a huge rope to get through a needle's eye than that well-known animal the camel! You must seek further to find a fit excuse to live secure, estranged from heaven's throne. Ships are no good to you, with their huge great fittings. If you want to exercise your ingenuity you had better investigate the weaving trade, and see if you can find some kind of thread called *camelus*. Such idiocy may amuse men ... but it will carry little weight with God. But, you quote ...'Things which are impossible with men are possible with God'. Of course it is possible for Him to let the rich into heaven, and to let them bring all their property and baggage and wealth with them; and possible to let the camels in too into the bargain. If it were just a matter of possibility, no one would be shut out of heaven, for we know that nothing is impossible for God.

This is fresh and lively language for fifth-century theology. But the ideas are not so new as the way in which they are expressed. Denunciations of wealth had been made before, if in more solemn words, in the name of evangelical poverty. It is when he turns to analysis of the origin and consequence of wealth that his thought becomes unusual, though not yet unique. Irenaeus had condemned property as the work of Mammon, but few later writers had built upon his text. Quoting Psalm lxii. 10, 'Trust not in oppression, and become not vain in robbery' (*Nolite sperare in iniquitate, et rapinam nolite concupiscere*), the author asks 'Are not "oppression" and "robbery" the main origin of wealth?', and faces a distinction between the new rich, made wealthy by 'oppression and robbery' and the 'born rich', 'who appear to possess their wealth not by "oppression" but by just inheritance'. He answers:

I am disputing the origin of wealth, not merely its possession. I find it hard to believe that it came down without some injustice. ... I infer the past from the present. When I see that a given cause has a given effect now,

I am sure that the same cause had the same effect then, even though I cannot observe it myself. . . . I do not say that riches necessarily are 'oppression', but I do say that they normally derive from 'oppression' (7. 2–5).

He also emphasizes the inescapable connexion between wealth and political power, public eminence, and unchristian cruelty.

Look you now, I pray you, at the pride and arrogance of those who would be rich where we know Christ was poor, who would take on the power of a master where Christ took the form of a slave (Philippians ii. 5). . . . With that proud ambitious spirit that covets all earthly glory for itself, the rich commonly seek worldly power, and sit themselves upon that tribunal before which Christ stood and was heard. What is this, Christian? . . . You sit upon the tribunal. . . . Under your eyes the bodies of men like you in nature are beaten with [whips of] lead, broken with clubs, torn by the claws, or burnt in the flames. And your pious eyes can bear to look on, your Christian compassion to watch. . . . To watch is horrible enough; what am I to say when you give the order? . . .
Any Christian feels such disquiet that he cannot sleep till he has brought the offices of mercy to those who have been so cruelly mangled . . . on your orders. . . . Yet you, who plead you were a servant of the law . . . were a little earlier claiming to live according to the Law of Christ. What is the explanation of this great difference between men who are described by the same word, Christianity, and are bound by the sacrament of the same religion? . . . It is worth inquiring closely into the reasons that produce such wide differences between men of the same religion. . . . It is the rich, dripping with excessive wealth, whom the will to cruelty leads into acts of such savage wickedness (6. 1–2, 3; 7. 1).

The tradition that Christians ought not to accept secular magistracies was deeply rooted in the experience and thought of the Church before Constantine; it was unusual to reassert it with such force a century after the triumph of the Church. Even more unusual is the inquiry into the causal connexion between wealth and political power, evident enough in practice, but rarely enunciated in theoretical argument.

It is this persistent inquiry into rational cause and effect that distinguishes the Sicilian Briton when he analyses the structure of his own society and urges remedies to reshape it.

'Tria enim ista sunt, in quae humanum genus dividitur: divitiae, paupertas, sufficientia.'
Mankind is divided into three classes, the rich, the poor, and those who have enough. . . . Wealth, as far as my weak wits carry me, means having more than you need; poverty means not having enough; and sufficiency, which occupies the middle place in moderation between the two, means having not more than you need (5. 1).
In comparison with those who love the affluence of wealth, and are not afraid to own too much while they see that many of their brethren are in want, we must praise the man who gives of his excess to the poor, and,

as the Old Testament commands, lives on what suffices him. Even greater praise is due to him who fulfils the commands of the New Testament as well as the Old, especially this statement of Our Lord and Saviour (cf. Luke xiv. 26, xviii. 22), that he taught by precept and example, 'No man who does not renounce all that belongs to him can be my disciple' (5. 3).

The mean between extremes was a virtue dear to the ancients. That society consisted of rich and poor was a platitude, and it was evident, though not often clearly expressed, that many men lay in the middle between the two extremes. But it was quite new to unite these concepts, to classify the human race into three distinct classes, and to praise the middle class above the others. It was also a novel and revolutionary conception that the structure of society should be changed, or could be. It is a curious irony that it should be this tract, the earliest extant work, apart from Pelagius's own Commentaries, to be published by a British writer, that should first proclaim the existence of a middle class, and advocate that the ills of society be cured by everyone attaining or accepting a middle-class standard of living.

The analysis and the remedy are surprising enough. Even more remarkable is the dialectical connexion that the Sicilian Briton observes. Castigating the plea of the 'defenders of property' that they could not be charitable to the poor if they had no 'substantia mundana' to distribute, he condemns their ignorance (12. 2):

> non intelligentes, idcirco egere alios, quod alii superflua possideant. Tolle divitem et pauperem non invenies. Nemo plus quam necessarium est possideat, et quantum necessarium est omnes habebunt. Pauci enim divites pauperum causa sunt multorum.

They do not understand that the reason why the poor exist is that the rich own too much. Abolish the rich and you will have no more poor. If no one has more than he needs, then everyone will have as much as he needs. For it is the few rich who are the cause of the many poor.

Caspari (p. v) commented that the ideas of the *de Divitiis* 'hie und da an die des Socialismus (*sic*) erinnern'. That seems to me an understatement. Before and since there have been plenty of egalitarian Utopias, usually set by classical authors in the mythical Golden Age of the past, by Christian writers in the coming millenium; and there have been plenty of philosophical and popular arguments in favour of the morality of social equality and a community of goods. Often these ideas 'here and there remind us of socialism'. But the crisp argumentation that wealth and property had arisen in the past through 'oppression'; that the existence of the rich, the fact that society is divided into such 'genera', is the cause of poverty, cruelty, and violence; and that society should be wholly reshaped, now and in this present substance, by abolishing the rich and redistributing their property to the poor—is by any textbook definition socialism. Further it is socialism of a coherence and urgency that was hardly to be met again before the nineteenth century, or at earliest the end of the eighteenth.

Augustine had cause for alarm. The words 'Tolle divitem' had the ring of a rabble-rousing slogan;[1] and the extreme views of the Sicilian Briton will be at least a part of the reasons that made the government support Augustine with unusual speed and decision. Augustine called these views Coelestian, and in the ten years after 417 the heresy is as commonly denounced as 'Coelestianism' as 'Pelagianism'. They are not, however, included among the charges on which Coelestius and Pelagius were condemned at the synods of 416 to 418, and are not again attributed to either of them, and it is therefore plain that it was impossible to make a convincing case that either of them had endorsed these views. But, in the works published in support of the charges, notably in the *de Gestis Pelagii* of the summer of 417, Augustine gives them prominence, as works that at any rate stem from Coelestianism.

It was by the intervention of the secular state, not by the full authority of the Church, that Pelagianism was decisively outlawed. Pelagius had been acquitted by the bishops of the East at Jerusalem and Diospolis, and Coelestius had been accepted as a priest in Ephesus. But both were condemned by the African bishops in 416,[2] and Pope Innocent confirmed their decision a month or two before his death. But they appealed, and his successor Zosimus summoned their accusers to Rome. The accusers did not appear, and in September 417 Zosimus addressed to the African bishops a stinging rebuke for their intemperate haste in trying to impose their own condemnation on the whole of Christendom without respect to the sovereign see of Rome; he described the condemnation of accused persons in their absence, with no opportunity for defence, as a violation of the elementary principles of civil and ecclesiastical justice; and denounced Augustine's Gallic witnesses as proven trouble-makers, with a long record of factious prosecutions against

---

[1] Fifteen years later Mercator concludes the *Liber Subnotationum* by applying to Julian Sallust's condemnation of Catilina, 'Vastus animus immoderata, incredibilia, nimis alta cupiebat' (5. 2). Julian was not accused of reviving the Sicilian Briton's argument; but the portentous name of Catilina carried only one connotation in antiquity, the archetype of the educated man who roused the ignorant poor against his own class and society. That the comparison is made at all suggests the emotional attitude adopted by the orthodox towards Pelagian extremism.

[2] The texts relevant to the years of controversy are conveniently assembled in *P.L.* 45. 1679 ff., and 48. 319 ff. (Synods 319 ff., Constitutions 377 ff.). The Constitutions are printed in *P.L.* 56. 490 ff., probably the best edition, and in Mansi, iv. 444 ff.

innocent clerics, notably against Brictius of Tours, Martin's successor, and as exiles justly condemned as political traitors, employed by the usurper Constantine as civil officials, and as ecclesiastical criminals, responsible for the false imprisonment and execution of Gallic priests, subsequently rehabilitated, under Constantine. At the beginning of 418, the Africans repeated their condemnation and demanded that Zosimus endorse Innocent's approval; but they refused to remit the case to Rome, or to send accusers to confront Pelagius and Coelestius. On 21 March Zosimus replied, insisting that the case be first referred to Rome. The letter reached Africa on 29 April, and two days later the General Council of the African bishops opened; but on the intervening day, 30 April, the government had intervened to order the arrest and exile of Pelagius, Coelestius, and their adherents. Zosimus did not endorse the condemnation of the Pelagians until after the state had intervened.

It was at this stage of the controversy that the *de Gestis Pelagii* was written, after Zosimus had succeeded Innocent and refused to endorse the condemnation without investigation, before the state was induced to intervene. It was in this context, and this alone, that Augustine gave publicity to the views of the Sicilian Briton. There is little evidence to show how seriously they were taken, how wide was their influence. They were plainly very far in advance of any contemporary ideas that have been preserved, and may very well have remained no more than the ideals of a few intellectuals, without effective appeal to large numbers. But they were potential dynamite, radical enough to upset any government, and to scare away more orthodox Pelagians. Augustine's concern was not to make his main attack on this alarming variant of Pelagianism, but to show that this sort of thing arose from the loose liberal premiss of Pelagius; and in this he succeeded.

The reasons that motivated the government are set forth, in the uncouth jargon and exasperating grammar of the administration, in five documents, the Emperor's rescript of 30 April 418 to the praetorian prefect Palladius, and his consequent edict (I and II), the emperor's rescript of 9 June 419 to the bishop of Carthage (III), and the rescript to the city prefect Volusianus, with his edict (IV and V). In 418 the emperor, in Ravenna, had been told that the city of Rome was 'scissis in partes studiis', 'split into struggling factions' by the new heresy (I); next year, it is to be fought in the provinces as well as Rome, lest the heretics 'ignorantium mentes saeva persuasione perverterent' by spreading their sacrilegious doctrine 'secretis tractatibus' (III). Despite the edicts it grew daily, 'quotidianis insinuationibus maiora fieri nuntiantur', causing public disturbances, 'discordia animos commovet populorum', that must be ended before public order could regain its old security 'concordiam tenere veterem firmitatem' (IV). The heresy sapped 'catholicae legis auctoritas' (I) and the Majesty of God, 'imperiique nostri auctor' (III). The anger of the government was directed not against Pelagius, but against Coelestius, 'divinae fidei et quietis publicae turbator', who remained with friends in hiding in Rome (V); it was 'Coelestium quoque magis ac magis ex Urbe pelli mandamus', and capital penalties were threatened against the prefect's staff if they failed to find and expel him (IV), as against any who gave shelter to the criminal, 'legibus divinis humanisque reum' (V). In 418 the Vicarius of Rome 'factione eorundem multa pertulit, quae illum sanctis confessoribus sociaverunt' (Prosper, *Chron.*).

This is strong language. It is also unusual. The western government forbade the adherents of persistent, long-excommunicated heresies to meet in *conventicula*, but it did not re-enact the much fiercer legislation that Constantinople directed against heretics. It was unprecedented to arrest and exile a man whom the bishop of his own city had refused to condemn, doubly so when that city was Rome. The government describes Coelestius as a rebel, who went into hiding in Rome, propagating his beliefs by secret pamphlets distributed by an organized faction; one phrase, whose reading is uncertain (see p. 17, n. 2, above), seems to imply that his party found a particular response among young people. His doctrine appealed to the 'ignorant', disturbed public order as well as the Christian faith, and spread in the face of repression. If Augustine is right that Coelestianism embraced the Sicilian Briton's slogan 'Tolle divitem', the government's unusual agitation is understandable.

The government had cause to be nervous of ecclesiastical disputes. When Zosimus died at Christmas 418, rival parties proclaimed rival popes. A fortunate chance has preserved the official reports of the Prefect of the City on the ensuing disturbances, with the replies of the government in Ravenna; we are therefore exceptionally well informed about the details of the disturbance, wholly ignorant of what it was about. Each side accused the other of enlisting riotous plebeians, and the government ultimately endorsed the less contumacious of the two, Boniface. There is nothing whatever to show whether Pelagianism and Coelestianism played a large part, a small part, or no part at all in the struggle. Boniface proved a strong supporter of Augustine, and if he already supported him before his election then it is quite likely that the Coelestians supported his rival, of whose views nothing is known; but it is also possible that neither side attracted their support. The incident, however, even if Coelestians had no hand in it, was sufficient to harden opinion against dissident sects whose agitation might imperil the public peace of the city.

Nothing more is heard of government action against Pelagians or Coelestians; in 418 they may or may not have been as serious a threat as the government feared, but it is quite clear that the agitation was short-lived, and no evidence extends it beyond the city of Rome. The Pelagian controversy went on for another decade; the champion of the heretics, Julian of Aeclanum, in the end forfeited his see, but suffered no harsher penalty. In his argument with Augustine there is no trace of the Sicilian Briton's extreme views. They were not the main stream of Pelagian thought, and Augustine's sure instinct led him to strike at the tree rather than the branch. The chaos that followed the fall of Rome was no time for a socialist revolution, and there can never have been a serious danger that the adherents of the Sicilian Briton, or of Coelestius, would threaten the fabric of the Roman world. The philosophy of Pelagius was in the long run a deeper threat, and Augustine's relentless attack has an historical as well as a theological justification.

There have been men in every age who found the harsh discipline of Augustine repugnant. The controversy was born when Pelagius read Augustine's *Confessions* and was repelled by the words, 'Da quod iubes et iube quod vis', proclaiming 'I cannot bear it' (Augustine, *de Dono Perseverantiae*, 53). In the middle decades of the fifth century, largely under the leadership of Faustus of Riez, another Briton, the theology of Gaul settled down to a position intermediate between Pelagius and Augustine, explicitly concurring in the condemnation of Pelagius and of his formulations without accepting or honouring the contrary dogma of Augustine; Augustinianism carried so little honour among the ordinary Christians of Gaul that the Chronicler who wrote in northern Gaul in 452 could set down, against the year 418, without any sense of controversy or fear of contradiction, the bald entry 'It is in this year that Augustine is said to have invented the heresy of Predestination'. By the sixth century the controversy was out of mind and Caesarius could lean heavily upon Pelagian texts without reviving it.

The issues that Augustine and Pelagius disputed aroused heat and passion in the critical age when they were debated, but partisan zeal dwindled as that crisis receded. Thereafter Christendom agreed to condemn the views Augustine attributed to Pelagius without too close inquiry into the nature and import of his philosophy. To many moderns the Augustinian picture of Pelagius is 'ein verzerrtes Bild' (Dinkler in Pauly–Wissowa, 19. 1. 239), and Bohlin (pp. 20–21) cites a convenient summary of modern theological judgements; to Harnack Pelagianism is 'im tiefsten Grunde gottlos', to Tixeront it 'ruinait l'idée même de la religion, qui repose tout entière sur le besoin que l'homme a constamment du secours de Dieu'. It is 'rationalist and moralist', 'eine aufgeklaerte, auf der blossen Natur und Vernunft fussende Sittenlehre', a 'verworrener, moralischer Humanismus'. Godless, rationalist, moral, humanist in the received tradition, a subtle dialectic to Bohlin himself. These are judgements not so much to be disputed or endorsed as to be set in context, and to be extended. The rationalism and the humanism are not to be separated from the 'Ciceronian' diction, the verbal ease of a man educated by older standards 'utriusque linguae'. The inheritance of Pelagius was fully classical; the morality of his teachings, that 'beziehen sich lediglich auf das Gebiet der Ethik', continues into the Christian future the ethical thought of Greek and Roman philosophy, within which Christian morality had been born. To Pelagius, his own views seemed orthodox, traditional, if not conservative; it was Augustine who was the innovator, importing at once into Christianity and into classicism the residue of his Manichee fatalism. In the theocratic and autocratic heritage of the Middle East, Zoroastrianism, Mithraism, Manicheism in the last analysis presented a dualism, wherein the equally balanced forces of Good and Evil, Light and Darkness fought their personified battles, with man as the passive and impotent subject of their struggle. In the monism of the Mediterranean, evil was but the negation of good; the Deity or the philosopher set an ideal or a standard of conduct which man strove to emulate as far as in him lay. In asserting that it was the responsibility of each individual to choose between good and evil conduct, Pelagius was quite ready to concede that man stood in need of the grace or aid of God, but that was to him a secondary issue. Augustine's insistence on the overriding priority of Grace, on the futility of human effort without the Grace bestowed by sacrament, seemed to him a humiliating degradation of the inherent goodness given by God to each individual, a blasphemous insult to the mercy of God. His morality was not merely rationalist and humanist; it was individualist, steeped in the sympathies that today we should term liberal.

It is no accident that the leading ideas of Pelagius reasserted themselves in the crisis of the Reformation, a thousand years later, when his name was all but forgotten. Then again the enthusiasms of men were moved by the text of James (ii. 14), on which the Sicilian Briton had glossed 'Faith alone is not enough . . . it is of no avail without works of righteousness' (*de Operibus* 22). With full justice de Plinval (1943, p. 405) exclaimed 'Combien d'éléments inconsciemment pélagiens ont reparu dans le protestantisme anglo-saxon ou scandinave'. It is not entirely chance that these ideas found their warmest welcome, in the sixteenth century as in the fourth, in the extreme north of Europe. From the outset, Pelagianism was British. Some half a dozen of its champions, a majority of the Pelagian authors that we can identify, were British,

Pelagius himself, perhaps Coelestius, the Sicilian Briton, the author of the *de Virginitate*, unless he be the same individual, Bishop 'Fastidius', and with them Faustus of Riez, the architect of 'semi-Pelagianism'. These writers comprehend almost the whole of the known literature of the Roman British before the English invasion. Pelagianism was not only of British origin; it was there that it persisted, for Britain had ceased to be subject to the government of the Roman empire before 418, and the edicts of Honorius were no longer valid in the island. There Pelagianism never became heretical; it was absorbed into orthodox thought, so that each time that British Christianity attracted the attention of European ecclesiastics, they found it Pelagian, and took steps to counter what they assumed to be a 'revival' of the heresy. At the height of the second stage of the controversy, when Augustine was writing the *Liber Imperfectus* against Julian, Germanus of Auxerre hazarded a voyage to Britain, the home and nursery of surviving Pelagianism. His biographer claims a splendid success, but he had to repeat his visit some fifteen years later; then he obtained a signal formal success, securing the co-operation of the government of Britain, hard pressed and in desperate need of Roman help, in the deposition and deportation of his leading opponents. Hitherto the gentler views of Pelagius had been helped to prevail in Britain because Britain had been spared the acute political convulsions that destroyed the political security of the Latin provinces of the continent; in the middle of the fifth century the devastation of the Anglo-Saxons destroyed the fabric of Roman life in Britain. But Pelagian concepts had taken too deep a root to die. A century after Germanus's last visit Gildas knew and quoted Pelagian theology in total ignorance that it was considered heretical; and several of his own expressions, used naturally in perfect orthodox confidence, for example his emphasis that sacramental validity is promised only 'omni sancto sacerdoti' (*de Excidio* 109), would have raised eyebrows in Europe. After another hundred years, when Pope John heard in 640 that Pelagianism 'denuo reviviscit' among the Irish, he explained to them that the heresy had been condemned, a fact that 'latere vos non debet' (Bede, *H.E.* ii. 19). It is doubtful if the Irish understood his complaint.

The language of the Pelagians perhaps shows some trace of Britain. Contemporaries were impressed with the unusual elegance and classicism of Pelagius's style; the modern reader of the Demetrias letter will share the same impression, and will observe the firm strength of the Sicilian Briton's rhetoric. Both show an older and more disciplined Latinity than Augustine or Hieronymus, Macrobius or Symmachus. In seeking the home of old-fashioned Latinity in the late fourth century or the early fifth, we are recalled to the conclusions of Kenneth Jackson:

The spoken Latin of Britain . . . differed completely from that of the western Empire in general. . . . The sound system . . . was very archaic. . . . To the ordinary speaker of vulgar Latin from the continent, the language from which the loanwords in Brittonic were derived must have seemed stilted and pedantic, or perhaps upper class and haw-haw (*Language and History in Early Britain*, pp. 86, 107, 108).

The style of the known British writers confirms Jackson's deductions from the nature of the later Celtic speech; some at least of their writings remained in Britain to continue to shape its Latinity. A generation later St. Patrick criticized the bishops of Britain as 'Domini ignari rhetorici . . . sapientes et legis periti et potentes in sermone et in omni re' (*Confessio*, fol. 23 a 1), and in the next century Gildas, despite his eruptive anger, cites twice as many classical writers as the whole ten books of Gregory of Tours' *History*, and cites them, unlike him, at first hand.

There is thus some evidence, external and linguistic, to argue that Pelagianism was predominantly British in origin and development; and that it became a majority trend in British Christianity, never successfully branded as heretical, leaving its imprint on Christian thought in Britain until well on in the sixth century, long after the name of Pelagius or the memory that it was a distinct trend had been forgotten Pelagian ideas were still accepted at the inception of the Celtic monastic movement of the middle decade of the sixth century,[1] and this movement was fully in tune with Pelagian concepts. Its direct inspiration was the precedent of the Egyptian Fathers, perhaps reinforced by the nearer and contemporary example of Benedict of Nursia. It was the first and only European imitation of the mass migration to desert regions of Egypt, Syria, and Cappadocia; for neither Martin in Gaul nor Benedict in Italy inspired such a following, and the somewhat analogous African tendency, most vividly portrayed in the life of Fulgentius, foundered in the wars of Vandals, Byzantines, and Arabs. The Celtic monks were intense individualists, who rejected the government of tyrannical unchristian secular rulers, and with them their kept bishops and corrupt priests. They admitted no sacerdotal authority between their own will and conscience and the will of God, revealed to them in meditation, prayer, and vision. One grouping among them, termed 'meliores' by their fellows, is typified by St. David and St. Samson. Like the Sicilian Briton, they insisted on the total renunciation of worldly wealth, both private and corporate. David refused to accept gifts of land or money for his monastery from pious benefactors, and carried the concept of absolute poverty to the extreme lengths of ploughing without oxen and pulling carts by manpower. Throughout the extensive literature of the

---

[1] Cf. pp. 1–15, above.

Celtic Saints there is little awareness of a problem of original sin, of the necessity for grace; even those who are rebuked for spiritual arrogance are merely counselled to prefer personal humility.

As with the first Egyptian monks, the desire of the first Celtic hermits was not to found monastic communities, but to escape from the trammels of an evil society and live as solitaries alone with God; like the Egyptians, they found that solitary hermits attracted devoted followers, and the hermits' Llan frequently grew to a substantial settlement requiring the organization and rule of a monastery. The impetus of the movement lasted no more than half a century in its homeland about the Severn estuary, or in Brittany. But in the different society of Ireland it took enduring root. The Irish tradition, as well as the British, is emphatic and insistent that the Irish monastic movement of the sixth century was wholly inspired from Britain, owing nothing to the episcopalian church of Patrick, with whose remnants it fused much later. This Irish movement was determinedly anti-sacerdotal. It took over the British ideal of apostolic poverty, and long preserved it. Here and there are slight connexions with Pelagianism. In the extant manuscripts of Julian of Aeclanum's translation of Theodore of Mopsuestia's *Commentary on the Psalms* (cf. *P.L.* Sup. i. 1572) the hand of Columban or one of his disciples may be traced. There are echoes of the Sicilian Briton in the 'prophet' Bec McDe, who, in the words of the *Annals of Clonmacnoise*, in the year 550, 'prophesied that lords would lose their Chiefries and seignories, and that men of little estate and lands would lose their lands, because they should be thought little'. It was this Irish monastic church that in 640 seemed to Pope John to be Pelagian in its theology.

Irish monasticism was not confined to Ireland. Early in the seventh century the monks of Iona converted Northumbria, and Bede's close portraits of Aidan, Chad, and their disciples emphasize the same picture of apostolic poverty, in contrast to the prelatical dignity of Wilfred. However direct or indirect their inspiration, they practised in seventh-century Britain the precepts which the Sicilian Briton had urged 200 years earlier. Missionary monks, Irish and English, with a few British, found an enthusiastic response in Merovingian Gaul and Lombard Italy, and were primarily responsible for the conversion of the heathen Germans and much of central Europe. Everywhere they brought with them a fresh and unrestrained enthusiasm, often mingled with a total disregard for secular and ecclesiastical authority thoroughly in keeping with the independent thought of the Sicilian Briton. Popes and archbishops found it hard to reduce their undisciplined successors to obedience to recognized rules or episcopal control. The boldness of the Sicilian Briton's imagination is well matched in the speculations of the eighth-century abbot Ferghil. Promoted to the bishopric of Salzburg, where he spelt his name Virgilius, he advanced the daring theory of the Antipodes, that there exist in the universe other solar systems besides our own, and withstood the efforts of his ecclesiastical superiors to excommunicate his heresy.[1]

There is little to show whether or not these self-confident Irish individualists knew or cherished Pelagian literature. Yet it is a problem that can be investigated. An inquiry into the place and date of composition of the numerous manuscripts in which the surviving Pelagian writings are preserved might show that the monasteries of Irish foundation play a considerable part in their transmission; for these monasteries appear quite frequently in the lists of those manuscripts which have not passed into larger collections. But whether or not there is a direct connexion between these monks and Pelagian literature, their movement originated in Britain, where Pelagian ideas were still prevalent, and the whole course of their movement lies much closer to the free thinking of the Pelagians than to the disciplined hierarchical church of the Mediterranean; and it is in the northern lands where these monasteries determined Christian thought that the Protestant conceptions of the Reformation, filled with unconscious echoes of Pelagianism, took strongest root.

In the fullness of the centuries, Pelagius and the Sicilian Briton did not write in vain. In their own day their achievement was negative; at best their protest somewhat limited the unqualified acceptance of those aspects of Augustinianism that they most resented. Their positive conceptions were born out of due time. If the Sicilian Briton's advanced views looked towards the thinking of the nineteenth century, or Pelagius's own conceptions towards the sixteenth century, neither of them had much to argue that could profit the early fifth century. For the year in which Pelagius was condemned, 418, was also the year in which the Visigoths were formally settled in Aquitaine, founding the first of the German successor states which replaced the western empire of Rome. As the old *Romanitas* split into fragments, Augustine concentrated on ecclesiastical discipline and unity of organization. The old-fashioned humanism of Pelagianism, a nursery of diversity and free thought, led directly towards a multiplicity of independent regional and national churches, that European Christendom was not strong enough to support for a thousand years. Augustinian discipline, founded on the subjection of the individual to the grace transmitted through the sacraments of an

[1] The relevant texts are listed and summarized in J. F. Kenney, *Sources for the Early History of Ireland*, i, pp. 523–6.

organized unified hierarchy, made it possible to christianize and romanize the barbarians, to curb the arbitrary licence of kings and nobles, to preserve through the Middle Ages something of the legality, of the sanctity of the individual, of the culture of antiquity. Some part of the humanist and rationalist values which Pelagius strove to defend entire against Augustine were preserved. But it was precisely Augustine's victory that preserved them. It is doubtful in the extreme if they would have survived had Pelagius prevailed; his successors would have been hard put to defend his values and the world which gave them life. Europe would have risked an eclipse of Roman thought and letters as total as in Britain, Pelagius's native land, where his views prevailed strongest and longest.

DARK AGE DATES[1]

There is a shocking contrast between our knowledge of Roman Britain and of the centuries that follow. Before A.D. 410 many reliable Roman writers mention Britain, and there is a very large amount of archaeological evidence, fairly well dated. Thereafter Roman writers rarely mention Britain, and the archaeology becomes dateless. The western mints ceased to issue small change, and there is no new standard to date pottery and structures. It is possible to recognise sites and objects of the latest Roman period, roughly between about 370 and about 450, only rarely possible to argue that any of them are nearer to the one than the other date; and when Roman commercial pottery ends, pottery of all kinds is rare for centuries.

New kinds of evidence replace the old, but they are much harder to interpret. There is abundant material, for the dark ages are dark not for lack of evidence, but because of its obscurity. Little of it is contemporary, and most of it is a distant echo of events its authors did not understand. Its greatest difficulty lies in its character and purpose. Roman historical writing at least purported to tell the truth, and copyists were expected to produce an exact copy of the text they reproduced. The documents that concern the fifth and sixth centuries, tracts, biographies, genealogies, poems, laws, charter memoranda, proverbs were written to edify and exhort, and they have a large influence on the few narratives and chronicles that survive. Copyists sometimes boast that they have turned a barbaric crude original to an elegant uplifting tale, and successive versions of the same story prove that they did.[2] In Europe the standards of accurate reporting survived, even though individual performance might betray them, and from Bede onwards English historians accepted these standards. Modern historians are soaked in material of this sort, but we are not trained to handle the peculiar literature of Celtic Britain, whose standards are poetry and romance, whose purpose is to exploit the past in the service of the present. Experience in the handling of rational sources can be a misleading guide to the interpretation of material that is

[1] Reprinted from *Britain and Rome. Essays presented to Eric Birley on his Sixtieth Birthday*, edd. M. G. Jarrett & B. Dobson (Kendal, [1966]), pp. 145–85.

inherently irrational; and modern attempts to compare one source with another, to change the date or meaning of one to square it with another, often increase confusion, sometimes crediting early medieval writers with a most unlikely faculty of invention. For, wherever the evidence is clear, we are dealing with misunderstanding, distortion, adaptation; invention is confined to recognisable limits, and needs to be studied no less scrupulously than fact. An undemonstrated modern assertion that a tale is 'invented', borrowed from 'folklore' or the like, is usually neither more nor less credible than the statement it rejects.

The heart of the problem lies in dates. History without dates is a jungle of speculation; and any historian, from Bede to the present date, who wishes to understand these centuries, must first establish a basic chronology. That means deciding which sources are 'basic', taking precedence over others. There can be no doubt that, first, contemporary continental evidence is to be preferred to later British evidence, however time-honoured or widely accepted in modern tradition; for however much a man may misunderstand the events of his own day, he is writing for readers who have some knowledge of them, and cannot be as wide of the mark as a writer who describes distant centuries. Second, nothing that rests on a single native source carries much weight, however plausible; what compels belief is the same event or situation described from different angles by different sources, even though at first sight it may seem improbable to our preconceived notions.

The story begins in the early fifth century; the central fact in the experience of that generation was Alaric's capture of Rome, in A.D. 410. Though the western empire lingered two generations more, the wound was mortal, and contemporaries knew it.[3] One detail in the dissolution of the empire was the abandonment of Britain; in 410 the emperor Honorius wrote to the 'cities of Britain', evidently in reply to a request for men and money, telling them to look to their own defence,[4] thereby legalising whatever form of island government they chose to erect. The British therefore

> took up arms and bore the brunt of the attack themselves, liberating their own cities from the barbarian threat. Armorica and the rest of the Gauls followed the example of the British, freeing their own territory in the same way and establishing native governments on their own authority.[5]

The history of the 'rest of the Gauls' is not simple. Much of the south and centre passed in the next few decades to German federates, governed by their own kings and their own laws, legalised as Roman allies by formal treaty that billeted them on Roman landlords. The Armoricans established a short-lived egalitarian peasant republic, and peasant rebels elsewhere had passing success; most of the north-west obeyed the *magister militum*, commander-in-chief, increasingly independent of the government in Italy; Aegidius, the last *magister*, was styled locally 'king of the Romans', for a period also enthroned as king of the Franks, and bequeathed his kingdom to his son. A similar hereditary kingdom emerged from the western Balkan command.

The form of native government established in Britain is not recorded; but the elements from which it was composed are clearly known, and they limit the possibilities. For centuries, in Britain as in Gaul, day to day government had been regulated by the *civitates*, a dozen or more states dominated by a capital city and controlled by their own magnates, among whom a single family or individual might not infrequently overtop his fellows. In early fifth-century Gaul, the greatest magnates from each *civitas* attended a periodical *Concilium Galliarum*, and it must have been a similar *Concilium Britanniarum* that wrote to Honorius and received his reply. But that reply thrust upon the British Council an immense new responsibility, the duty and the power of making governments and unmaking them; for hitherto the states had been co-ordinated and their external affairs controlled by representatives appointed by the emperor. The *vicar* of Britain was a deputy of the *praetorian prefect* of the Gauls, and supervised the *rectores* of the five provinces of Britain. Defence was divided between the *Dux Britanniarum* at York, many of whose northern forts had grown into substantial towns, and the *Comes Litoris Saxonici*, in command of the massive coastal forts between the Wash and Southampton Water, with perhaps a field force, in billets rather than in forts, under a *Comes Britanniarum*.[6] What happened in 410 was that the imperial government declined to make new appointments to these offices or to pay their salaries. There was no 'evacuation of Roman Britain', no 'withdrawal of the legions', beyond the substantial withdrawals of the previous thirty years. What ended was the apparatus of central government; the *Concilium*

Britanniarum, hitherto without executive authority, and the then holders of the civil and military offices, were constrained to fill vacancies and to find some substitute for the authority of the emperor. The history of the next two centuries is the history of the failure of the British to replace that authority with a central government that could achieve permanent and general respect.

From the beginning there was discord and violence. The tract *de Vita Christiana*, published in or about 411, almost certainly in Britain,[7] describes a recent violent change of government.

> We see before us plenty of examples of wicked men, the sum of their sins complete, who are at this present moment being judged, and denied this present life no less than the life to come . . . Those who have freely shed the blood of others are now being forced to spill their own . . . Some lie unburied, food for the beasts and birds of the air. Others . . . have been individually torn limb from limb . . . Their judgements killed many husbands, widowed many women, orphaned many children. They made them beggars and left them bare . . . for they plundered the children of the men they killed. Now it is their wives who are widows, their sons who are orphans, begging their daily bread from others.[8]

This is an actual event, and a recent one. Plebeian violence doubtless explains the lynching of leaders of an unpopular government, but does not suggest a peasant rising on the Armorican model; for the author, approving the new government, counsels the rich to use their wealth in charitable kindness to the poor. One group of magnates had ousted another. The occasion is not explained; it may be that the party which inspired the appeal for help to Honorius was overthrown when that help did not materialise, but there may be other explanations.

The account hints faintly at the nature of the government; it was *'iudices'*, magistrates, who were overthrown, not, as in every other condemnation of a defeated government in the late empire, a *'nefandus tyrannus'*, a rival emperor. At much the same date a young Briton, writing home from Sicily to an elder wealthy relative who sat on a tribunal and inflicted capital punishment, ends with the odd greeting 'Opto te semper Deo vivere et perpetui consulatus honore gaudere'.[9] It is just possible that the council of the magnates attempted some form of aristocratic government, alternative to the appointment of an emperor. If so, they did not achieve permanent success; for one at least of the early fifth-century notables 'wore the purple',[10] a phrase that can only express the title Emperor. But the landed nobility was not the only political force; throughout the later Roman empire political struggles turn upon the antagonism between the army, resentful of rich civilians too mean to pay for their defence, and the aristocracy, fearful of an undisciplined army. In Britain, the genealogies trace the authority of the later kingdoms of the north to a common 'ancestor', Coel the Old. Among them one line ends with Eliffer (Eleuther(us)) of the Great Army and his son Peredur of York, Peredur of the Steel Arms.[11] It is not impossible that the last *Dux Britanniarum* bequeathed a kingdom to his sons, like Aegidius in Gaul.

Political history cannot be reconstructed from such fragments; but they combine to outline a situation, an age of violence and bitter division, of short-lived experiment in the face of novel need. The economy is better witnessed by archaeology; the familiar life of Roman Britain continued, its towns, villas, farms, its forts and garrisons, its manufactures, roads and distributive trades. Here and there, a chance find demonstrates its survival for some generations after the later fourth century, and there is rarely evidence of an earlier end. The evidence tells more of place than of date, for prosperity and economic vigour were uneven. The London region was in decline, but Verulamium was not [12]; the latest coins, with pewter, silver, and elegant buildings, are commonest in the Cotswolds, among the potteries of the Peterborough region, in east Kent. As throughout the empire,[13] there was an acute shortage of manpower, partially made good by the importation of half-barbarian foreigners. In Gaul, numerous settlements of *Laeti* and *Gentiles*, groups of German families, had for four generations tilled the soil of great estates and provided local defence;[14] in Britain they probably existed, and may have included numerous Saxons,[15] not to be confused with later fifth-century federates of the same nation. As elsewhere, there were many Germans in the army, though nothing suggests that they formed a majority among the officers or other ranks, in Gaul or Britain.[16] Besides individuals in regular older formations, there were some purely German units; two or three are named in inscriptions on Hadrian's Wall[17]; Ammian[18] mentions an unsuccessful Alaman kinglet, Fraomar, who took service as a tribune somewhere in Britain, in command of a substantial force of his fellow countrymen, and a Germanic officer buried near Dorchester-on-Thames[19] may have held a like command. On the west coast there was heavy Irish settlement from Cornwall at least to north Wales,[20] imperfectly obedient to the Roman government,[21] while the peoples of the northern borders south of Clyde and Forth, assimilated in speech, economy and interest to the British, were ruled by *praefecti gentium*, apparently established by Valentinian in 368.[22] A few contemporary notices date the continuance of Roman civilisation; in 429 Germanus found a flourishing *martyrium* at Verulamium, and about the same time Patrick's anxious parents urged him to stay at home in safety and accept *munera*, public office. A dozen or so years later, in the early 440s, Germanus encountered civil magistrates and well dressed prelates, and Patrick denounced the same bishops as 'learned, skilled lawyers, powerful at public speaking and all else'.[23]

Patrick's is the last voice of Roman Britain. Soon after, its civilisation was annihilated, and the sequel is told by men barbarised in speech and understanding by the violence of the explosion. Chief among them is Gildas. His date is well established; Columban, writing to Gregory the Great about 595,[24] cites him as an authority of the recent past, and makes credible the Cambrian Annals date for his death, 570. His principal work, the *de Excidio Britanniae*, attacks five western rulers, chief among them Maglocunus. The Cambrian Annals, at 547, enter 'Mortalitas magna, in qua pausat Mailcun, rex Genedotae'. There were many plagues in the sixth century, but only one 'mortalitas magna'. Procopius[25] fixes its outbreak to 541/2, its arrival at Byzantium to 543, whence it 'affected the whole Roman empire'. Gregory of Tours, then a child in the Auvergne, escaped it in November, probably of 544,[26] and recalls its ravages as far as Arles, Rheims and upper Germany. These, and the places named in the lesser later outbreaks,[27] lie in southern Gaul or on the trade routes to the upper and middle Rhine. It is not recorded in northern or western Gaul, and presumably reached Britain not across the channel, but in the ships that brought imported pottery from the Mediterranean to western Britain and Ireland.[28] It might have reached Britain one or two years before 547, but no date in the fifth and sixth centuries can hope for a much closer approximation. Procopius and Gregory confirm both this date in the Annals, and the date of Gildas' work. It was written before 547; but not long before, for Maelgwn had a long eventful life behind him, and Gildas gives a vivid description of contemporary Britain, wherein the monastic movement for which he spoke was in being, not yet triumphant. Its initial triumphs are dated[29] by a few continental records and a mass of native traditions to the three or four years before the plague; Gildas will have written about 540 or a little before.[30]

Gildas begins with a loaded and selective account of how the evils he attacks came to be. His narrative is widely familiar in an abridged version, placed by Bede at the beginning of his *Historia Ecclesiastica Gentis Anglorum*. Bede's History begins in 597, but is prefaced by a summary of British history from Julius Caesar to the end of the fifth century, leaving a century's gap before 597. This preface consists of the abridgement of Gildas, supplemented by verbatim extracts from Constantius' *Life of Germanus* and notices from continental chronicles. Bede is one of the world's great historians, widely read for twelve centuries, whereas Gildas and all other native writers are known to few but specialists; it is therefore necessary to stress that for the fifth century Bede is a secondary, not a primary source; independently of him, we possess every source that he used, and we also possess many that he did not know.[31] We must admire the masterly scholarship with which he handled difficult and limited sources; but we may not legitimately cite him as an authority for any event in fifth-century Britain, and may not ignore or undervalue the sources he was unable to consult.

Gildas wrote without written record, from the memories of old men, which included what they had heard from their fathers. The limits of his information are 'living memory', a period that in any age covers hardly more than a century. Beyond the horizon of living memory, his information is slight and misconceived. He had heard of Boudicca's revolt, of Diocletian's persecution, which he wrongly supposed to have occasioned martyrdoms in Britain, of the Arian controversy, and of Maximus' rebellion (A.D. 383-388), which he mistakenly took for the end of Roman rule. He saw the two northern walls, and explained their construction by a triad of enemy invasions, separated by two Roman expeditions, placed after Maximus, at the end of the fourth century. All this was long out of memory, and it is somewhat idle to relate the walls or the raids to actual events. Gildas' living memory begins in the early fifth century, at the point where continental record ceases, when, after the break with Rome, the British repelled their enemies. There followed a period of great prosperity 'of which no after age remembered the like'. Then came the dreadful rumour that the old enemies were come again, and then a plague. Thereafter the 'members of the council' and the 'proud tyrant' in their blind folly invited the unspeakable Saxons to defend them against Picts and Scots. The first 'three keels' (*cyulis*) were followed by larger numbers. Subsidies kept them quiet 'multo tempore', but they eventually rebelled, mastering the island and destroying its civilisation. Some of the survivors emigrated overseas, taking with them whatever written records may have existed, but those who stayed were rallied by Ambrosius Aurelianus, son of an emperor, and, after a long war of alternating victory and defeat, finally overcame the enemy at the siege of Mount Badon. Orderly government endured in the lifetime of the men who had won the war; but as they died out, it was subverted by a new generation who had known nothing of the troubles, and had experienced only 'our present security' (serenitas).

The main events, the coming of the Saxons and their rebellion, the migration, the resistance and its victory, have been accepted as fact by later historians from Bede to the present day; and rightly so, both because they are confirmed and dated by contemporary continental evidence, and because the experience of Gildas' first readers imposes its own limits. If a present day historian wrote for a public like Gildas', that had never seen a newspaper or a line of written history, he might freely abuse the distant past. If he chose to make Marlborough defeat Napoleon at Minden, he would meet no effective protest; if he confused the battles of Sedan and Verdun, only the very old would object. But if he congratulated his twentieth-century readers on their freedom from war in their own lifetime, or praised the long unbroken democratic record of modern Germany, he would not be believed. Living experience may be misinterpreted, but it may not be invented.

But, though the sequence of the main events is beyond dispute, the narrative based on living memory is dateless. Beside this undated oral record, Gildas shows knowledge of only one document, a single date, a letter addressed by unspecified 'British' to the Roman commander Aëtius 'ter consul' (between 446 and 454), asking for help against unnamed barbarian enemies. He took the enemies for Picts, and placed the letter at the very beginning of his narrative of the fifth century, after the third of his triad of raids, before the British success, before the long period of prosperity and subsequent events. He had nothing to guide him on the context of the letter, for he had no means of knowing either the date of Aëtius or the date of the events he narrated. He had to guess where he should place it; and his guess was certainly wrong. For between the letter and the Saxon rebellion he places events that fill at least a generation, the British victory and long prosperity, the rumour and the plague, the arrival of the Saxons and the 'long time' of quiescence before their rising. If all these events followed after about 450, the first Saxon rebellion would have occurred within a few years of his own lifetime, the wars of the resistance and the battle of Badon well within his adult experience.

His mistake caused abiding confusion. Bede, editing Gildas two centuries after he wrote, had not the means to correct the error, though he detected a problem. He makes plain his evidence, and the conclusions he drew from it, for he made two separate attempts to date Gildas' narrative, and reached widely different results on the two occasions. The first attempt is in the Chronicle, issued as an appendix to his *de Temporum Ratione* in 725. The Chronicle is arranged under the reigns of emperors, and under each emperor the events are set down strictly in chronological order, according to the dates given by his continental sources, which are in almost all cases readily identifiable. The events set down under 'Theodosius minor . . . annis XX et VI' (423-449, rightly 450), are

Proclamation of Valentinian	Marcellinus (425)
Vandal conquest of Africa	Isidore (*c.* 427)
Death of St. Augustine of Hippo	Possidius, etc. (430)
Palladius' mission to the Scots	Prosper (431)
Third Pictish raid on Britain	Gildas, 19
Epistola . . . ad Aëtium ter consulem	Gildas, 20
Prosperity, plague, invitation to Angli	Gildas, 20
S. Maria Maggiore dedicated	Liber Pontificalis I, 232 (432/440)
S. Stephen's relics brought from Jerusalem	Marcellinus (439)
Huns waste Thrace	Marcellinus (442)

Bede here dates the Aëtius letter to the 430s.

Under the next reign, 'Martianus et Valentinianus annis VIII' (449-456, rightly 450-457), the first event is the landing of the English, 'tribus longis navibus', to be followed by larger forces. The visit of Germanus and Lupus is misdated to 453/4 (rightly 429), and the resistance of Ambrosius, with alternating war extending to the final victory of the English, is placed in the reign of the emperor Zeno, dated between 484 and 491.

By the time he published the History in 731, Bede had acquired more information. In particular, he had secured the full text of Constantius' Life of Germanus, and learnt that there were two visits of Germanus, not one; but he still had not discovered Prosper's date for the first visit, so he transcribed Constantius out of temporal order, at the end of his fifth-century narrative, because he did not know where it fitted. He had also learnt the date of Aëtius' third consulate, 446, the 23rd year of Theodosius, reckoning from his accession as senior emperor in 423. His first dating had allowed a proper interval between the letter, at the beginning of Gildas' narrative, and the Saxon landing twenty years later. Now that the letter was dated, the interval could be no longer maintained. He refrained from shifting the whole of his dates, and made as few changes as possible. He left out most of his continental events, and jumped straight from Palladius' mission in 431 to the letter of 446, following it with two new items, Attila's wasting of Europe and the Constantinople earthquake (both from Marcellinus, 447), thereafter the prosperity, the plague and the rest of Gildas' narrative. The English landing is given a slightly looser date (450/7 instead of 450/453) and Badon is for the first time admitted, and precisely dated by the emendation of a corrupt passage in Gildas to 44 years after the English landing.

The text of the Chronicle also needed correction; but it was already published, and it was not possible to change the order of events. Our manuscripts contain a striking peculiarity; with two exceptions, no event is given a precise year date within a reign, though the order is always chronological. These two exceptions are the Palladius' mission and the Aëtius letter; after the first come the words 'anno Theodosii VIII' (431), after the second the words 'XXIII Theodosii principis anno' (446). The second of these is certainly a correction to the original text, for the letter is placed before numerous events that Bede certainly knew were much earlier than 446. The first was presumably inserted to provide a date bracket for the sequence of British events. It is quite clear that Bede had no independent authority whatsoever for his date of 449 (450); he had to do the best he could with Gildas' text, and he went wrong because Gildas' single date was misplaced, an error which he had no evidence to correct. But because Bede is the greatest of English historians, his date has passed into our received tradition, and, until quite recently, has blocked the search for further evidence.

Such evidence exists, known to us but not to Bede; and once the false light of the date 450 is put out, it is not difficult to detect. A Gallic Chronicle,[32] published in 452, observes, under the year 441/2.

> Britain, which had hitherto suffered various disasters, passed under the control of the Saxons.

Something happened which, ten years later across the Channel, seemed to be a Saxon mastery of Britain; of course, that mastery did not literally extend to the whole island, but it did extend to most of the civilised lowlands that faced Gaul. In the event, it was not to prove permanent, but in 452 that was not yet evident. In its own day, it seemed as final and decisive as the mastery of Visigoth or Burgundian; doubtless as in Gaul, German control did not mean the total immediate annihilation of every city and every regional government, but it did mean the political predominance of the Germans. In 452, the Gallic Chronicler could not foresee that the normal course of western European history was in the future to be arrested in Britain, its fulfilment delayed for over a century. Gildas, who knew that future, describes the mid-fifth century Saxon revolt that destroyed the civilisation of Roman Britain, the 'fire of righteous vengeance . . . burning almost the whole surface of the island', comparable with the Assyrian destruction of Judaea. It is the same event.

The revolt occurred 'multo tempore' after the first landing of three keels; Nennius' Kentish Chronicler supplies some detail of events between. They cannot easily be compressed into less than ten or twelve years, and the date of the first Saxon keels will be hardly later than 430, perhaps a year or two earlier. Nennius' Chronographer preserves an elaborate series of calculations that make the date 428, in the third year of Vortigern[33]; they may have some basis, but they may equally be elaborations of the round figure 40 years after Magnus Maximus, 388. In any case, it would be unwise to press any date over precisely, and these calculations add little to the date of roughly 430 indicated by the contemporary Gallic Chronicle.

The second fixed point in Gildas' narrative is the migration to Gaul. Twelve thousand British were engaged on the middle Loire by 464[34]; expelled by the Goths, they fought in a three-cornered war in Anjou with Aegidius and the Romans, in the course of which Childeric's Franks expelled Odovacer's Saxons from 'their islands', and then made a treaty with them. The new allies moved to Italy,[35] where Odovacer formally ended the western empire. But the British remained, and, about four years later, were settled 'north of the Loire',[36] under the leadership of Riothamus, owning estates and enticing their neighbours' slaves.[37] They had arrived some years before 464, for the minutes of the Council of Tours in 461 were signed by the Bishops of the five eastern sees of Lugdunensis Tertia, with the Bishops of Rouen, Chalons and Bourges and 'Mansuetus, Bishop of the British'.[38] The title is unique and arresting; the immigrants were numerous enough to warrant a Bishop, on a par with diocesan Bishops; and they were too recently arrived to have been assimilated into territorial dioceses. The migration is to be dated to 460, or a year or two before.

The third point approximately fixed is Badon. Procopius and Gregory date Gildas to about 540 at latest[39]; and Gildas wrote a long time after Badon. Those who had witnessed the wars and the final victory preserved orderly government: 'at illis decedentibus, cum successisset aetas tempestatis illius nescia et praesentis tantum serenitatis experta, ita cuncta veritatis ac iustitiae moderamina concussa ac subversa sunt.'[40] Since the wars, wherein Badon was 'almost the last' engagement, a new generation had grown up that had known nothing of the troubles, experienced only 'our present security'. It was not a generation of dissidents in their twenties, but of mature rulers; and the men who had fought in their vigour were dead. This is a contemporary statement, whose truth or falsity was apparent to the readers to whom it was addressed; its plain meaning is that the wars ended more than a generation since, something like forty years or more ago, that Badon was fought about 500, or a little before. It is to be preferred to brittle manipulations of crude figure dates.[41]

Three dates in a century are not many. But they are enough to make sense of the main outline of fifth-century history, dividing it into four main periods, the first from the break with Rome in 410 to Vortigern's enlistment of Saxons, about 430; the second from about 430 to the first Saxon revolt about 442, the third from the revolt to the migration, about 459, the fourth being the period of British resistance and counter-attack, a full generation from about 460 to about 495/500. These clearly marked periods proved a context and a measure whereby later native evidence may be assessed.

Dates make early medieval writers easier to interpret; for they give a context to several main sources, as well as to the separate items contained within them. The principal supplement to Gildas is a collection of historical documents brought together in the eighth century, known under the name of Nennius.[42] A few of these documents have been closely investigated,[43] but most have not. For the fifth century, the most important items are a coherent rational narrative of events in Kent, falling wholly within the second and third periods, between about 430 and about 460, best known as the 'Kentish Chronicle'[44]; and an elaborate series of date reckonings, best described as the 'Nennius Chronographer'.[45] A second main source comprises the Annals[46] of the English, British and Irish. Events drawn from different sources were in each case tabulated in relative order, and the absolute A.D. dates that strike the eye in modern printed editions were added very much later, often taking some particular dateable event as the starting point. The Anglo-Saxon Chronicle began from the equation of the Saxon landing with Bede's 449; and, since that date is some twenty years too late, it follows that, to recover the original form and intent of the compilers, all fifth-century entries must be set back about twenty years. The principal base of the Irish reckoning is the arrival of Patrick in 432,[47] and most of the early entries in the Cambrian Annals derive from the Irish. None of the annalistic dates receives positive external corroboration before the mid-sixth century[48]; earlier events and the dates assigned to them inspire belief only in so far as they are buttressed by other references to the same events in sources independent of the annals.

The British and English genealogies[49] trace the descent of early medieval kings back to the rulers of the fourth, fifth and sixth centuries, and beyond them to English Gods or Roman Emperors, occasionally to the family of the Virgin Mary or the pre-Roman British king (Cuno) Belin(us). What is contrived and distorted is the links in the middle, usually marriages with an heiress, often many generations amiss; the latest stages are contemporary, and the late Roman or post-Roman founders are persons at least believed to have existed independently of the genealogies; for it was the author's business to connect his patron with known heroes, not with figments of his own imagination. Many lines are confirmed from the eighth century onwards; Gildas confirms four, and there is a probable fourth-century context for three more, with one inscription and one German saga also relevant.[50] One among them, that of Wessex, is demonstrably false[51]; its marked difference from its fellows argues the antiquity of the rest, though again they have little weight by themselves. Where dates permit control, they conform to the rules of human biology that govern all pedigrees; though individuals may beget children at 20 or at 60, an average interval between generations over a long period lies between 25 and 35 years, always probable, never certain; and they are also subject to textual corruption, leaving out a generation, or inserting a place or title as an extra name.

Many of the kings in the genealogies occur in old Welsh poems,[52] whose text and date has been established comparatively recently. A few of the poems were set down quite close to the events they sing; others, including the few which concern the fifth century, may be as nearly related to the events they describe as 'Don John of Austria' to the battle of Lepanto, or may be as distant as Homer from the siege of Troy. Their historical value lies not in the date of the poem, but in its relation to evidence from quite different sources.

Few of the other written sources concern the fifth century; but there is a great deal of archaeological evidence, a little relevant to the British, the greatest bulk excavated from Anglo-Saxon pagan graves. The dating of Anglo-Saxon ornament has suffered from Bede's 449; until quite recently, specialists strove to reconcile their discoveries with this date[53]; the attempt proved impossible, and there is a tendency nowadays to recoil to the opposite extreme, pushing the pagan cemeteries in England well back into the fourth century,[54] on the basis of a typology of pottery that makes sense in Germany, but altogether lacks external control. Some historians, intolerant of the confidence with which such diverse dates are assigned to the same objects, understandably dismiss archaeological evidence as not yet usable. The detail study is forbidding, but its grammar is somewhat simpler. It rests upon two related principles. First, that an uncontrolled typology cannot pretend to date the beginnings of Germanic cemeteries in England; unless and until the dates are made watertight by firm associations, the date of federate settlement in England dates the graves. Second, the only associations that can securely date Germanic ornament are Roman. These associations are of two kinds; the character of the cemeteries, wherein men and women are buried according to their national customs with wholly Germanic ornament, unmixed with Roman, is akin to the federate cemeteries of the fifth-century Franks and Visigoths in Gaul, wholly different from the mixed Romano-German cemeteries of the fourth century, attributable either to some kind of *Gentiles,* or to German officers in the Roman army like Fraomar or the Dorchester German.[55] The first such federate settlement in the western provinces was that of the Visigoths in Aquitaine in 418; it would require weighty evidence, and a considerable revision of our understanding of the policies of later fourth-century emperors, to establish such settlement a generation earlier in Britain. The second association is that of objects. It must be stressed that in assessing the date of a grave, the brooches date the pots, not the other way round; both because some of the brooches, unlike the pots, can be dated by Roman associations, and because the nature of many of them lends itself to a simple evolution of form, in contrast to the manifold variety, conservatism, and baffling mixture of throw back and experiment that bedevils the study of the pottery on its own. The earliest brooches found in English cemeteries derive from prototypes in use at the end of the fourth century, and are sufficiently developed therefrom to imply an interval of not much under a generation.[56] Recent work upon buckles and similar small metal-work[57] presses the same general date; the types used by Germans in the Roman provinces in the late fourth century are quite different from those found in Anglo-Saxon graves. Such evidence is, however, too fragile to provide safe dates, for a brooch or buckle may be old or new when buried, early or late in its own fashion when made; but, though archaeological evidence is weak on dates, it may readily be plotted on a map, and has much to say on where the first English settlements were located.

These varied sources have much to say about the 430s, somewhat less about the 440s and 450s, very much less about the second half of the century. Their notices fill in the detail of Gildas' bare outline; but they have a very different use and value from the contemporary dates that fix that outline. Their interpretation, and often their dating, are much more open to argument, conclusions based on them much more tentative. Very few single statements can by themselves arouse more than a subjective response, of belief or disbelief. They cannot wisely be used except in combination, when a number of independent fragments say substantially the same thing, after each has been scrutinised in relation to its own origin; nor fairly considered unless the whole of the major items are surveyed. Their story begins with the invitation to the Saxons.

The Kentish Chronicle names the 'proud tyrant' Vortigern, and so do many other documents. It summarises his problems under three heads, 'In his reign he was threatened by the Picts, and by the Scots, and by a Roman attack and fear of Ambrosius'.[58] The headings are convenient. He met the Pictish threat by enlisting three shiploads of Saxons, soon heavily reinforced, under Hengest and Horsa, nicknames meaning stallion and mare. German saga[59] remembered a mercenary captain of the early or mid fifth century named Hengest, a Danish exile from Sweden, the then home of the Danes, who commanded a force of Jutes in Frisia. The Kentish Chronicle, the genealogies, and Bede locate Hengest's immediate personal followers in Kent, and Bede calls them Jutes. Archaeologically, much of the earliest material is closely paralleled in Frisia, and a number of English villages are named from Frisians. Gildas located the first settlements 'in the east of the island'; the earliest cemeteries lie about the Humber, on both sides of the Wash, in Lincolnshire and north Norfolk, and about the Thames estuary, with three cemeteries guarding the southern approaches to London, and a tail running down the Icknield Way, in north-west Suffolk, about Cambridge, Dunstable and Abingdon. There is of course no archaeological 'route' whereby the 'invaders' 'penetrated' to their new homes; they were placed where Vortigern needed them, and it is a sound military maxim that a commander's estimation of the situation may be judged from his dispositions. These dispositions clearly have nothing to do with a Pictish raid by land; but they are an intelligent answer to an invasion expected by sea along the east coast, directed towards the riches of the south and the Cotswolds, whose easiest landfall would be the area of the Wash, with the Humber and Thames as alternative possibilties. Gildas calls the Picts, as well as the Scots 'transmarini', people who come across the sea, and the earlier siting of the Yorkshire signal-stations, to the north of the prosperous Wolds, also argues that they were built against sea-borne Picts who had learnt to by-pass the northern defences and weary overland march[60]; and Gildas also asserts that it was the intention of the Picts to 'inhabit the land from end to end'. Invasion and conquest, not merely another plundering raid, was threatened. Even the dim and twisted memories of the Picts record that something was afoot at this time; the first name in their king-lists of whom anything beyond the name is stated is Drust mac Earp, who 'fought a hundred battles and reigned a hundred years'. Other notices assign him more credible and more precise dates, 414 to 449.[61]

Few of these scraps of information have any serious worth in isolation; each can be explained away, for Gildas, writing a century later, might have misunderstood, and so might the Kentish Chronicle; sagas and Pictish king-lists are at best remote and fanciful echoes of reality. Yet the cumulative weight of a dozen separate items arrests attention; the story they combine to tell is intelligible. In retrospect, Vortigern's decision was fatal. At the time, it was not so foolish. The threat of sea-borne invasion was wisely countered by enlisting the ablest seamen of the age, known to the Gauls as 'masters of the sea'.[62] The federates were first invited in numbers small enough for safety, and they did the job for which they were paid. The Picts did not conquer the lowlands; whether they were met and defeated, on land or on sea, or were deterred from their enterprise, we do not know. But they were never again a serious threat to southern Britain.

A similar array of fragmentary detail concerns the western danger. There is solid continental evidence for warfare in the west in these years; the first visit of Germanus of Auxerre, with Lupus of Troyes, is dated to 429 by his exact contemporary, Prosper, and is described half a century later by his biographer Constantius, who knew Lupus personally. Guided by Germanus, the British won a bloodless victory in mountainous country by a large river, against Picts and Saxons. This is a fact that cannot be dodged; it is not credible to pretend that Lupus' memory betrayed him in old age, or that Constantius misunderstood him. He was there, and what we have is an eye-witness account at one remove. The locality suggests itself; mountains and a big river are no nearer to the lowlands than the northern Welsh borders, where the Dee and the Severn leave the hills; and a very considerable local tradition,[63] already old by the eighth century, brings Germanus to the Vale of Llangollen on the Dee. Picts and Saxons in north Wales seem odd to us; contemporaries would probably have been less surprised, for the Saxons who followed Odovacer in Anjou and Italy[64] are no more out of place, and, if the Picts could form a 'barbarica conspiratio' with Saxons and Scots in 367,[65] they probably did so on several other occasions thereafter. There is no reason to connect the Saxons with Hengest and Horsa, and the Picts might or might not have anything to do with the shadowy 'Irish Picts' of Powys.[66]

The substance of the tradition is that Germanus, associated with Vortigern and a Cornovian chief, recovered the upland territory of the Cornovian *civitas* from a tyrant with an alien name and formed it into a separate kingdom called Powys, in Latin 'Pagenses'. Nor was this the only disturbance of the Cornovii; at some date in the first half of the fifth century[67] a number of Cornovii moved south to rule Dumnonia, where later history attached the name of the dynasty to the extreme west of the old *civitas*, Cornwall, confining the territorial name, Devon, to the eastern part. The two events may have been contemporary and complementary.

There was a similar movement of peoples further north. Cunedda, grandson of the *praefectus* instituted over the Votadini, probably by Valentinian in 368, was moved to north Wales with his 'sons',[68] where, in the next few generations, they subdued the Irish colonists. Here there is an apparent conflict of date; a dozen genealogies make Cunedda great-grandfather of Maelgwn, whose active manhood lay about 520 to 545; two generations of thirty years each from his grandfather give a date about 430, and three from his great-grandson also give 430. But a northern document in Nennius[69] gives the figure date of 146 years before Maelgwn and Ida, evidently intended for 547, which would put Cunedda a generation earlier, about 400. In such a conflict, it is sounder to value a controlled and frequently repeated genealogy to a date in Roman numerals, liable to corruption. At much the same time Vortigern settled Saxons in or near the territories vacated by Cunedda.[70]

The movements of the Votadini and the Cornovii and the separation of Powys may or may not have been contemporary, but they had a common purpose, the reduction of Irish colonists in western Britain. That involved relations with mainland Ireland. The 'High-king' received Patrick,[71] and with him the religion of Britain; therewith the long record of Irish raids on Britain abruptly ends.[72] He also married his son to a daughter of the 'king of the British', who named her child Fortchern, which is an Irish rendering of Vortigern.[73] It is likely that she was Vortigern's daughter, giving her son her father's name. These are political arrangements; in the early fifth century, among Romans and barbarians alike, a dynastic marriage often sealed a treaty.[74] Patrick claimed 'friends in Gaul', and was probably a pupil of Germanus; his appointment must have had the backing of at least some Gallic bishops and the blessing of the Pope. His own words seem to mean that it was approved by the bishops of Britain, though he denies their ecclesiastical jurisdiction,[75] and was apparently later exempted therefrom by Leo the Great[76]; and such an appointment could not have been made without the active interest of the government of Britain. The neutralisation of Ireland deprived the colonists of effective support from the homeland; and it was achieved by virtue of superior force. About 434 the Annals note 'the first booty of the Saxons[77] from Ireland'; whether or no Vortigern and his federates were involved, Vortigern was plainly in a position to loose his seaborne federates upon an Ireland that interfered in Britain.

Again, a multitude of dubious fragments combine to depict a situation, an answer to the Irish problem as effective as the ending of the Pictish threat. In the middle of the 430s, Vortigern had succeeded where Rome had failed; the frontiers and coasts were safer than they had been for two hundred years, and the long standing threat from the foreign barbarian was over, not to be renewed till the coming of the Northmen three hundred and fifty years later. But the hard-won security was to be destroyed by enemies within. The

Picts and Scots, two of three dangers listed by the Kentish Chronicle, had been contained; the third, 'fear of a Roman attack and of Ambrosius', concerned internal discord. Again, a few twisted uncomprehending notices bear upon events.

From Gildas onward, later writers describe Vortigern as 'tyrannus' or 'rex' of all (Roman) Britain, acting with his 'seniores' or 'concilium', plainly the *Concilium Britanniarum* of the notables. His authority, ranging from the Wall to Wales and Cornwall, was imperial, whether or not he used the title Emperor[78]; and must have commanded at least the acquiescence of the bulk of the notables. But it was a precarious authority resting on continuing consent; it lacked the four hundred years of traditional acceptance and the obedience of distant provinces that strengthened the emperors of Rome, but it inherited their historical experience, that an emperor could be unseated by those who had created him, unless he commanded a sufficient military force bound to him by personal loyalty.

The genealogists[79] make Vortigern a 'son' of Vitali(nu)s of Gloucester, himself a magnate of one of the greater civitates. The traditional outlook of Roman nobles, provincial or Italian, did not welcome the permanent sovereignty of one among their peers; and in their historical experience, only a real or fictitious dynastic origin protected an emperor against rivals after the emergency that enthroned him receded, and new problems divided his original supporters. The Kentish Chronicle[80] states the issues that divided Vortigern from his council. 'The British' resolved to discontinue payments to the federates as their numbers increased, and dismissed them, now that their job was done. Vortigern's response was to enlist many more federates to 'fight against his enemies', to marry the daughter of their commander, and to cede Canterbury and east Kent over the head of its then ruler.[81] Similar conflicts had divided the governments of both the eastern and western empires in the previous generation, and underlain the fall of Gainas and of Stilicho; for over and beyond the immediate causes of dispute, governments relied upon barbarians, but magnates detested their manners and their expense, and patriotically deplored dependence on the foreigner, though their patriotism did not provide the men and money to maintain an adequate native army.

It was a situation that threatened civil war, and a solitary unconfirmed notice in the Nennius Chronographer asserts that it did; 'there are 12 years from the (beginning of the) reign of Vortigern (425) to the quarrel of Guitolin and Ambrosius, that is Guoloppum, the battle of Guoloph'. Identities are, as always, a matter of probability. The odds are against the prominence of two people called Vitalinus in the same generation, and Guitolin is probably Vortigern's Gloucester associate. Ambrosius might be identical with the hero who headed a resistance a quarter of a century later, but the interval of time makes it more likely that he was the hero's unnamed father, who 'wore the purple'. An emperor who raised an army against Vortigern's adherent cannot but have sought aid, with or without success, from Roman Gaul, threatening a 'Roman attack'.

Whoever won the battle of Wallop, the ultimate gainer was the Saxon. The date assigned is just before the revolt that confounded both parties. A paragraph of Gildas[82] dramatically generalises the destruction of the cities and civilisation of Roman Britain, some of whose survivors emigrated, after which the 'raiders' (*praedones*) returned 'home', presumably to the settlements beside the early cemeteries. As far as Gildas knew, they raided and destroyed but did not yet extend their homes. But his 'tempore . . . interveniente aliquanto' covers a period of some fifteen years at least, roughly 442 to 457, and the severity of the destruction varied, leaving some damaged *civitates* unoccupied. Other evidence agrees. Unburied bodies on a mosaic floor at Caistor-by-Norwich mean the end of Roman life; the date is uncertain, the occasion probable. Next year's seed cabbage abandoned at Great Casterton, numerous coin hoards, and many other small signs at various places argue a panic flight with no return, at some time about the second quarter of the century. But at Canterbury, already ceded to the federates, Roman and Saxon lived side by side with no sign of violence, and at Verulamium a corn-drying oven built within the walls implies survival in a time of insecurity, and is followed by more substantial building before the end of the city. Only a minority of excavated buildings show evidence of physical destruction; most were abandoned and rotted by the weather. For what was destroyed was the sophisticated economy upon which town and villa rested; in most parts of Britain, the highly organised commercial pottery industry ends sharply and suddenly, without a gradual decline or admixture of poorer local vessels; and the indestructible products of the potter serve as index to the perishable products of other crafts. The state of lowland Britain in the 440s and 450s will have had some similarity with the decline of Roman Noricum[83] in the same age, where for several decades the cities of the Danube survived in a countryside already dominated by barbarians, each cultivating the lands immediately outside the walls, concentrating their crops, their tools and their cattle within the walls in emergency, until they were abandoned one by one over a considerable period of time.

Little enough can be made of the fighting. A muddled notice in the genealogy of Deira records that Soermil, about the middle of the fifth century, 'first separated Deira from Bernicia'; 'separation' from the authority of the northern British could mean revolt, but a revolt that was not permanently successful. The two large cremation cemeteries outside York seem to end within the fifth century, earlier than those of the Wolds, while Anglo-Saxon burials at a number of northern forts nowhere suggest a community comparable with those of the south, and may be later in the century. There is no record of fighting in the midlands, but the cemeteries in and about Leicestershire have not yet produced objects as early as the earliest burial grounds, and may have been established during the fifth-century wars. Norfolk and East Kent seem to have passed wholly to federate rule, but about 445 in one area, perhaps the *civitas* of the Belgae of Hampshire and Wiltshire, Germanus encountered (A)elafius 'quidam regionis illius primus' attended by 'provincia tota', and prosperous bishops.[84] Detail comes only from Kent, where the Kentish and Anglo-Saxon Chronicles record the same battles, with different names, in a different order, and from a different standpoint.

Nennius 44	*Anglo-Saxon Chronicle*
I. Battle of Derguentid (Darent). No claim of victory.	Battle of Crayford (two miles from Dartford and from the confluence of Cray and Dart). British defeat, flight to London. (457 = *c*. 437.)
II. Battle of Episford (or Rithergabail, 'Horseford'). Death of Hors and of Vortigern's son Categirn. No claim of victory.	Battle of Aylesford, near Maidstone. Death of Horsa. (455 = *c*. 435.) No claim of victory.

III. Battle 'iuxta lapidem tituli, qui est super ripam Gallici maris', a 'portus'. British victory; expulsion of the enemy from Kent.	Battle of Wippedesfleot (Wipped's estuary, creek, inlet). Death of twelve Welsh chiefs and of the *thane* Wipped. (465 = c. 445.) No claim of victory.

There were doubtless many stone inscriptions in Roman Kent; only one is known, impressive enough to name a port, the pedestal of the great monument at Richborough. Though the monument may well have vanished long before the fifth century, parts of the inscription remained for twentieth-century excavators to unearth.[85] The names and form of entry make the two accounts independent of each other, their common origin fact. They record a strategic victory of the British, the repulse of a Jutish attempt to break out of Kent and join forces with the east Angles. But London evidently held them apart. The dates, tested by the Gallic Chronicle seem five or six years too early; which is not far out for so distant a record.

The British victory was not final. The Kentish Chronicle makes Vortigern recall his federates, presumably against internal enemies, while the English claim another victory in 473 = c. 453. The Kentish Chronicle sets down a vivid story. Both sides agreed to a treaty, presumably accepting a fixed frontier. Vortigern came to ratify it with 'three hundred elders', presumably the magnates of the Council of Britain; and Hengest treacherously assassinated all but Vortigern. It is a familiar and simple tale, more easily paralleled in history than in legend and folklore. It was thus that Tissaphernes had entrapped twenty-five commanders of Cyrus' Greek mercenaries, in the vain hope of leaving them leaderless; and thus more recently that Count Lupicinus had tried to assassinate the Gothic 'elders' before Adrianople. Neither Lupicinus nor Hengest needed to have read their Xenophon to prompt so elementary a ruse. Hengest differed only in that he succeeded. The discredited Vortigern signed away Essex and Sussex, and 'wandered from place to place', hated by all, till 'his heart broke and he died without honour'.[86] The cession of Essex is not confirmed, but the Anglo-Saxon Chronicle dates the settlement of east, not west, Sussex, to 477 = 457, and the cemeteries, confined to east Sussex, suggest a beginning in the mid rather than early fifth century,[87] with a large Kentish element among the first settlers; a notice in the Anglo-Saxon Chronicle may indicate a definite agreed frontier.[88]

These events describe the destruction of the organised central government of Britain in the late 450s, immediately before the attested migration to Gaul. They provide a credible occasion. But throughout this third period, *c.* 422 to *c.* 460, the sources are no longer a mass of separate detail, but two documents only, the Kentish and Anglo-Saxon Chronicles, supported only by their independent agreement, and by a faint corroboration from archaeology. In the ensuing fourth period, the sources for events in Britain are even slighter. But, after the cession of Sussex, the war was no longer confined to Britain, and its extension to Europe is reported by contemporaries and echoed in later tradition. For it was only in the decades after 460 that Gaul remembered a Saxon threat; to which the Saxon possession of good harbours on the south coast of Britain will have contributed. Gregory of Tours knew Saxons in Anjou, based on islands in the Loire,[89] by 464, and others, established then or later, at Bayeux, and perhaps elsewhere.[90] The continental British placed the 'devastation of the Frisians' immediately before the arrival of 'Riathan' (also called 'John Regula' and 'John Reith'), who sounds very like Sidonius' Riothamus, and made Gradlon of Quimper defeat 'the keels of five chiefs' in 'many battles' on the Loire.[91] By 478 Sidonius recognised the Saxons as 'masters of the sea,'[92] terrorising the Biscay coast,[93] and it is to 474 that the Irish Annals date the 'second Saxon booty from Ireland'. No source says whence these Saxons sailed; but English harbours, probably from Thames to Solent,[94] may well have served their fellow countrymen from Germany as well as colonists, and it is more than coincidence that their raids are no more recorded after the British recovered their shores and Clovis the Frank mastered the continental coasts from the Elbe to Contentin.[95]

The second phase of the wars began with Ambrosius; it ended with Arthur, the most elusive name in British history. There is just enough evidence to show that Arthur existed, the earliest of it dating from about a century later; and to show something of the different attitudes that later centuries took towards him.[96] Only one engagement of Arthur's wars is recorded, again separately in a British and an English version, both of them set down, in their present form, several centuries later. Most of the Welsh battle poems deal with the northern wars of the late sixth century; one only concerns the south and the fifth century, the Lament for Geraint.[97]

Before Geraint,	the enemy's scourge
I saw white horses	tensed, red
After the war-cry	bitter the grave . . .

In Llongborth	I saw the clash of swords
Men in terror,	bloody heads,
Before Geraint the Great,	his father's son.

In Llongborth	I saw spurs
And men	who did not flinch from spears
Who drank their wine	from glass that glinted . . .

In Llongborth	I saw Arthur,
Heroes	who cut with steel,
The Emperor	ruler of our labour.

In Llongborth	Geraint was slain
Heroes	of the land of Dyfnaint
And before they were slain	they slew.

Under the thigh of Geraint	swift chargers
Long their legs	wheat their fodder
Red, swooping	like milk-white eagles . . .

When Geraint was born	Heaven's gate stood open
Christ granted	all our prayer
Lovely to behold	the glory of Britain.

Llongborth means 'port of the warships'; a naval station where a prince of Dumnonia fell is probably the westernmost Saxon shore fort, Portchester, at the head of Portsmouth harbour. The date lies late in the wars when Arthur had replaced Ambrose, somewhere about the years 470/490. A prosaic entry in the Anglo-Saxon Chronicle, dated to 501 = c. 480, reads

> In this year Port and his two sons, Bieda and Maegla, came to Britain at a place which is called Portsmouth, and slew a young Welshman, a very noble man.

It would be fatuous to suppose that the British poet was inspired by the English Chronicle, or that the Chronicler read the foreign poet. Two independent traditions tell the same tale, a battle on Portsmouth harbour where the principal casualty was a British leader. Their common origin is an event, not an invention.

The battle is a single incident, but it was part of a situation.

Bieda is a Saxon name, Maegla British.[98] It is not usual in Europe to find all the Romans on one side, all the Germans on the other, and such simple divisions had not been found in Vortigern's time in Britain. The distorted tradition of Wessex echoes this inter-racial alignment. The later kings claim descent from Cerdic; but he had a British name, and, alone among the founders of Saxon dynasties, he is given ancestors and descendants who were consciously invented.[99] He lived in changeful confusing times, and recalls his older contemporary Aegidius, *magister militum* of Gaul, who was for a time king of the Franks.[100] It is probable that he was master of the *civitas* of the Belgae of Winchester,[101] at war with Ambrose and Arthur, employing federates from Kent and Sussex,[102] Cynric, Stuf, Crioda and Bieda, whom later ages made into relatives.[103] The Anglo-Saxon Chronicle dates their coming to 494/5, the mid 470s. They will have added Solent and Spithead to the Saxon waters.

At Llongborth, the British used spurs and swords against spears; later, the men of the Gododdin rode to Catraeth, Cyndylan's men wore plumes and owned forty horses, and throughout the poems, men fight on horseback with little sign of infantry. Procopius[104] and archaeology agree that the English were as yet ignorant of cavalry.[105] The picture dimly outlined of the British-Saxon wars is of cavalry bands[106] engaged against footfolk; the peculiar circumstances recall the exploit of Ecdicius at Clermont-Ferrand in 474, when eighteen determined horsemen routed a thousand startled Goths.[107] The mobility of cavalry, free of slow moving infantry, gave the initiative, the ability to find the enemy unawares, to charge without warning and escape when worsted, to limit the enemy's forays by threatening homes left unprotected. But unaccompanied cavalry is vulnerable when it is dismounted, at night or between campaigns; the protection of horses may well explain the frequent post-Roman reoccupation of ancient hill-forts.[108]

The last great battle was Badon. British tradition made Arthur the victor, and the English remembered his enemies. Of the three southern kings, Cerdic of Wessex is said to have died in 516 = c. 496, Aesc of Kent, perhaps identical with Osca Bigknife, who 'fought with Arthur at the time of Badon',[109] in 512 = c. 492, while the eldest among them, Aelle of Sussex, was known as the first 'Bretwalda',[110] overking. It is very unlikely that he fought and conquered his English neighbours, quite possible that he commanded their joint forces at Badon.[111]

After Badon, evidence gradually becomes more plentiful, and dates become easier. The Peace of Badon lasted two full generations; for fifty years the Anglo-Saxon Chronicle has no entries save repetitions of fifth-century events and a couple of eclipses, while the British know security and remember no wars against the English. Their interest concentrates on the monastic reformers,[112] hermits who rejected their society as thoroughly as their Egyptian exemplars two centuries earlier, and founded new settlements in large numbers in Britain, Ireland and Brittany. Many scores of separate accounts place the first flush of their success in the few years immediately before the great plague. After the plague, their dates are attested in Europe; many lives denounce the tyrant Cunomorus, also called Marcus, 'rex transmarinus' in Brittany, whose name may still be read on his son's tombstone near Fowey.[113] Gregory of Tours dates his death to December 560, and the Councils of the Church record the presence of two of the British monastic Bishops, Samson and Kentigern in 547 and *c.* 557.[114] Thereafter, native dates become reliable; Gregory of Tours[115] notes the marriage of the daughter of Charibert (561-567) to the king (Ethelbert) of Kent, thus confirming the dating of the Anglo-Saxon Chronicle, while the careers of Columcille, and then Columban and many later saints abroad confirm the Irish and British annals. From the end of the century, Bede's narrative gives a yardstick to other sources.

The second Saxon revolt began, slowly and locally, about 550, gathering momentum until between 570 and 600 it conquered permanently most of what is now England. The first half of the century is harder to comprehend. Gildas is a contemporary witness, chief authority for the shape of the post-war world fashioned by the victors of Badon. He regretted the 'lugubrum divortium barbarorum'[116] that made some of the holy places inaccessible. The words imply frontiers as recognisable as the later Danelaw, and one Irish saint experienced their reality; Columba Terryglass, who died in the plague of the 540s, passed on his way home from the continent through 'that part of Britain which the Saxons rule', where the dead were cremated,[117] perhaps Norfolk or Lincolnshire. Anglo-Saxon burials clearly of the early sixth century are confined to half a dozen areas (East Anglia, East Kent, East

Sussex, the East Riding, south of London, parts of Lincolnshire and Leicestershire, the Dunstable, Aylesbury and middle Thames regions) separated from each other by territory where burials of this date have not yet been recognised[118]; and these areas show less sign of intercourse with one another than in earlier or later generations. Grave goods offer little comment on the political allegiance of their owners, and it is likely that the status of these communities varied. The Norfolk dykes[119] suggest independence in East Anglia, as does the Frankish influx in Kent.[120] On the other hand, a British power still needed to be beaten in the south-east midlands in 571, and the apparent end of burials at York[121] suggests British authority in the north. Some at least were 'foederati' in Gildas' time,[122] and some of the 'foederati' may have directly served British rulers. All observed their frontiers, tacitly acknowledging a superior British power. They expanded in Europe, not England.[123]

Among the British, greater *civitates* seem to have swallowed up their smaller neighbours. In the lower Severn lands, the Silures of Monmouth and Glamorgan disappear from record, and the earliest post-Roman memories of their territory are of an eponymous ruler 'Gliuis' and a territory named 'Glevissicg', linguistically not Glevum, but still a puzzle. The Dobunni also disappear, and there is some sign of Cornovian rule in their territories in the middle Wye. To the south, the Durotriges and Belgae disappear, and Dumnonia alone survives. The massive linear earthwork known as the Wansdyke,[124] with its disconnected eastward extensions as far as the neighbourhood of Silchester, encloses the territory of all three *civitates*; the Cornovian rulers of Dumnonia, Geraint who fell at Llongborth and his successor Cato, appear as the principal associates of Arthur in war and peace, and may well have been rewarded with the kingdom of Cerdic. Faint memories locate Calchvynydd, land of the limestone hills, between Trent and Thames, including Dunstable and (Nort)-Hampton, perhaps the power that fought the English in 571, while one dubious late notice names the territory between Dumnonia and Kent Caledin (from Calleva?).[125] Gildas, the genealogies, the poems and saints' lives describe the political geography of the highlands more plainly.

The English 'brought over kings from Germany to rule over them',[126] and their cemeteries show an increasing differentiation between rich and poor throughout the sixth century, culminating in chieftain's barrows towards the end of the century, and the great royal tombs early in the seventh century. The institutions of the British are harder to determine. Nennius calls Arthur 'dux bellorum', and Welsh poets call him 'Emperor', a 'Briton of the nobility of Rome'.[127] The seventh century north remembered a great warrior of the recent past,[128] and the biographers of highland saints in Scotland, Wales and Cornwall knew him as a lecherous foreign tyrant, violently asserting his authority from beyond their borders, a 'great king of all Britain'.[129] The Cambrian Annals date his death at Camlann twenty years after Badon. These distant broken memories indicate a sovereign of the lowlands, whose most probable title was Emperor. A curious phrase in Gildas concurs; apologising for his impertinence in speaking out, he admits 'Habet Britannia rectores, habet speculatores', but their burden is too heavy for them.[130] The words have a precise technical meaning; *rector* means Roman provincial governor, except when applied to the deity, in contrast to military *duces*, and so Gildas uses it elsewhere,[131] and *speculator* is the executive officer of the rector, 'policeman'.[132] At first sight, it appears absurd that provincial governors should persist in sixth-century Britain; yet the absurdity lies more in the preconceptions of the twentieth century than in the thinking of the sixth. A government that had fought to preserve and restore Roman Britain could hardly avoid attempting to revive its institutions; emperor was the natural title for the head of the government, prefect, vicar and *rector* for its civilian officials, *magister militum* and *duces* for its military officers. 'Duces patriae' is the official title that Gildas accords to those he abuses as 'tyranni' or 'reges'.

It was a restoration that could not endure. Two generations of war had wasted the lowlands, and altogether snapped the relationships that held society together; scraps of evidence demonstrate the survival of an impoverished British peasantry in the Fenland and Hertfordshire,[133] and their like were doubtless to be found in most of the lowlands.[134] But no power could induce poor subsistence farmers to resume the rents their grandfathers had paid to landlords who fled half a century before; and even in the west, far from the battle zone, where rents survived,[135] landowners had neither the income nor incentive to maintain or repair their country houses or their towns. The economy of Roman Britain was gone beyond recovery. It is hard to see that any government could do more than extract supplies in kind for the maintenance of its officers and its armed forces.

The essence of Gildas' complaint is that civilian *rectores* were unable to control military *duces* and their licentious *commilitiones,* who in his day had usurped the function and perhaps the title of civilian 'kings'; and the distant sources of the hagiographers consistently mirror the same antagonism of civilian landowner and peasant towards the arrogant armed princes. It was one of the factors that impelled the rich to grant land to hermits, and to join in their migrations. For the warbands had not demobilised with victory; with no foreigner to fight, they fought each other; their children were the *commilitiones* of Gildas' *duces,* their grandchildren the followers of the chieftains honoured by the Welsh poets. The poems give a melancholy picture of their decline, deeply moving in its awareness of inevitable tragedy and irrevocable failure. Hard-drinking warriors, living by the score or hundred in ancient hill-forts, demanded wheat for their horses, barley for their beer and much else beside from a countryside to which they brought nothing but the destruction of mutual raids. 'Oed gnodach y guaet ar wyneb (y) gwellt Noc eredic brynar' sang one poet,[136] 'Commoner was the blood upon the grass Than the furrow of the plough'. By the middle of the sixth century they were a more present burden to their countrymen than the distant Saxon. When, after the plague, the English were emboldened to risk a second revolt, the war-bands were doomed; for a single defeat meant the end of a force that could no longer coerce its peasantry into replacing its horses or recruiting new warriors, whereas the English were a people in arms, well able to replace the fallen.

The history of the fifth and sixth centuries must needs handle two unequal themes; the bare outline, secured by a minimum of fixed dates, derived from sources akin to those which inform us of Roman and of medieval history; and the much more doubtful relationship of the mass of ill understood garbled information supplied by medieval writers to this outline. The single gospel that is here preached is that the two be not muddled; it is legitimate to dispute the meaning of medieval writers; it is not legitimate to argue from interpretations of them for or against the basic chronological pattern determined by contemporary and continental sources.

The study of these centuries is a study of a society wholly different from that of Europe; there the Germans settled in Roman territory relatively peacefully, with little resistance, fusing with the Roman population, producing the society we call feudalism and maintaining a continuity of institutions. One result of this fusion was to end the native speech, and with it the folk memories, of the Celtic peoples of Europe. In Britain a bitter war forbade such fusion, and ended with half the island in the power of Germans, almost entirely free of native Roman influence, the other half a rundown limb of the Roman empire, almost uninfluenced by German custom. The comparison provides a laboratory control on those ideas, laws, social and political patterns which may be ascribed to the 'Germans', and those which derive from the economy, whatever its past. In Britain, institutions did not continue; but there is continuity of peasant speech and culture, so that even today in western Britain, as nowhere else in Europe, the language is substantially that which was spoken in Roman and pre-Roman times; and with the language survives a significant trace of its prehistoric and Roman past.

In their own day, the tragedy of the British was that victory was won at the cost of all that the victors had taken arms to defend. The dim outline of Arthur is of a Roman gentleman, the last Roman emperor, and at the same time the first medieval king. The earliest traditions remember a ruler who commanded the obedience of the whole of what had been Roman Britain; but who left no successor, and not even the possibility of a successor. The epitaph on his success and failure, and on the two centuries that he bridges, is best expressed by the wisest and kindliest of Norman historians, William of Malmesbury:

> This is that Arthur of whom modern Welsh fancy raves. Yet he plainly deserves to be remembered in genuine history, rather than in the oblivion of silly fairy tales; for he long preserved his dying country.[137]

FOOTNOTES

[2] Cf. e.g. Jocelyn of Furness, *praefatio in vitam Kentegerni*. 'Quaesivi . . . vitam si inveniretur . . . stilo cultiori . . . quam vestra frequentat ecclesia; quia illam . . . tincta per totum decolorat unculta oratio . . . abhorret . . . quiddam . . . catholicae fidei adversum . . . Codiculum autem alium, stilo Scottico dictatum, reperi, per totum soloecismis scatentem . . . Quo circa sedit animo ex utroque libello materiam collectam redintegrando sarcire; et iuxta modulum meum, et preceptum vestrum, barbarice exarata Romano sale condire. Absurdum arbitror thesaurum tam preciosum tam vilibus obvolvi semicinciis . . . Adhibui etiam operam ex veteri vase in novum vivificum liquorem ita transfundere, ut simplicioribus sit appetibile, mediocribus non sit inutile, sensu locupletioribus non sit contemptibile, pro vasis mediocritate haurire.'
This is typical of hagiographers. Our business is to keep our wits from being fuddled by the edifying liquor, and to try to reconstruct the typological evolution of the vases.

[3] See above, pp. 17–51. Cf. especially a young Briton, writing home from Sicily about 411 (Migne, *PL Sup*. I, 1690=C. Caspari, *Briefe, Abhandlungen*, p. 7): 'Dices mihi illam vulgi sententiam "Ergo totus mundus periit" . . . . quid mirum, si, quod iam factus est, fiat? Recordare, temporibus Noe totum periisse mundum, et nonnisi (paucissimos) iustos salvari? Et si idem Deus nunc, qui et tunc, cur, quod iam experimento probavimus, non credamus?' (*Ep*. 1, 1 *ad fin*.). Within months of Alaric's sack of Rome, he is virtually saying 'The Roman Empire is over; welcome to the post-Roman world.'

[4] Zosimus 6, 10.
[5] Zosimus 6, 5.
[6] *Notitia Dignitatum*, most recently discussed by A. H. M. Jones, *The Later Roman Empire*, vol. 3, 347-80.
[7] Migne, *PL* 40, 1031=50, 383; cf. above, pp. 23–6.
[8] Ch. 3.
[9] Sicilian Briton, *Ep*. 2, 7=Migne, *PL Sup*. I, 1380=Caspari, p. 21.
[10] purpura indutis, Gildas, *de Excidio* 15.
[11] Eliffer (Eleuther) and Peredur; Bonedd Gwyr y Gogled 5; Harleian MS. 3859, 12. Peredur arueu dur, *Canu Aneirin* 359; Peredur (mab) Evrawc, Mabinogion, Peredur; cf. also *Annales Cambriae* 573, 580. Peredur becomes Perceval in legend.
[12] Proportionately, much more of the first two centuries A.D., much less of the fourth century, is found in London and the London region than in most Romano-British towns and their hinterlands. Recent excavations have emphasized the scale and long duration of prosperity in the central shopping area and public amenities of Verulamium, cf. *Ant. J*. 36-41 (1955-60).
[13] Cf. now A. H. M. Jones, *The Later Roman Empire* 812 ff.; 1040 ff.
[14] Cf. Eumenius, *Panegyrici Veteres* 8, 21, 1; cf. 6, 6, 2.
[15] J. N. L. Myres (*Dark Age Britain* 16-39) established the existence of 'Romano-Saxon' pottery, made on the wheel in Roman commercial kilns but imitating the forms of decoration of the handmade vessels in use among the barbarian Saxons of north-western Germany. It has been identified on some fifteen sites in East Anglia and north Kent, including four of the eleven Saxon Shore forts, and on nine or ten inland sites, and dates from the end of the third century to the end of the fourth. Its existence is not universally accepted; S. S. Frere (*Med. Arch*. VI-VII (1962-3) 351-2) thinks it 'quite likely that such things will turn out to have a respectable native pedigree', and suggests that the decoration was originally Roman, later copied by the Saxons. Since the pottery which uses this decoration has a long ancestry in Germany, it will not be easy to endorse this view until the alleged British ancestors have been properly published.
It is, however, not possible to accept the hypotheses about its users advanced by Myres (p. 37) and adopted by D. A. White, *Litus Saxonicum* (Madison, 1961), and others, that the Saxon Shore means a shore inhabited by Saxons, either as late third-century invaders, as recruits serving in the garrisons or supplementing them as 'federates', or that imitation is explained by 'trade'. Five-sixths of the find-spots are not Saxon Shore forts, and two-thirds of the Saxon Short forts have not yet produced this pottery; and 'federates' are a phenomenon of the fifth century, not the fourth. 'Trading contacts' might be tenable if there was

evidence of the export of objects in either direction; but the commercial Roman vessels are not found in Germany, nor the handmade Saxon pots in Roman Britain; neither are the brooches or other marketable metal wares found overseas.

The facts are fortunately clear; the pottery was made by commercial kilns whose aim was to sell it; and it caters for the taste of German Saxons, who must therefore have had money to buy it. It is found on Roman sites, not found in pagan Saxon cemeteries. In Europe the purchasers of such wares would create no problem. The *praepositurae* of the *magister militum praesentalis* include the *praefecti* of a dozen groups of *laeti*, mostly drawn from German peoples of the lower Rhineland, in Gaul; and of twenty-one groups of *Sarmatae gentiles*, fifteen in Italy, six in Gaul; and there the list breaks off, with its last sheet missing (*ND Oc.* XLII); the missing sheet will have contained the remainder of the *gentiles*, Sarmatae and perhaps others, in Gaul, Britain and Spain. There is a little evidence for the presence of such *gentiles* in Britain in the fourth century; the unsuccessful emperor Magnentius was British born, and his father was a German settled in Roman territory by Constantine, his mother a Frank (Zonaras 13, 6; Julian, *Or* 1, 27; *Cod. Voss.* cf. Rev. Ét. Anc. 27 (1925) 312); at the end of the century Fraomar's Alamanni (cf. below and n. 18) will have been such *gentiles**; so will two men buried in the Roman cemetery at Colchester with colour-coated ware of the mid or late fourth century and German, probably Saxon, spears (Colchester Museum). The *Notitia*, for reasons not wholly clear, distinguishes *gentiles* from *laeti*. Both of them were commanded by regular Roman *praefecti*, and differed radically from fifth-century federates, national groups under their own laws whose chiefs achieved treaty status, equivalent to the *Bucellarii* of the eastern empire; the earliest such federate settlement in the west was that of the Visigoths in 418.

* German *cohortes* and *alae* are found only in Syria and Egypt.

[16] Of the fourth-century officers whose origin we know, about a third were barbarian; the vast majority of the rest have Roman names. A few Germans took Roman names, but it is not wise to assume that more than a small proportion of the men with Roman names were German. Evidence for the rank and file is much weaker; what there is suggests that the barbarian element was considerably smaller than among officers. The view that the fourth-century Roman army was mainly composed of barbarians is a modern myth.

[17] e.g. RIB 883; 1576; 1594.

[18] 29, 4.

[19] *Oxoniensia* 17-18 (1954) 63 ff.

[20] So far as I know, the very numerous references to Irish settlement have not yet been collated and critically evaluated. Among the most important are *Sanas Chormaic*, ed. Stokes (Calcutta, 1868) 110, s.v. Mug-eime; Nennius 14; YC 14 (1901) 112, cf. *Eriu* 3 (1907) 136, and also the genealogies of Demetia; Ogham inscriptions in ECMW and CIIC; raths on OS sheets (1 inch) nos. 138 and 151, of varying dates; RCHM (1937) xxxvi; I. A. Richmond (1958) 113. Scandinavian and English conquest have wiped out what traces of Irish settlement may have existed in Lancashire and much of Cumberland.

[21] Valentinian recovered a province that had surrendered to enemy rule ('quae in ditionem concesserat hostium'). Ammianus 28, 3, 7. Archaeological evidence is decisive that disputed territory on the Pictish frontier was abandoned, not recovered, by Valentinian; the province was therefore somewhere in the west, the enemy Irish. The expeditions of Cunedda and the Cornovian princes demonstrate that the Irish did not remain subdued in at least the southern part of the west coast; and Irish memory asserts that they did not. Cf. J.R. Soc. Ant. I., 90, 133 ff.

[22] The evidence rests almost entirely upon genealogies; principally upon Harleian MS. 3859, 5 (Altclyde); ibid. 1; Jesus MS. 20, 6; *vita Cadoc* 47; *vita David* (Latin) 68, (Welsh) 1 (Votadini).

The first recognizable names begin with the grandfathers of Ceretic, Patrick's contemporary in Altclyde, and of his contemporary, Cunedda (cf. p. 162 below). They are Cinhil< son of >Cluim< son of >Cursalem and Patern Pesrut (scarlet cloak) son of Tacitus< son of >Ceint (variant Cein). Quintilius Clemens, of a place whose name is corrupted, and Tacitus of Kent bear Roman names, and names that in the later fourth century are proper to the decurial classes of Britain, Gaul or Africa, not to the aristocracy of Italy, to the army or to border peoples. Elsewhere Valentinian sometimes installed Romans of such station as *praefecti gentium*, not to be confused with *praefecti gentilium* (n. 15 above), over border peoples, while sometimes he recognized border *principes*; earlier emperors had done the same.

²³ Patrick, *Confessio*, Book of Armagh, fo. 23a r°; emended p. 360, Stokes' Tripartite Life.
²⁴ MGH *Epp*. III 158-9; the letter of 'Giltas' that he cites is perhaps Gildas' extant fourth letter.
²⁵ *Persian Wars* 2, 22 ff., where the plague is characterized by the swelling in the groin (bubon).
²⁶ *de Gloria Mart.* 50.
²⁷ 571, 582, 587, 590. *Hist. Franc.* 4, 5; *vita S. Galli* 6; *de Gloria Confess.* 78; Narbonne, Marseille, Albi, Vienne, Viviers, Avignon, Trier, Lyons, Bourges, Chalon-sur-Saône, Dijon (*Hist. Franc.* 6, 4; 7, 1; 4, 31; 9, 21; 10, 1; 10, 23; *vitae SS. Patrocli, Nicetii, Iuliani*). To Gregory the plague is *lues inguinaria*, groin plague.
²⁸ C. A. Ralegh Radford in *Dark Age Britain* 59 ff.
²⁹ Cf. p. 79.
³⁰ The date 'about 540' is upheld by Mommsen, Gildas' principal editor (MGH 13, 1-85) and almost all other scholars. Dissentients are A. W. Wade-Evans (*Nennius' History of the Britons*) and P. Grosjean (Bull. du Cange 25 (1955) 155-187, cf. *Anal. Boll.* 75 (1957) 185 ff.) who regard ch. 3-26 with, doubtfully, 27-36 as a later addition. The starting point is the subjective impression set down by C. E. Stevens (EHR 66 (1941) 353, cited by Grosjean, *Anal. Boll.* 223) that the 'chapters of historical narration fit somewhat loosely into the general scheme'; an impression that not all readers of Gildas will endorse. The arguments differ; Wade-Evans makes Gildas' Badon the *bellum Badonis secundo* of *Ann. Camb.* 665, adds Gildas' 44 years and dates the work to 708/9. The identification of the battle is neither evidenced nor probable, and it is hard to credit that Bede in 725 was fooled by a work published sixteen years before. Grosjean relies on a Leyden glossary that confines its selections to the early chapters, and on a number of parallels between Gildas and 'Hisperic' Latin, though the chronological inference drawn therefrom is not clear. There are plainly many reasons why the glossarist, like Bede, might choose his limits of citation. No linguistic or stylistic comparison has yet been attempted; in its absence it is only possible to rely on subjective impressions, as Grosjean and Wade-Evans do. To most readers the mentality, purpose and character of both sections appear identical, and wholly different from any other medieval writer, while the historical chapters form an integral part of the scheme, not to be separated without very serious and strong evidence.
It must be observed that while Columban places the person Gildas, and perhaps one of his extant letters, well back in the sixth century, Bede is our earliest prime authority for attributing the *de Excidio* to Gildas. He took it for granted, and there is no reason to believe him wrong.
³¹ The observation (HE 1, 15) that the Angles came from Anglia, the Jutes from Jutland, the Saxons from Saxony hardly presupposes a source; nor does Bede's information about where they lived in the eighth century. The Kentish genealogy is preserved independently of Bede.
³² MGH 9, *Chronica Minora* 615 ff.
The Chronicle was actually written in 452; the length of reign is given for all rulers but the last, Marcian and Valentinian (450-457, or, better, 450-455), and only the events of the first two years of their reign are noted. Later events and the length of their reign are not reported because they had not yet happened.
³³ The name means 'top tyrant' (tyrannus superior). Gildas' 'tyrannus superbus' is one of his frequent puns.
³⁴ Jornandes, *Getica*, 45.
³⁵ Greg. Tur., *Hist. Franc.* 2, 18-19.
³⁶ Sid. Apol., *Ep.* 1, 7, 5.
³⁷ Ib. 3, 9.
³⁸ Mansi 7, 941.
³⁹ Cf. p. 58 and nn. 25-28, above.
⁴⁰ Ch. 26.
⁴¹ Gildas 26, 'quique quadragesimus quartus, ut novi, orditur annus, mensa iam uno emenso, qui et meae nativitatis est'. Since he knows the date because he knows his own birthday, the commonsense meaning is that the battle was forty-four years ago; but Bede amended to give a meaning forty-four years after the Saxon landing; and, as we do not know the exact year in which he wrote, the statement adds little. Nennius' Chronographer reckons 69 years from 428, *adventus Saxonum* 'ad Decium et Valerianum'; 'Valerian' is probably added

because it goes with Decius, as the genealogists turned Cl(audius) to Cl(eopatra) and added Antun (*vita Cadoci* 45; Harleian MS. 3859 xvi; cf. above, p. 3). A palaeographically possible emendation of 'ad Decium' at the end of a faulty original is 'ad bellum (Badonis)'. The *Ann. Camb.* 516 is 69 years from an *adventus* date reckoned at 446/7, as in Bede's subsidiary approximate datings (HE 1, 23; 2, 14; 5, 23; 5, 24).

[42] MGH 13, 111 ff. The most useful edition is E. Faral, *La Légende Arthurienne* III, 4-62 (=Bib. de l'École des Hautes Études, Sections des Sciences historiques et philologiques, fasc. 257, Paris, 1929), printing side by side Chartres MS. 98 (IX/X) and Harleian MS. 3859 (XI/XII). A great deal of work has gone into the analysis of the stemmata of later MSS., less into the isolation of the ingredients. The work consists of six main sections:

I. Ch. 1-5. World Chronology, based on Jerome-Eusebius and Bede.

II. Ch. 7-18. Early British History; (a) Brutus the Trojan, descended from Noah or from the kings of Rome, based on Jerome-Eusebius (ch. 7; 10-11; 17-18); (b) Geography of Britain, related to Gildas (ch. 7-9); (c) Origins of the Picts and Scots, mainly from Irish tradition (ch. 12-15), with notes, some dated '858', on the coming of Cunedda, Patrick and the Saxons (ch. 15-16).

III. Ch. 19-30. Roman Britain, based on a late Roman *breviarium*, supplemented by Orosius, Prosper and Vergil, with two enterprising exercises in epigraphy (21; 25), apparently original hypotheses of the author.

IV. Ch. 31-56, with 66. Fifth-century Britain, the core of the compilation, consisting of seven separate documents, the first three of them chopped into segments interspersed with one another.

(a) A devolved miraculous life of Germanus; (ch. 32-35, 39, 47-48).

(b) A fairy tale of Embreis Guletic; (ch. 40-42).

(c) A straightforward narrative of British-Saxon wars in mid-fifth-century Kent (ch. 36-38, 43-46, integrated by 31). The treatment is rational and coherent, different in concept and style from other British and Gallic accounts of the long distant past composed in the seventh or later centuries. Its merit escapes attention until it is disentangled from the surrounding fantasies; it is best described as the 'Kentish Chronicle'.

(d) The genealogy of Vortigern's descendants, to *c.* 750/800; (ch. 49).

(e) An abridged life of Patrick, derived from Muirchu and Tirechan (late seventh or early eighth century); (ch. 50-55).

(f) A list of Arthur's 'twelve battles' (ch. 56).

(g) A set of elaborate calculations, best described as the 'Nennius Chronographer', dating the arrival of the Saxons to 428; (ch. 66). A few notes inserted into these documents are mainly concerned with equating British and English place-names.

V. Ch. 57-65. Sixth- and seventh-century Britain, consisting of two main documents:

(a) Anglo-Saxon genealogies, in eight branches; (ch. 57-61).

(b) An account of British-Saxon-Pictish wars in the north from *c.* 550; (ch. 62-65).

VI. Ch. 67-75. The Miracles of Britain

and

VII. Later documents, found only in Harleian and related MSS., best edited by Phillimore, YC 9 (1888) 141-183:

(a) *Annales Cambriae*.

(b) Twenty-nine British genealogies.

[43] e.g. Kenneth Jackson, 'The Northern British Section in Nennius', in N. K. Chadwick, *Celt and Saxon* (Cambridge, 1963) 20-62.

[44] Ch. 36-38; 43-46, with 31; cf. n. 42 above.

[45] Ch. 66, cf. n. 42 above. The bulk of these calculations may well be no more than an elaborate illustration of the approximation 40 years after Maximus (d. 388); but the fact that this date is near right entitles the Chronographer's other dates (Guoloppum, cf. p. 165; and 'ad Decium', cf. n. 41) to more respectful study than they would otherwise receive.

46 The handiest edition of the Anglo-Saxon Chronicle is the Everyman (G. N. Garmonsway), with a full bibliography; the origins of the texts are discussed pp. xix ff.

The principal *Irish Annals* (*Tigernach, Inisfallen, Clonmacnoise, Ulster, Four Masters* and *Chronicon Scottorum*) have been published in texts of varying value, but not yet collated or critically edited; they are therefore frequently undervalued or misquoted. In particular, minor confusions in the transmission of the text, of the kind long since ironed out by the intensive study of the separate texts of the Anglo-Saxon Chronicle, are easily abused to sustain historical and chronological theories. In the main, the separate versions are consistent with each other; they are sometimes inconsistent with a variety of alternative chronologies asserted by modern critics, cf. n. 47. None of the external controls is beyond dispute; but the Irish Annals cite continental events more frequently and more accurately than the Anglo-Saxon Chronicle. Distortion is not invention.

The *Annales Cambriae* (YC 9 (1888) 152-169) also lack a critical edition comparing them with later interpolated MSS. and with the Irish Annals, from which most of their early entries derive.

47 The heated atmosphere that surrounds the study of St. Patrick in Ireland is lucidly depicted by D. A. Binchy, *Studia Hibernica* 2 (1962) 7-173. It is not wholly immune from the impact of modern ecclesiastical and political concerns. Oddly, the controversy pays little attention to Aed of Sletty, the seventh-century promoter of the cult of Patrick and patron of his biographer, Muirchu, whose interest was the strengthening of a disciplined hierarchical and unified church, accepting the Roman Easter, at the expense of the independence of the monasteries, in whose tradition Patrick played little or no part; nor does it place weight on the most solid-looking of all the annalistic dates, the *Probatio Patricii* under Leo the Great, an event the annalists did not understand, but which is a natural and expected consequence of Patrick's own implied threat (*Confessio*, Cotton MS. fo. 172, b. 1, p. 370, Stokes' Tripartite Life) to the British bishops that he could appeal to 'friends in Gaul'.

Dr. Binchy ruthlessly destroys the arguments of those who have produced chronologies alternative to the Annals; but rejects the Annals. His main grounds (112 ff.) are that the Patrician documents associate Patrick with many persons who lived on into the early and mid sixth century; yet these associations are the most dubious of all the statements in these documents. His argument is that usually hagiographers bring in important earlier notables to honour their hero; 'but since they (Muirchu and Tirechan) were writing a life of Patrick, there was no reason whatever why they should reverse the process by making him associate with persons who actually lived one or two generations later.' This curious reasoning arises from the omission of Aed of Sletty, and of a serious analysis of why the documents were written when they were. Patrick is made to ordain or consecrate a number of saints who were infants or not yet born in his lifetime because, at the time the documents were written, the heirs of these saints did not admit the primacy of Patrick. The tradition of Patrick's stay at Auxerre, and the modern work of Père Grosjean and others thereon, is also dismissed by a serious misconception; 'during these 15 years (or more) he must have spoken . . . read . . . heard nothing but Latin', yet his Latin is rough and unfamiliar. This is quite contrary to what little we know of the language of early fifth-century Gaul; it is probable that he spoke and heard both vulgar Latin and Celtic; if he read or wrote, he would have used Latin; but he asserts that he did little of either. A man may speak a tongue he cannot write.

The root of the matter is that the Annals, and the whole of the early Patrician tradition, bring Patrick to Ireland in or about 432; though his death dates vary, there is no other tradition of arrival, though a secondary stage equates him with Palladius. The confusion arose early, when, by the eighth century, Patrick was credited with the lifespan of Moses, 120 years, given as 60 in Ireland and 60 before. A sixty years stay meant a death in the 490s; and rational scholars, who doubted the long life, turned two death dates into two Patricks. The dates 432 to somewhere in or about the 460s fit well with the chronology of Britain and with the events and situation in Europe; a later fifth-century date does not; these dates are approximately established by Leo's 'probatio'. I hope to discuss the problem more fully elsewhere in the near future (cf. pp. 95-144, below).

48 Columba's dates confirm the Irish and Cambrian Annals; Ethelbert's marriage (Greg. Tur. *Hist. Franc.* 4, 26; 9, 26) to a daughter of Charibert of Paris (561-7)

confirms the Anglo-Saxon Chronicle, as, approximately, does Bede's knowledge of Ceawlin.

[49] The principal collections of British genealogies are Harleian MS. 3859 (YC 9 (1888) 169-183); Jesus MS. 20 (YC 8 (1887) 83-92); Bonedd y Sant and the Brecon documents (A. W. Wade-Evans, *Vitae Sanctorum Britanniae et Genealogiae*, B.C.S. History and Law Series 9 (Cardiff, 1944), pp. 313-323); Bonedd Gwyr y Gogled (Skene, *Four Ancient Books* II, 454) and numerous versions embedded in the lives of particular saints. They await collation. The English genealogies are recorded in the Anglo-Saxon Chronicle, Nennius, Florence of Worcester and other later Chroniclers, and in a few separate documents.

[50] Mailcun, Cunglas, Vortipor and Constantine are denounced by Gildas; Vortipor's tombstone survives (ECMW 138); the *Widsith* concerns Offa of Angel; the dynasties of Altclyde and the Votadini have a fourth-century context (n. 22 above); and so perhaps has Tutwal of Galloway, patron of Ninian.

[51] K. Sisam, *Proc. British Academy* 39 (1953) 287-348.

[52] Notably the northern kings of Altclyde, Eitin and of the family of Coel.

[53] e.g. Nils Åberg, *The Anglo-Saxons in England* (Uppsala, 1926) 13: 'the brooch from Dorchester (cf. n. 19 above) represents a precedent stage of the cruciform types, and might therefore possibly be dated to the time around the year 400. However, the deposition of the find may have been considerably later, and to judge from its geographical situation, this will probably have been the case.' The Dorchester burial is now known to date before rather than after 400.

[54] e.g. R. R. Clarke, *East Anglia* (1960) 130: 'there can be little doubt about the Germanic character of the *foederati* brought in c. 390-400 from Schleswig-Holstein and north-west Germany. This dating of the foundation of our earliest Anglo-Saxon cemeteries is based on the work of continental archaeologists, which places the beginning of these Anglo-Saxon communities half a century earlier than the traditional date of 449.'

[55] The present state of evidence, and of archaeological thinking about its meaning, is clearly and concisely set down by Sonia Hawkes and G. C. Dunning in *Med. Arch.* 5 (1961) 5-10. Some confusion is created by the belief that 'fourth-century . . . German noblemen usually had the status of chieftains of tribal groups of *foederati*' (7-8) and that 'We know that the Roman army at the end of the fourth century recruited its forces almost entirely from . . . barbarian peoples', cf. n. 16 above. The date and distribution of the Gallo-Roman cemeteries do not correspond to those of the *Laeti*.

[56] The most numerous and most important are the cruciform brooches, whose beginnings Åberg placed 'just before the middle of the fifth century' (36), making them as late as he could, in view of the then prevailing misunderstanding of the date of the Dorchester burial (n. 53 above). Two examples of the prototype of the equal-arm brooches (Åberg 13, fig. 11, from Kempston and Luton) are quite as early as the earliest cruciforms. Pots of course have a shorter life than brooches; a brooch may be old or new when buried, but an unbroken pot is not likely to be many years old. The forms however persist; it is noteworthy that virtually identical vessels are buried in Germany with the latest 'crossbow' brooches, which are never found in England, and the earliest 'cruciforms'; the same types clearly spanned the period when the one brooch replaced the other. In England there are about fifty burials which contain both a brooch and a pot, half of them from two unpublished cemeteries in Norfolk. The study of pottery will not make great advances until these fifty associated burials are published.

[57] Sonia Hawkes and G. C. Dunning in *Med. Arch.* 5 (1961) 1-70.

[58] Nennius 31.

[59] *Beowulf* 1083 ff. Finnsburg Fragment. cf. H. M. Chadwick, *Origin of the English Nation*, 44 ff.

[60] These signal-towers were violently destroyed in the early fifth century; the date was earlier than the earliest Anglian settlement in the Scarborough area (Crossgates, Scarborough Museum).

[61] Patrick landed (432 is intended) in the 19th year of his reign, *Pictish Chronicle* (Skene, *Chronicles of the Picts and Scots*, 6) and related documents; his death, *Annals of Clonmacnoise*, p. 71.

[62] Sid. Ap., *Ep.* 8, 9, 5.

[63] Pillar of Eliseg (ECMW 182); Nennius 32-5; the place-names Moel Fenlli and Moel Geraint, etc.

[64] Greg. Tur., *Hist. Franc.* 2, 19, cf. n. 35 above.

[65] Ammianus 27, 8, 1.

66 Most of the references to the Gwydyl Ffichti of Powys are late and dubious; but not 'Didlet brenhin Gwydyl Fichti ym Pywys', Jesus MS. 20, 23.

67 Gerontius. a Dumnonian chief of the second generation. is said to have fallen at Llongborth about 480 (n. 97 below). St. Kebi was of the same family; his 'consobrinus senex', Cyngar or Docco, founder of St. Kew and of the Llandoughs, inspirer of the late fifth-century saint Enda, is said to have died as early as 472 (*Annals Ulster*, cf. *Clonmacnoise*, 471/480) 'Doccus Bushopp of the Brittans dyed'; he also perhaps founded Congresbury in north Somerset. Their fathers will have been the migrants.

68 Tradition credits Cunedda with a dozen or more sons, most of them named from various districts of North Wales. Three only, Typipaun, Ceretic and Enniaun are sufficiently remembered outside genealogies to suggest that early tradition saw them as real sons; though the reality of some of the others might be possible.

69 Nennius 62. Several emendations are possible; 'an x or two too many in cxxxxvi' (Morris Jones, YC 28 (1919) 202); or, in place of CXLVI, the substitution of CXVI or CXVII, or perhaps better, CXIIII (cf. e.g. XXII for XXV in the *editio princeps* of Pliny, *Ep.* 10, 79-80, cf. *Classical Review* 17 (1903) 54). The choice among emendations is trivial; the essential is that the figures are corruptible, and are probably corrupt. Understanding has not been advanced by translating 'atavus', ancestor, as specifically 'great-great-grandfather', and using this misleading translation to rebut the genealogies.

70 Ochtha and Ebissa (Nennius 38), given regions in the north *iuxta murum qui vocatur Guaul*, sailed about the Picts, raided the Orkneys and settled 'ultra mare Frenessicum usque ad confinium Pictorum'. A few unfurnished cemeteries of the north Northumberland coast may be recognized as Saxon by the presence of a stray knife; several more, with no such handy knife, look otherwise like them. It is not impossible that Dumfries also bears their name.

Their presence doubtless influenced Cunedda's nephew to join his uncle in Wales; for the provenance of this second migration of the Votadini, the curious may compare CIIC 514 (Liddelwater) with ECMW 283-5 (Caer Gai; Llanymawddy; Tomen-y-mur).

71 Cf. n. 47 above.

72 The settlements of Brychan in Wales and Cornwall and of the Argyll Scots two generations later belong more to an age of dynastic wars than to an age of conquest and colonization akin to the fourth century.

73 *Book of Armagh*, folio 16a; *Bethu Phatraic* I, 43. Two inscriptions bearing the name (CIIC 97; 297) are of course later than Fortchern and are no evidence that the name existed in Ireland before him.

74 So the marriage of the emperor's sister Placidia to a Gothic king; of the emperor to the daughter of his barbarian general Bauto; the romantic tale of Honoria's betrothal to Attila; Childeric's Thuringian marriage, etc.

75 I cannot see that the *Confessio*, despite its obscurities, can have any other purport. Patrick's mission was inspired by Germanus and the Gallic bishops, necessarily endorsed by the Pope. He says that he was proposed by a friend, apparently a British Bishop. The mission could hardly have gone ahead without seeking the approval of the British episcopate. It is fully in accord with the ecclesiastical history of the century that they should claim jurisdiction, and Patrick refuse the claim. The only way to resolve the dispute was by appeal to the Pope, which Patrick could properly make, without leaving Ireland, only through the Gallic bishops. Such an appeal was predestined to success; Popes in general, and Leo in particular, were apt to welcome a request for direct rather than indirect submission to Rome.

76 *Inisfallen, Ulster, Clonmacnoise*. Cf. n. 47 above.

77 *Inisfallen, Ulster, Chron. Scot*. 'Prima praeda Saxanorum ab Hibernia'; by misunderstanding *praeda* as raid rather than booty, the Irish language *Annals* (Cetna brat Saxan di Ere) and some modern writers have conceived raids based on Ireland; cf. also *Annals of Roscrea*, PRIA 59 (1958) 145. There is no warrant for emending *Saxanorum* to *Sanctorum*.

78 There are numerous possibilities; emperor (princeps, Caesar Augustus) is the most natural; but he might have called himself *praefectus praetorio*, possibly beginning as prefect to an emperor whom he later replaced. The most likely status of Hengest will have been *magister militum*.

79 Nennius 49, 'filii Guitaul, filii Guitolin, filii Glovi . . . qui aedificavit urbem magnam . . . britannico sermone Cair Glovi, saxonice autem Gloecester'; cf. Jesus MS. 20, 15. The eponymous frequently appears elsewhere in a clearly fifth-century

context; the 'filius' (map) is probably intrusive; Vitalis is either a doublet, or possibly Vortigern's Roman name; he will certainly have had one.

80 Nennius 36; cf. Gildas 23; the British contributed 'annona'; the Saxons demanded increased 'epimenia', threatening 'rupto foedere'. These are technical terms.

81 Nennius 37. The marriage echoes that of Arcadius and Eudoxia, cf. n. 74. 'Guoyrancgono regnante in Cantia' implies a *de facto* monarchy, as in some other *civitates*.

82 Ch. 24-25.

83 Eugippius, *vita Severini* 4, 1.

84 Constantius, ch. 26=Bede, HE 1, 21; for the date, see *Anal. Boll.* 75 (1957) 180 ff., cf. 135 ff.; cf. *Ant.* 30 (1956) 167.

85 J. P. Bushe-Fox, *Excavations at Richborough*, no. 2, pl. xiii; 3, pl. vii; 4, pl. lxx=RIB 46 ff.

86 Nennius 45-48.

87 The earliest datable objects are five-scroll saucer brooches, which might be of any date in the fifth century, cf. *Surrey Arch. Coll.* 56 (1959) 81-83. A sufficient number of graves have been excavated at Alfriston, High Down, Lewes, etc., to give some weight to negative evidence, of early fifth-century objects not found there.

88 e.g. *Anglo-Saxon Chronicle* 485, Mearcredsburna; there may have been a person called Mercred, but English rivers are not commonly named after people; the natural translation is 'river of the frontier agreed by treaty'.

89 Greg. Tur., *Hist. Franc.* 2, 18.

90 Ibid. 5, 26; 10, 9. They had been converted to Christianity by the British well before the 570s. The sees of Bayeux, Seez and Lisieux were held by bishops with German names a generation earlier than in the rest of Frankish Gaul (Mansi, Councils of 538, 549, 556, etc.). This might be chance; or it may be that there Germans settled and were converted earlier than the Franks. Other evidence of Anglian settlement in the area (place-names and brooches) relates as well to the sixth century as to the fifth.

91 Frisians, *vita Melori*, 1; Gradlon, Wrdestan, *vita Winwaloe* 2, 15.

92 Sid. Apol., *Ep.* 8, 9.

93 Ibid. 8, 6.

94 See p. 78.

95 Clovis in north-west Germany; Daeghafn the Frank (Beowulf 2500 ff., etc., cf. 2340 ff.) was general of the Frisians against Hygelac, to be equated with Gregory's Chlochilaicus (*Hist. Franc.* 3, 3) dated to 516. The Franks had evidently mastered Frisia some time previously.

96 To the author of the Gododdin (1242 (cii), cf. 1217) he was a mighty warrior of the past; the name Arthur was given to three princes born in the mid sixth century (Arthur son of Aedan mac Gabran: Arthur map Pedr, great-grandson of Vortipor: Artuir f. Bicoir Brito (*Annals of Tigernach*, p. 178): cf. also Arthur Penuchel, *Achau'r Sant* 5, 5) and was not again recorded until after Geoffrey of Monmouth. In the highland areas he was a brutal foreign enemy, successfully exerting an authority they resented; in Scotland (*vita Gildas* (Caradoc) 5) he was 'rex rebellis' who killed a 'noble youth' who 'raided and burnt with honour'; in mid-Wales (*vita Paterni* ch. 21) he was 'tyrannus altrinsecus', raving with fury; in south Wales (*vita Cadoci* prologus: ch. 22) a lecherous supreme ruler, the great king of all Britain who invaded Gwent from beyond the Usk; in Cornwall (*vita Carantoci prima* ch. 4) the ally and patron of Cado, interfering with the saint's altar.

The battles in Nennius 56 may rest on a Welsh poem; if we had the poem we might better estimate its value. Some of the sites are identifiable; Linnius is Lindsey, its river presumably the Witham; Celidon is the forest of Peebles; Urbs Legionis is Chester or Caerleon, Guinion some Roman town or fort beginning with Vin-. But identifications help little when we know nothing of the source whence they come.

97 *Black Book of Carmarthen* 22=*Red Book of Hergest* 14=*Four Ancient Books* I, 37 and 274; II 266. A translation appears in Gwyn Williams, *The Burning Tree*, 43-45.

98 K. Jackson, *Language and History in Early Britain* (Edinburgh, 1953) 463, 466, n. 1.

99 Ancestors, cf. n. 51 above. His descendants are given in the Anglo-Saxon Chronicle Parker preface, and in the Annals of 597, 611, 648, 674, 676, 685, 688,

728, 855. The discordant lists, unlike those of other dynasties, are evidence that a king of Wessex needed to be provided with a descent from Cerdic, because a genuine descent was lacking.
100 Greg. Tur., *Hist. Franc.* 2, 12.
101 Possibly the successor of Elafius.
102 Such are the affinities of Droxford and the Isle of Wight cemeteries.
103 'Stuf and Wihtgar' of 'Wihtgaraesburg' are evidently a misunderstanding of Stuf of Wihtgar; Annals of 514, 531, cf. 530.
104 8, 20.
105 A few later sixth-century chiefs are buried with horse trappings; at best the horse was the property of a commander who rode while his men walked.
106 Where numbers occur, they are commonly 300 or multiples thereof; each war band was probably quite small. Cyndylan had 40 horses.
107 Sid. Apol., *Ep.* 3, 3; cf. Greg. Tur. *Hist. Franc.* 2, 24.
108 e.g. Castle Dore, *J. Royal Institution of Cornwall*, n.s. 1, 1951, Cadbury Castle, *P. Somerset A.N.H.S.*, 99-100 (1954-55), 106-113.
109 Vaughan, Hist. MSS. Commission, *Report on MSS. in the Welsh Language* (1898) 1, 63, cf. *Ant.* 10 (1936) 96.
110 Bede, HE 2, 5: *Anglo-Saxon Chronicle* a. 827.
111 If the place be Bath, it will represent a last attempt of the English to smoke out the heartlands of the British.
112 Cf. pp. 1-15 above and 95-144 below. Editions of the lives are listed in *Bibliotheca Hagiographica Latina*.
113 'regis Marci . . . quem alio nomine Quonomorius vocant', *vita Pauli Aureliani* 8; *vita Samson, Acta SS* 586 F; *Anal. Boll.* 6 (1887) 2; 3; 17; *vitae Gildae* (Ruis) 20 ff.; *Goueznou passim*; *Huerve*; *Leonori*; *Melori*; *Arthmael* (Albert le Grand 522); *Teilo* (Liber Landav. 115), etc. Greg. Tur., *Hist. Franc.* 4, 4 (Chonomoris); 4, 20 (Chonoober). Inscription, C. A. Ralegh Radford, *J. Royal Institution of Cornwall*, n.s. 1 (1951) 117-9, emending CIIC 487; cf. above, p. 14, n. 13; Drustanus hic iacit Cunomori filius. The historical king Mark was father, not uncle, of Tristan.

114 Mansi 9, 743, *Concilium Parisiense III, c.* A.D. 557.
Signatory no. 9: Gonothigirnus, ep. Silvanectensis; no. 14: Sampson ep. Mansi 9, 127, *Concilium Aurelianense V*, A.D. 547.
Signatory no. 44: Gonotigirnus Silvanectensis (variant, Cunautigernus). The name is British, not Gallic; though its constituent elements are common enough, it is not recorded for any other man than St. Kentigern. Jocelyn's *Life of Kentigern* unwittingly preserves an incident from the episcopate of the Bishop of Senlis. While abroad (ch. 28) Kentigern was called upon to consecrate a learned and elegant 'clericus . . . ad sacerdotium promovendus'. But flames of sulphur and the filthy smell of evil exposed the man as a sodomite. He was 'natione Britannus, sed in Galliis educatus'; the plural 'Galliis' argues a source far older than Jocelyn. I know of but one other reference to homosexuality in sixth-century Gaul; the second Council of Paris (Mansi 9, 739) in 555 deposed Bishop Saffaracus on a proven and admitted charge. Gonotigirnus was then Bishop of nearby Senlis.
115 Cf. n. 48 above. A close date, 561/565, since father and father-in-law were alive.
116 Ch. 10.
117 *Vita Columba Tirdeglas, Acta SS. Hiberniae.* Smedt and De Backer (1888) 449, ch. 10; cf. also Ibar (died *c.* 503) and Abban at Abingdon, Plummer, VSH 1, 12.
118 Cf. *Surrey Arch. Coll.* 56 (1959) 155.
119 Cf. *Norfolk Arch.* 31 (1955) 178 ff.; cf. 419; cf. *Ant.* 3 (1929) 135 ff. There is no evidence of date; but the dykes enclose all the fifth- and early sixth-century burial grounds of Norfolk; those beyond are not earlier than the later sixth century.
120 Cf. especially C. F. C. Hawkes in *Dark Age Britain* 90 ff. There is no contradiction between the Frankish and Frankish-inspired art of Kent and the Jutish origin of Kent. Bede's statement of the race of the settlers has no bearing on the jewellery their granddaughters favoured, or on the degree of later Frankish settlement.
121 York and British Museums, cf. YAJ 39 (1958) 427; *Med. Arch.* 1 (1957) 149; Mearney, *Gazeteer.* 303; Baldwin Brown 802.
122 Ch. 92.
123 Evidence summarized *Surrey Arch. Col.* 56 (1959) 155.

124 The Wansdyke and its extensions, with hypothetical forest in the gaps between them, constitute a continuous geographical boundary, whether or not all sections were dug at the same time. The securely-dated portion, the massive central section, is post-Roman.
125 Iolo MSS. 86; Peniarth MS. 135.
126 Nennius 56.
127 'Emperor' at Llongborth, n. 97 above: Guledic, wearing the purple: Taliessin 34-35, lines 6, 8, 9. 'Briton of the nobility of Rome': Taliessin 76 (Darogan), cf. *Four Ancient Books* II, 210; I, 274; Arthur seems to be intended.
128 Cf. n. 96 above.
129 Cf. n. 96 above; 'rex totius maioris Britanniae' (*vita Gildas* (Caradoc) 5); 'rex illustrissimus Britanniae' (*vita Cadoci* 22); in *vita Illtud* 2 he is overking.
130 Ch. 1.
131 Ch. 6; 14; 15.
132 Cf. e.g. *Acta Appiani* (*Acts of the Pagan Martyrs*, XI, ii, 12, p. 65); *St Mark's Gospel* 6, 27; Gildas 91, like the Vulgate, uses the word for 'watchman' in Ezechiel 33, 2, applied to the protective role of the priest.
Augustine, *de civ. Dei* 1, 9, 3, glosses 'speculatores, hoc est populorum praepositi', and in the eighth and ninth centuries the word became an alternative to *episcopus* (cf. P. Grosjean, *Anal. Boll.* 76 (1958) 379 ff.).
133 The Hertfordshire river Bene appears as Beneficce in the Anglo-Saxon Chronicle, a. 913, evidently Bene Fychan, Welsh not earlier than the seventh century; howling Britons annoyed the holy Guthlac in the Fens (Felix, *vita Guthlaci* 34); sites like Thorley, Herts. (unpublished: noted in JRS 44 (1954) 196, n. 37) may well have lasted into the sixth century.
134 As attested by Anglo-Saxon laws concerning Wealas, and the numerous Waltons and similar place-names.
135 *vita Samson* 1, 1 (*Anal. Boll.* 6 (1887) 83): 'tributa servorum levigantes'.
136 *Canu Llywarch Hen* 11, 56.
137 ed. I; 1, 8.

THE DATES OF THE CELTIC SAINTS*

THE history of the British Isles in the fifth and sixth centuries remains obscure. Uncertainty is not due to a lack of sources, but to the difficulty of interpreting the very full sources. Most of them were written long after the events they concern, by men who had no understanding of the past, and no wish to understand it; their concern was to exploit the past in the service of the present. The modern historian is at a disadvantage in dealing with them, for his training is designed for the study of easier evidence; nearly every other age has left a framework of chronological history, set down by a contemporary or near contemporary, a Thucydides, a Tacitus, an Ammian, a Gregory of Tours, or a Bede, a series of medieval chronicles, around which the rest of the evidence may be arranged, and by which it may be judged. Without such a guide he is at a loss, exposed to a double temptation, either to select items of evidence and try to fit them together as though they were pieces of a jigsaw puzzle, or to avoid difficulty by denouncing the evidence as not worth studying. It is fatally easy to surrender to both temptations at once, writing off such items as do not seem to fit the jigsaw.[1]

It is easy to scoff at these temptations; but anyone who has seriously wrestled with these sources has experienced their power, and needs to steel himself against them. For the simple techniques appropriate to a jigsaw puzzle do not help to explain the complex, flexible human relationships that constitute history; they lead to arid misconception. Nor is it sufficient to express an opinion that a source is wholly wrong because much of what it says is demonstrably false. Fancy and invention require just as much proof as fact; and it is oversimple to seek a 'reliable' source whereby 'unreliable' sources may be judged, to try to distinguish 'fact' from 'hypothesis'. All that may legitimately be attempted is to establish degrees of probability, from that which seems virtually certain to that which seems wildly improbable. The yardstick is common sense, and its first precept is that overriding priority must go to the interpretation of contemporary statements, second priority to those which link events in the British Isles with datable and intelligible events in Europe. The contemporary may be wrong, but only within narrow limits; the Continental connexion may be misplaced, but the history of Europe is well enough documented to limit the areas of displacement.

[1] The analogy is sometimes expressly stated; e.g., D. A. Binchy, *Studia Hibernica* 2 (1962), p. 8.

* Reprinted from the *Journal of Theological Studies*, N.S., 17 (1966) 342–91, by kind permission of the publisher.

But throughout, the historian has to deal much more with statements that are half-truths and misunderstandings than with statements that can be accepted as they stand or rejected *in toto*.

The sources are of many different kinds, each with its own particular bias and distorting pressures, that must be investigated before the particular documents, and the statements they contain, can be profitably assessed. The main sources for the Christian experience of the age are saints' lives, annals, particularly Irish, and genealogies.[1] The purpose of the genealogist was to link his patron with heroes believed to have lived in the past. His distortion lies in the links in his chain, not at the two ends; one end is contemporary, the other is at least what was in his day received opinion. The British genealogies are comparatively simple; they comprise no more than a few score names in the fifth and sixth centuries, a fair proportion of which are also found in contemporary or near contemporary documents, occasionally on inscriptions. The Irish genealogies are more difficult. The number of names is vastly greater, and they have been tapered to converge, not in the intelligible context of the sixth century, but in a legendary remote past located vaguely about the middle of the second millennium before Christ. In addition to these inherent distortions, they suffer the ordinary textual perversions of names misread, omitted, inserted. Over and above these general sources of error, two particular corrupting tendencies need emphasis. Later Irish thinking applied to the descent of political power the practices of family inheritance; in simplified terms, a man might claim full inheritance back to his great-grandfather, but not beyond, and genealogists were tempted to foreshorten royal and princely pedigrees, particularly of the fifth century, to conform to these conceptions. The second particular tendency concerns the ancestry of saints; since many saints were in fact of high birth, monastic interest naturally claimed royal origin for its patron. While the genealogies of saints are often good evidence for the secular pedigree to which the saint is attached, they are in themselves no evidence for the origin of the saint.

The Annals[2] constitute a problem whose elements are simpler, but

---

[1] The principal British collections are Harleian MS. 3859, published in *Y Cymmrodor*, ix (1888), pp. 169 ff.; Jesus MS. 20, in *Y Cymmrodor*, viii (1887), pp. 83 ff.; Bonedd y Saint (with the Brecon documents) in Wade-Evans, *Vitae Sanctorum Britanniae et Genealogiae* (Cardiff, 1944); Bonedd Gwyr y Gogled, in Skene, *Four Ancient Books of Wales*, 2, p. 454. The principal accessible Irish collection is M. A. O'Brien, *Corpus Genealogiarum Hiberniae*, vol. i (Dublin, 1962); numerous other texts are published elsewhere. Neither British nor Irish genealogies have yet been collated.

[2] The principal editions of Irish Annals are those of *Inisfallen*, ed. Sean MacAirt (Dublin, 1951), (composed *c*. 1092); *Tigernach*, ed. Stokes, in *Revue Celtique*, xvi (1895), pp. 375–419; xvii (1896), pp. 6–33; 120–263; 337–420; xviii

whose solution is harder to determine. The Irish Annals are extant in half a dozen versions. Their entries imply the form of their origin; items taken from native tradition were inserted into a copy of the *Chronicle* of Isidore of Seville,[1] that ends in 612. The entries are very numerous, and present a full account of the political history of the fifth and sixth centuries, but they have little or no external confirmation before the middle of the sixth century. They pose two related questions: what is the validity of the native entries; and what evidence had the annalists to guide them to the places in Isidore's *Chronicle* at which they were to be inserted? Further inquiry into both these questions is possible. It is commonly assumed, by ancient and modern writers, that writing with pen and ink did not reach Ireland until the coming of Christianity in the fifth century; the earliest written authority cited in the Annals is Mocteus of Louth who is said to have died in the early sixth century. But pen and ink were not the earliest writing materials in Ireland; the peculiar incised script known as Ogam[2] appears on stone in the later fourth century, and was first developed on wooden sticks, evidently by the *filid*, the scholars of pagan Ireland. There is room for further inquiry into what the *filid* wrote on their wooden sticks, and when they began to use them. The question of the synchronism between native and Continental dates is more complicated; numerous, and discordant, synchronisms survive from the eighth or ninth century onward, with little to show the worth of the evidence on which they were based. More important is the preservation of a number of oral verses, giving lengths of reigns, intervals between events, and the like; and it is virtually certain that the manner in which the annalists worked was to try to relate such native interval dates to absolute dates contained in Continental

(1897), pp. 9–59; 152–98; 267–303; 374–91, (composed *c.* 1110–20); *Ulster*, ed. W. M. Henessy (Rolls Series, 1887–1901), (composed before 1498); *Clonmacnoise*, ed. D. Murphy (Dublin, 1896), (composed *c.* 1408, but surviving only in the forceful English translation of MaGeoghagan, 1627); *The Four Masters*, ed. J. O'Donovan (Dublin, 1851), (composed *c.* 1632–6); and the *Chronicum Scotorum*, ed. W. M. Henessy (Rolls Series, 1866), (composed 1660–6). To these main versions should be added Stokes's *Annals from the Book of Leinster* (*Vita Tripartita*, 512 ff.). The British *Annales Cambriae* (ed. E. Phillimore, *Y Cymmrodor*, ix (1888), pp. 152 ff.; E. Faral, *La Légende Arthurienne* (Paris, 1929, III, pp. 44 ff.)) draws most of its early entries from the Irish Annals.

[1] So cited in *Inisfallen*, a. 612. References to a Chronicle of Eusebius elsewhere refer to the same or a similar chronicle.

[2] What is known of the origins of the script is summarized by Kenneth Jackson in *Language and History in Early Britain* (Edinburgh, 1953) (cited hereunder as *LHEB*), pp. 151 ff. Cf. Ifor Williams, *Cymmrodorion Transactions* (1943–4), pp. 153 ff. It is held to relate to the Latin alphabet as taught by Donatus in the fourth century; not enough is known, however, of third-century grammarians to warrant the conclusion that these correspondences must date after Donatus.

writers. There is not much doubt that the starting point of their absolute dates, both backward and forward, was the arrival of Patrick, placed at about 432. The dates of Patrick are therefore of cardinal importance, for the secular as well as the ecclesiastical history of Ireland.

The present state and direction of the study of the Annals cannot be regarded as satisfactory. The main texts have been printed, in editions of varying quality; but they have not yet been collated. In the absence of deep inquiry, most writers until quite recently tended to assume without argument the general validity of their account, and to discuss detail adjustments. Latterly it has become fashionable to reject them with equal lack of argument; in a formal sense, they have no significant external confirmation before the mid sixth century; in practice it tends to be asserted that dates after 500, or after 400 or 450, according to the taste of the individual critic, are to be accepted as valid, those earlier as invalid, and such statements are often made in support of particular arguments, concerned with the date of Patrick or the like. Subjective judgements of this sort are plainly no substitute for the detailed study which the Annals deserve. But, pending such study, it is not possible to use the Annals dates in evidence, unless it can be shown that a particular entry is of exceptionally early origin. It is, however, scarcely proper to suppress their evidence; a date from the Annals is to be cited as a plain statement of what the Annals say, without judgement as to whether that date is approximately right or wrong.

The Annals give dates to many churchmen; their doings are related in many scores of biographies.[1] Though their authors had little interest in

---

[1] Saints' Lives. Editions are catalogued alphabetically in *Bibliotheca Hagiographica Latina* (Brussels, 1898–1901, and *Novum Supplementum* by Henri Fros, 1986), cited here as *BHL*. The main accessible collections of Irish Latin Lives are the *Acta Sanctorum Hiberniae ex codice Salmanticensi*, ed. de Smedt and de Backer (Bruges 1888), newly edited as *Vitae Sanctorum Hiberniae*, ed. W. W. Heist (Brussels, 1965), here cited as *CS*; and C. Plummer, *Vitae Sanctorum Hiberniae* (Oxford, 1910), here cited as *VSH*; of Lives in Irish, Whitley Stokes's *Lives of the Saints from the Book of Lismore* (with translations) (Oxford, 1890), here cited as *Lismore*. Plummer's *Miscellanea Hagiographica Hibernica*, Subsidia Hagiographica 15 (1925, photostatically reproduced 1965), here cited as *MHH*, contains a full bibliography of Lives in Irish, and of Lives in Latin supplementary to *BHL*. J. Colgan's *Acta Sanctorum Hiberniae*, vol. i, January–March (Louvain, 1645, photostatically reproduced by the Irish Manuscripts Commission, 1947), here cited as *ASH*, and *Trias Thaumaturga* (Patrick, Columba, Bridget) (Louvain, 1647, not reproduced), here cited as *TT*, both contain material not published elsewhere.

The British Lives are less conveniently published. A. W. Wade-Evans, *Vitae Sanctorum Britanniae et Genealogiae* (with translations, for whose inaccuracies cf. *Cymmrodorion Transactions*, 1943–4, pp. 157, etc.) (Cardiff, 1944), here cited as *VSB*, supersedes Rees's *Cambro-British Saints*. Other texts are widely scattered in the Bollandist *Acta Sanctorum*, cited as *ASS*, and *Analecta* chronology, they bring their heroes into contact with one another, and with lay princes who are dated in the Annals, and related to one another in the genealogies. The whole, therefore, forms an interlocking corpus, no part of which can sensibly be studied in isolation. Most of the saints' lives are unattractive documents, sensational popular literature that assumes the values of their own day, alien to the taste of a rational humanistic society and offensive to every canon of ancient and modern scholarship. To the modern student they have their easy deceits, negative as well as positive. It is tempting to assume that an early manuscript is more 'reliable' than a late one, a simple sober account more solid than a florid account full of wonders. It is sometimes so; but once a life passes out of direct contact with contemporary sources, oral or written, usually when it was written more than a century after the death of its hero, such assumptions prove fallible. Baldric's[1] twelfth-century life of Samson is, for example, much less devolved from its extant original than the eighth-century life of Germanus of Auxerre used by Nennius,[2] and Jerome's fourth-century life of Paul[3] is more fanciful than many medieval lives. It is also easy to be unwarrantably deterred by the quantity and character of miracles. In an age of superstition, the degrees of sobriety and fancy are much more qualities of the individual writer than indications of date. Jonas[4] describes in detail the physical appearance of St. Peter to his own abbot; he was present in the room at the time, though unfortunately asleep. Adomnan[5] was born within about thirty

Bollandiana, cited as *AB*, and elsewhere, those prior to 1911 being listed in *BHL*. Capgrave's *Nova Legenda Angliae* (London, 1516), ed. Horstman (Oxford, 1901), cited as *NLA*, and Leland's *de Scriptoribus Britannicis* (Oxford, 1709), cited as *SB*, contain material not elsewhere published.

The principal collections of summaries of lives are Albert le Grand, *Les Vies des Saints de la Bretagne-Armorique* (Nantes, 1634–6, republished ed. Kerdanet, Saint-Brieuc, 1837), cited as le Grand; S. Baring-Gould and J. Fisher, *Lives of the British Saints* (London, 1907–10), cited as *LBS*; and G. H. Doble's Cornish Saints series, republished in part as *The Saints of Cornwall*, ed. D. Attwater (Truro, 1960–5), cited as Doble. Le Grand is bedevilled by the importation of exact dates, more entertaining than misleading, but had access to many manuscripts which perished in the French Revolution; *LBS* has curious identifications, and makes no attempt to differentiate the absurdly devolved from the plausible and possible, but is a mine of information; Doble is more concerned with topography than with chronology. The works starred list their lives in alphabetical order; most of the others are adequately indexed. I have not been able to consult Ussher's works or O'Hanlon's *Lives of the Irish Saints*.

[1] Cf. p. 101, n. 3 below.
[2] Chs. 32–35; 39; 47–48; cf. Constantius, *Vita Germani*, *MGH.SRM.* vii. 259 ff.   [3] *PL.* 23. 17 ff.
[4] *Vita Columbani*, 2. 23a; *MGH.SRM.* iv. 146.
[5] Bull: Adomnan 2. 17; cf. Fechin, ch. ix (*VSH* 2. 79). Resurrection 1. 1; 2. 32. Voyages 2. 42. Foresight and demons, *passim*.

years of Columba's death, but brings into his story the standard wonders of medieval folklore, the milking of a bull, the resurrection of the dead, as well as fabulous voyages, quantities of telegraphic foresight, and visible aerial conflicts with demons. The source of one of the more dramatic water engineering miracles of late medieval Irish hagiography is Gregory the Great,[1] to whom the neighbouring bishop had at once told the story 'ante biduum', the day before yesterday. No account could be more contemporary, and it is plain that credibility has little to do with date.

The positive element embedded in the saints' lives is well delineated by the French scholar, Fustel de Coulanges.[2]

> Saints' lives are also history. . . . They were certainly not compiled as works of history; . . . their aim was rather to demonstrate the sanctity of their hero . . . in the interest of the church or abbey that had taken him for patron. A large number . . . of these lives have been preserved. Unfortunately, they have rarely been studied from the point of view of textual criticism, or of testing their validity.
>
> It can be said in general that the life of each saint was written by one of his disciples, or by a man who knew him, or at least on the evidence of his acquaintances. But this primitive version has hardly ever come down to us. . . . Each century re-copied it, making changes and additions. . . . It is very difficult to distinguish what belongs to this first text from what has been added.
>
> The use of documents of this kind therefore demands considerable prudence; but once that has been taken, they are of high value. . . . We may be certain that the author did not invent; though he added virtues to his hero, he did not imagine the small details of his life. . . . What interests us is not the miracle, but the details that surround it. . . .
>
> Though there are often errors of date, transpositions of proper names, facts distorted by the hagiographer's preconceived ideas, that is unimportant. What we need to look for are the . . . facts that the hagiographer had no incentive to change.

The essence of the matter could not be put more clearly; the problem is to distinguish 'changes and additions' from the 'first text'; the well worn principle of 'cui bono' is the method; the 'facts that the hagiographer had no incentive to change' must be isolated from distortions due to his interest, carelessness, or preconceptions.

Fortunately, we do not have to rely on guesswork. A number of lives exist in successive versions, which enable us to see what later versions changed and what they did not change. The student is immediately struck by the difference between Latin Irish lives and British lives.

---

[1] *Dialog.* 3. 9; cf. Fridian (Finnian Magbil.), *ASH* 638, cf. 634–5.
[2] *Histoire des Institutions Politiques de l'ancienne France: la Monarquie Franque* (Paris, 1888), pp. 9–12, cited *Lismore*, xci–xcii.

Adomnan[1] ends his life of Columba with an injunction that his text be exactly copied. In general, he was heeded. His work is extant in a dozen or more manuscripts, written between the eighth and the sixteenth centuries. Some copy an abridged version, and many offer variant readings, but none show any serious devolution from the original. There are also several other lives of Columba; though his exceptional eminence caused many wonderful tales to be attached to his name, and these lives contain some stories not reported by Adomnan, few of them offer violence to the substance of Adomnan's account or its date. So with Muirchu's Life of Patrick;[2] the Book of Armagh leaves out much found in the Brussels manuscript that did not appeal to its scribe; the Novara manuscript varies the wording and makes mistakes, but does not alter the story. Exceptionally, the Armagh legend added an immense quantity of material contrived for the particular interests of its church, but little that did not serve that interest directly and recognizably. The lives of Columban show equally little devolution, and the numerous lives collected in the Rawlinson, Salamanca, and other manuscripts have much in common. Unlike the British lives, they show no sign of a break in the continuity of their tradition. Their form is close to Adomnan's, save that their language and outlook is flat and jejune where his is vigorous and compelling, and that they commonly arrange their miracles in chronological framework rather than by subject. They name a vast number of persons or places, and numerous princes and saints occur many times over in different lives. As yet, these relationships have not been systematically studied; Patrick and Gregory the Great appear out of due time and place, and a few saints are given a life span of up to 300 years. Occasionally persons of the same or similar name are confused; evident additions are miracles that name no place or person, many of them borrowed from the lives of other saints. Otherwise they contain few obvious misplacements of time or place; the quantity of persons named and the degree of interlocking is so great that it cannot be attributed to invention or late addition.

A few British lives show a similar close continuity from their originals, occasionally evidencing a contemporary original source. The life of Samson[3] exists in three main versions, the seventh-century original citing a written contemporary text, a tenth- or eleventh-century version copied into the book of Llandaff, and Bishop Baldric's Norman twelfth-century version. Rough offensive detail is toned down; in the first version

[1] 3.23 (136a).
[2] Cf. p. 111, n. 3, and p. 118, n. 3, below.
[3] *BHL* 7478 ff. with R. Fawtier, *La Vie de Saint Samson* (Paris, 1912), a fresh text of the *vita prima*, with a somewhat naïve introduction.

the Abbot of St. Kew rejects Samson's request to stay with him. In Baldric, Samson rejects the abbot's invitation to stay, and Llandaff omits the story. In the first version, Samson 'in a fury' threatens king Childebert; Baldric replaces the furious threats with an edifying homily borrowed from Cyprian, and Llandaff again omits the incident. Baldric emends the account of Samson's consecration to conform with canon law, adds stories about Normandy and leaves out some set in Wales. Llandaff epitomizes, adds only the title 'archbishop', assigned to Dubricius. This is the general tendency; in British lives, Patrick and Gregory also appear out of due time, with them Arthur, Martin of Tours, Germanus of Auxerre. Apart from these few great names, few are added, and few appear in the wrong time and place. But later versions are much modernized; and the principles are explicitly stated. Vitalis of Fleury,[1] abridging Wrmonoc's Paul Aurelian, was offended by its 'Britannica garrulitate' and boasted of omitting many 'absona ... et ... barbara Britonum nomina'. But he adds nothing. Jocelyn of Furness[2] found one old life of Kentigern 'sanae doctrinae et catholicae fidei adversum', and a 'codiculum ... alium stilo Scottico dictatum ... per totum soloecismis scatentem'. He judged that his hero's life, 'signis et prodigiis gloriosam', was degraded by such 'relatu perverso, et a fide averso', and so made it his business 'ex utroque libello materiam collectam ... sarcire, et ... barbarice exarata Romano sale condire'.

Jocelyn in the twelfth century wrote after a break in continuity; needing a life, he had to root out old forgotten manuscripts. Eleventh-century Welsh monks had the same problem. Ricemarchus[3] concludes his David with an apology

hec ... ex plurimis ... in unum collegimus, que in vetustissimis patrie, maximum ipsius civitatis, sparsim inventa scriptis, que, assidua tinearum edacitate ac annosis evi terebraminibus per horas et cardines corrosa, ac ex antiquo seniorum stilo conscripta nunc usque supersunt.

His manuscripts, their margins eaten away, written by long dead ancients, had mouldered through a considerable period when no one wanted to read a life of David. Two, perhaps three, of the main texts he conflated may be distinguished, and chance preserves a sixth-century confirmation[4] for part of one of them. His more elegant

---

[1] *BHL* 6586.   [2] *BHL* 4646, pr.   [3] *VSB*, ch. 66.
[4] Ricemarchus, ch. 22, cites David's rule: 'iugum ponunt in humeris; suffosoria vangasque invicto brachio terre defigunt ... boum nulla ad arandum cura introducitur'. Gildas, *Ep*. iv, criticizes 'aratra trahentes et suffosoria figentes terrae cum praesumptione et superbia', in contrast to those who 'habent pecora et vehicula' with humility. *Ep*. iii castigates other practices of David's rule, as described by Ricemarchus. The words 'suffosoria figentes terrae' are distinctive enough to require a common origin, earlier than Gildas' letter and, therefore, in

contemporaries, Lifris[1] and Caradoc,[2] swell their text with unctuous reflexions and sugared adjectival clauses; but their task was like his and Jocelyn's, to write a new life on the basis of fragmentary originals alien to their taste. These are long lives; most British lives are abridgements, often abridgements of such twelfth-century re-editions, sometimes later expanded versions of such abridgements; so that in general the British lives show a far greater degree of devolution than the Irish lives. But none of them offer significant evidence of the invention of persons or places, other than those that are crudely and obviously coined to meet the needs of their own monastery in their own day. They frequently mistake names; but many such errors may be corrected from other lives, from inscriptions, genealogies, annals, and the like.

This material cries out for detailed study. Without it, any penetration beyond a broad outline of events is blind and tentative. The essential tools of such study are a dictionary of persons, listing what is said about each individual in which source; and a dictionary of British places, to match Hogan's *Onomasticum Goidelicum*. With this equipment, it should be possible to study the separate lives, the annalistic texts, the genealogists, with the thoroughness that so far has been restricted to Reeve's edition of Adomnan.

These are the limitations that hinder an assessment of the evidence for the fifth and sixth centuries in the British Isles. I have elsewhere[3] attempted a summary of the evidence for the political history. In brief, the imperial Roman government withdrew its support from Britain in 410, the year when the Goths took Rome, and thrust upon the islanders an unwilling independence. The British prospered, to their neighbours' surprise; against their ancient enemies, the Picts of northern Britain, they hired Germanic federates, Saxons, Anglo-Saxons, or English, but against the Scots of Ireland they employed diplomacy and native forces. Towards the middle of the fifth century, the Saxons rebelled, and half a century of bitter fighting in the rich lowlands destroyed the economy and civilization of Roman Britain. The British won the war, and defeated the Germanic settlers, as nowhere else in contemporary Europe. For two generations, from about 500, native governments controlled most of the island. A second Saxon revolt broke out sporadically about 550, soon

the lifetime of David. Since Gildas does not name David, it is not reasonable to suppose that Ricemarchus quoted Gildas, turning his abuse of anonymous arrogance to praise of David. He used the same sixth-century source as Gildas.

[1] *Vita Cadoci*, VSB.
[2] *Vita Cadoci*, AB 60 (1942), pp. 45 ff. *Vita Gildae*, BHL 3542 sup.; Williams, *Gildas*, 2, pp. 394 ff.
[3] 'Britain and Rome', in *Essays presented to Eric Birley*, ed. M. G. Jarrett and B. Dobson (Kendal, 1966), pp. 145–85, reprinted above, pp. 53–93.

after the great plague, gathering momentum after 570, until it mastered most of what is now England, by the early years of the seventh century. The monastic movement of the Celtic saints took shape in the first half of the sixth century, during the years of British political dominance.

The early history of Christianity in the British Isles naturally divides into three main periods; the urban episcopacy of the late Roman Empire; the bishops and early ascetics of the later fifth century; and the monastic explosion of the sixth century. British Christianity is feebly evidenced in the fourth century. A few British bishops attended conferences in Gaul,[1] and were praised for their steadfastness in the Arian controversy. There is a considerable Christian archaeology,[2] but few dates to show whether any significant part of it belongs to the fourth century rather than the early fifth. The structure and extent of the religious as of the secular life of Britain must in the main be inferred from the practice of Gaul. The emperors governed through four prefects; each prefecture contained a number of provinces, five in Britain, governed by *rectores*, brigaded into dioceses, each administered by a vice-prefect or vicar. Britain formed one such diocese. But the foundation of government was the self-governing *civitas*, a political state shaped from a pre-Roman people, now, in the lowlands, subsumed in its principal town. Each *civitas* had its bishop, and the bishop of the chief town of each province ranked as metropolitan. There are no grounds for supposing bishops anywhere but in the chief towns of *civitates*. The church was a hierarchy based on towns, with comparatively little impact upon country folk before the last years of the century. Even within the towns, it was a quite recent growth; in Tours, a city about which we are well informed, thanks to the researches of Gregory of Tours,[3] the first effective bishop took office about 340, convening his congregation in a private house, until they grew too numerous to be accommodated therein, and rich enough to build a modest church. The next bishop, Martin, elected in 372, built a second and larger church, his successor a third. The faint uncertain archaeological traces of urban churches in Britain, notably in Verulamium,[4] suggest some parallels with the recorded

[1] The references, from Mansi, Hilary of Poitiers, Athanasius, Sulpicius Severus and others, are conveniently assembled in Haddan and Stubbs, *Councils*, i (1869), pp. 7 ff.

[2] The evidence is assembled by W. H. C. Frend, *J.B.A.A.* 18 (1955), pp. 1–18; the principal subsequent discovery is the splendid pavement from Hinton St. Mary, now in the British Museum, cf. J. M. C. Toynbee in *J.R.S.* liv (1964), pp. 7 ff.; *Proceedings of the Dorset Natural History and Archaeological Society*, lxxxv, 1963 (1964), pp. 116–21.

[3] Greg. Tur. *H.F.* 10. 31; cf. 1. 48.

[4] Cf. pp. 145–53, below.

evolution of Tours. Tours was typical, for, though Christianity was stronger in Trier and a few other great royal and military centres, the number of sees whose existence is credibly attested in northern and central Gaul before the middle of the century is exceedingly few.

The laymen whom the church served in lowland Britain, south and east of the Trent and Severn, in the East Riding and on the south Welsh coast, shared a civilization very like that of northern and central Gaul. All were Roman citizens, the earlier distinction between native and foreign Roman long forgotten. Their upper classes were at least as wealthy and well educated as their cross-Channel neighbours. But the highland zones, the moors of Devon and Cornwall, mountainous Wales, and the Pennines, were too poor to have much part in the material civilization of Rome. The north was overshadowed by a considerable standing army; beyond it, British border states reached to the frontiers of the alien Picts beyond the Clyde and Forth. The name of Scot was still restricted to the inhabitants of Ireland, who had recently by force of arms established numerous colonies on the coasts of western Britain. Most were to be subjugated during the fifth century, save in Demetia, south-west Wales; though new emigrants were to follow in some areas.

The intelligible history of British Christianity begins with the visit of Victricius,[1] bishop of Rouen, about 396. He was invited by his 'worthy fellow bishops to make peace', and was satisfied with the result. He 'filled the sensible with love of peace, taught the teachable, overbore the ignorant, and attacked the unwilling'. Though he believed that his views prevailed, he admits a strong opposition. He described the visit in a letter to Ambrose of Milan and others immediately on his return to Europe. Though he gives no detail of points at issue, he says that he took to Britain 'the precepts of the martyrs'; and makes plain what he understood those precepts to be. He, and Amator[2] of Auxerre, were the most prominent of Martin's pupils. Martin, who was still alive, stood out in men's minds as the plebeian bishop who spoke to and for the conscience of ordinary men. He had won fame as the first anchorite of Gaul; he was disliked by his gentlemanly fellow bishops[3] as 'shabbily dressed, with unbrushed hair'; he treated emperors[4] as equals, neither less nor greater than other men, with as little respect as 'other bishops accorded to minor court officials'. He refused to live in the bishop's house, and in his cell outside Tours established a monastic school; and he was the first to preach extensively to peasants.

[1] Victricius, *de laude Sanctorum* 1.
[2] Sulpicius Severus, *Dialogi* 3. 1. 4.
[3] Sulpicius Severus, *Vita Martini* 9; cf. *Dialogi* 1. 26. 3.
[4] Sulpicius Severus, *Vita Martini* 20. 2; 20. 5–7; *Dialogi* 2. 5. 5.

Martin became a legend in his lifetime, and Victricius followed his example, and extended it. He expressed in principle the contempt for earthly dignity that Martin practised:[1] 'Divinity spits upon degree, breaks beyond time and place. . . . Men differ not by nature, but in place and time, in their occupations and ideas. (Social) difference is foreign to (divine) unity.' He preached not only to peasants, but also to the border peoples[2] of the barbarian frontier, as none before him; and he embraced eagerly the newly devised cult of the martyrs, Christian heroes who had defied unjust authority. He was a controversial figure before his visit, more so thereafter. Pope Innocent[3] sent him a dozen rulings. One, forbidding the ordination of baptized soldiers, touched him, for he was an ex-soldier and conscientious objector. Two more may have derived from the British visit; a bishop may not ordain on his own, or without the metropolitan's licence; appeals from a provincial synod lie to Rome alone, not to other provinces. Though we do not know what was discussed, nor the strength of the opposing parties, we do know that the causes Victricius favoured prospered in Britain in the next few years. Half a dozen British monks[4] are known, though western monks were still rare, and known British individuals rarer still; one of them, Pelagius, who moved to Rome by A.D. 400, became the outstanding champion of the older, humanistic, and classical values within Christianity against the harsh logic of Augustine. His essential view, man's right to reach direct communion with God through good works, lies close to the heart of monasticism. It was not seriously impugned until after the fall of Rome in 410, nor outlawed before 418; and by that time the writ of Rome had ceased to run in Britain, so that his outlook continued to prevail widely among the Christians of Britain, without sharp awareness that Europe treated it as heresy.

The cult of martyrs was also a novelty when Victricius came to Britain; but within thirty years the relics of St. Alban[5] were the centre of a national cult of importance. Few but Victricius had bothered in the west with border barbarians, but in Britain someone had converted some of the Picts,[6] well before the time of St. Patrick; and early tradition, older than Bede,[7] calls the missionary Ninian, a Briton operating

[1] *de Laude Sanctorum* 6–7 (*P.L.* 20. 448 f.).
[2] Paulinus of Nola, *Ep.* 18. 4 (*P.L.* 61. 239).
[3] Innocent, *Ep.* 2 (*P.L.* 20. 472).
[4] Pelagius; Coelestius, the Sicilian Briton, the author of *de Virginitate* (cf. pp. 17–51, especially 32, 28, 27); Faustus of Riez; Constans, son of the emperor Constantine III (Orosius 7.40); perhaps also Antiochus and Martyrius, named by the Sicilian Briton, monks, but possibly not British.
[5] Constantius, *Vita Germani* 16.
[6] Patrick, *Ep. ad Coroticum* 2 and 15 (*VT* 375, 379).
[7] *H.E.* 3. 4: 'Predicante eis verbum Nynia episcopo . . . de natione Brettonum,

from a church named after Martin at Whithorn in Galloway, whose excavated remains are of early but uncertain date. Another church, at Canterbury,[1] was named after Martin, and built 'while the Romans were yet in Britain'; it may not be the only one, for archaeologically it cannot be distinguished from many other simple early churches in Roman towns, whose first foundation neither Bede nor anyone else records. The name of Martin,[2] not of Victricius, is associated with these churches and with the barbarian mission; but Victricius was the eager advocate of Martin's views, himself the pioneer of barbarian missions, and it is his name that Patrick[3] cites as the inspirer of his undertaking in barbarian Ireland.

Little else is known of the British church for a generation, beyond the fact that Victricius' ideals made headway, and that Pelagian views remained prominent. In 429 they were noticeable enough to cause Germanus of Auxerre, Amator's successor, to visit Britain; he is said[4] to

qui erat Romae regulariter ... edoctus; cuius sedem episcopatus sancti Martini episcopi nomine et ecclesia insignem ... nunc Anglorum gens obtinet; qui locus ... vulgo vocatur ad Candidam Casam' (Whithorn). For the excavations, cf. especially *Transactions of the Dumfriesshire Natural History and Archaeological Society*, xxviii (1957).

[1] Bede, *H.E.* 1. 26: 'Ecclesia in honorem sancti Martini antiquitus facta, dum adhuc Romani Brittaniam incolerent, in qua regina ... orare consuerat.' Roman towns with ancient Martin churches include also Chester, Chichester, Colchester, Exeter, Leicester, Lincoln, London, York, as well as Ancaster and many other smaller towns. Ancient churches named after Martin's favourite saints, Peter and Paul, are found in Cambridge and many other smaller Roman towns.

[2] Considerable confusion has been created by arguments as to whether or no churches could be 'dedicated' to living or recently dead persons. It largely arises from misuse of the modern word 'dedication'. In the fourth and early fifth centuries churches were 'dedicated' to God; they were commonly named after, or in honour of, their builders, or their builders' masters. Thus the first basilica on the Esquiline was the Basilica of Liberius; its fifth-century successor, S. Maria Maggiore, was named in honour of the Virgin. The first church of Tours was the Basilica of Litorius; Martin's church in the *monasterium maius* was named 'in honour of' the apostles Peter and Paul; his successor Brictius built a third church 'above the body of Martin' (Greg. Tur. *H.F.* 10. 31). The fifth- and sixth-century British continued the practice in vogue in Rome and Gaul at the time of the separation of Britain from the empire. In the life of Samson, echoing a sixth-century original, a monastery on the Severn was known as 'the monastery held to have been built by Germanus'; Paul Aurelian's churches in Brittany, attested on equally early authority, were usually known by his name, sometimes in honour of his teacher Iltut. None were 'dedicated' to Martin, Germanus, Samson, Paul, or Iltut. Bede's language, describing two churches 'in the name of', or 'in honour of' Martin, is entirely correct. In common parlance, and later usage, they were known as 'St. Martin's, Germanus', Samson's church'. Ailred's story, *Vita Niniani* 3, that Ninian decided to name his church after Martin when he heard of Martin's death (397) during the construction of the church is wholly unconfirmed, but is fully in accord with the usage of his time.   [3] See p. 112, n. 4, below.

[4] Sent by Gallic bishops according to Constantius, *Vita Germani* 12; by Celestine on Palladius' suggestion according to Prosper, *Chron.* a. 429.

have come at the instance of the bishops of Gaul, and on the authority of Pope Celestine, instigated by his deacon Palladius. The two traditions are complementary rather than contradictory, for the Pope's authority outweighed objections to bishops who meddled abroad. Half a century later in Gaul, Germanus' biographer regarded his visit as wholly successful; in Rome at the time success seemed less than complete, for the chronicler Prosper makes no such claim, and two years later Celestine sent Palladius in person to Britain.

These visits are precisely dated by an exact contemporary. They seemed to have coincided approximately with a critical change in the secular politics of Britain; the then British government, headed by Vortigern,[1] put a final end to the two major foreign dangers that had beset Roman Britain for centuries. A threatened Pictish invasion was averted with the help of Saxon, or English, federate troops, and the Picts were never again a serious threat. Other means were used to contain the Irish; native forces began a long methodical reduction of the Irish colonies established in western Britain, while mainland Ireland made no detectable effort to help them. Later Irish tradition believed that the then king of Ireland[2] married his son to the daughter of the king of Britain; and their child was given the name of Vortigern. It is a tradition of a marriage alliance, sealing a treaty, for the Irish raids that had plagued Britain for two hundred years ended abruptly.

Secular and religious developments went hand in hand, for the same men took part in both. The detail is irrecoverable; but some of the tendencies are plainly visible. In Europe, a powerful section of the magnates angrily resented Germanic settlement; but the strongest adherents of

---

[1] Cf. pp. 53–93, especially 60ff., where the sources are listed.

[2] *Additamenta ad Collectanea Tirechani* (Book of Armagh 16ʳ (ed. J. Gwynn, p. 31); *AB* 2 (1883), p. 214; *VT* 334–5), and derivative sources. The king's son Fedelmid married 'filiam regis Brittonum' and named their son Fortchern. The dates assigned in Irish tradition to the king, Laoghaire, *c.* 428–*c.* 465, almost exactly coincide with those indicated in British sources for Vortigern, *c.* 425–*c.* 457. Even without the grandson's name, he is the king implied. Fortchern is an Irish transliteration of Vortigern. The name exists in Ireland, but is extremely rare; it occurs on two inscriptions, *CIIC* 97 and 297, and twice among the 13,000-odd persons indexed by O'Brien, *CGH*. The dramatic date in both genealogies is later fifth century, and both are northern. The inscriptions are southern; 97 looks early, but is the second inscription on a re-used stone. These four instances do not demonstrate that the name existed independently of the king's grandson; they suggest that it had a short-lived popularity, in his time or soon after. The story of marriage was set down more than three hundred years after the event, and is unconfirmed. It is, however, an incidental notice, neither designed nor used to foster the author's purposes, and may echo genuine tradition. It makes sense in the circumstances of its own day.

Augustine championed the policy of accepting, baptizing, absorbing the barbarians. In Britain, a large party among the magnates[1] also opposed barbarian settlement; and in Britain Pelagian views, outlawed in Europe, were also strong among the aristocracy. We do not know how far these views coincided, how strong were the various parties; but we do know that these tensions existed. Further, the policy of Vortigern brought a new dimension into foreign relations and attitudes thereto, an alliance with the Irish, a problem of friendly relations with at least some of the Irish, and therewith a problem of Christian attitude towards a pagan people.

The words of Prosper, written two or three years after the event, illustrate the complexity, as it was seen at the time. In the *Chronicle*, he states that Celestine in 431 'sent Palladius as first bishop to the Irish who believed in Christ'. In the *Contra Collatorem*,[2] he sums up Celestine's achievement with a slightly different emphasis; after expelling the Pelagian leaders from Italy, he 'took no less care to free the British Isles from the same disease; ... in consecrating a bishop to the Irish, while he was striving to keep the Roman island catholic, he also made the barbarian island Christian'.

These Irish who were already Christian need explanation. Their probable location stands out clearly; in most of western Britain, the Irish settlers were reduced in the course of the fifth century, subdued, expelled, or absorbed. But in their strongest settlement, in Demetia, south-west Wales, emerged a bilingual state, its Irish element on a par with the British, in an area richer in the material civilization of Rome than other western regions where the Irish had settled. The principal

---

[1] Cf. p. 72, above.

[2] Ch. 21 (*P.L.* 51. 271) 'Coelestinus ... Coelestium (Pelagianum) ... totius Italiae finibus iussit extrudi. ... Nec vero segniore cura ab hoc eodem morbo Britannias liberavit, quando quosdam inimicos gratiae solum suae originis occupantes etiam ab illo secreto exclusit oceani, et ordinato Scotis episcopo, dum Romanam insulam studet servare Catholicam, fecit etiam barbaram Christianam.'

Prosper could hardly have made it plainer that in his view the consecration of a bishop to the Irish was one among the measures Celestine took to combat Pelagianism in Britain. This was a considered estimate of Celestine's efforts, set down a few years later, after Celestine's death, in the pontificate of his successor, Xystus, who was reported to have been at least lukewarm in his pursuit of Pelagians. Prosper was a zealous Augustinian, visited Celestine in Rome in 431, and became *notarius* to Xystus' successor Leo in 440, who renewed the anti-Pelagian campaign. He asserts that Celestine excluded some Pelagians from Britain, and strove to keep the island Catholic; but does not say that he succeeded. The statement that he incidentally 'made Ireland Christian' addressed to southern Gauls and Italians, partially offsets the limited success of the main objective. It is to be observed that Patrick's writings show no sign of Pelagian views, or of any urge to combat the heresy. There is no reason to suppose that his appointment was anything other than a straightforward mission to the Irish.

settlement of Demetian Irish was drawn from the Dessi of south-eastern Ireland, and there alone in Ireland survived a faint distorted tradition of a Christianity earlier than Patrick. It is probable that Irish Christianity in 431 was principally located in Demetia, and in the homeland of the Demetian colonists, carried thither by the colonists to their relations in Ireland.

But Palladius' mission[1] had more than one purpose. There was as yet no papal policy of missions to barbarians beyond the frontier; no bishops were sent to the Rugii or Langobardi, Alamanni or Franci, though they mattered more to Rome than Ireland, and had colonies enough on Roman soil as fully exposed to Christian influence. It is quite inconceivable that the sole, or even the principal purpose, of the consecration of a Roman deacon, one of the Pope's principal confidants, a leading figure in the campaign against Pelagian heretics throughout the Roman world, was the spiritual need of a small remote barbarian community of recent converts. Hundreds of humbler priests were available for this modest enterprise, had anyone considered it worth consecrating a bishop. So Prosper emphasizes the main purpose of consecrating an eminent ecclesiastic from the Pope's entourage to the Irish; it was while he was striving to keep Britain Catholic, that he also made Ireland Christian. The principal object was the fight against Pelagianism in Britain. In authorizing the short visit of a Gallic bishop, Celestine had exerted his authority to the full. His was not yet an age when the Pope might send his deacon as a legate[2] or nuncio to whom incumbent bishops must defer. To complete the work of Germanus, he needed a trustworthy orthodox bishop on the spot to co-ordinate and lead the Catholics; he could not intrude upon an existing see, nor yet create a new territorial see among the British, but in appointing a bishop to the Irish he established in Britain a representative whom the native bishops could not refuse to accept.

But Palladius could not neglect his official responsibilities, in Ireland

---

[1] Prosper (*Chron.* a. 429) 'ad insinuationem (variants: ad actionem, actione) Palladii diaconi, papa Caelestinus Germanum ... vice sua mittit'; the words, and Prosper's usage elsewhere, mean a deacon, more properly, the deacon of the Pope at Rome. P. Grosjean (*AB* 63 (1945), pp. 76 ff.) has put out of court the ill-informed suggestion that he was a deacon of Auxerre, or of any other place than Rome; to which may be added that the concept of a 'stirps Palladiorum', a family bearing this name, cannot commend itself to anyone acquainted with the prosopography of the Later Empire. The name is a *signum*; though the usage of *signa* is not understood, they were certainly not family names, and in the fourth and earlier fifth centuries it does not follow that two men sharing the same *signum* are related to each other, while relatives often used different *signa*.

[2] The function already existed; Celestine sent Germanus *vice sua*. What was lacking was the papal authority that could compel submission.

as in Demetia. His was an uncharted undertaking, for the experience of western barbarian missions was as yet limited to the work of Martin's pupils, in the Low Countries and among the Picts, and Palladius was no radical disciple of Martin. Prosper is content with the bald statement that he 'converted Ireland'. From the sequel, it is plain that the words oversimplify; at best, some people were converted in some part, presumably the south. The later Irish[1] believed that the 'fierce and stubborn people did not easily receive his doctrine, nor did he wish to spend time in a foreign land', so that he went back to Britain, and there died.[2] The Roman and the Irish versions are not so much contradictory as different views of the same event.

Palladius was followed by Patrick,[3] and Patrick speaks for himself.

[1] Muirchu 7.

[2] Palladius' death. A group of manuscripts of Prosper's *Chronicle*, a. 431, read 'Palladius ... moritur' in place of 'mittitur'; meaning not that he was sent in 431, but at some unstated previous time, and then died. He was, however, certainly not sent earlier than 429, when he was still in Rome, and the reading, credible because it is a *lectio difficilior*, does not make such good sense as 'mittitur'. It is not excluded that both readings descend from an original 'mittitur et statim moritur'. It is to be noted that Prosper twice names Palladius in the *Chronicle*, going out of his way to do so in the 429 annal, for it is not usual to name the adviser who prompted the Pope's decision, but pointedly omits his name in the *Contra Collatorem*, where it might be expected as naturally as in the 431 entry, more so than in the 429 entry. If the works had been written under different popes, the reason might have been that Palladius was a powerful figure under Celestine, in less favour with Xystus. But both works were published under Xystus, the *Chronicle* (first edition) about 433, the *Contra Collatorem* one or perhaps two years later. It is a strong possibility that Prosper left his name out of the later work because he had in the meantime died. Muirchu's two statements (ch. 7) that he set out to return 'to him who sent him', and that he died *en route*, in Britain, well fit what Prosper says of his office and his mission, and his implication of an early death. The Irish tradition that his successor was consecrated before the death of Celestine (27 July 432), while quite possible, may well rest on an assumption, drawn from the knowledge that Palladius was sent by Celestine, and the belief that Patrick was sent very soon after.

[3] Patrick's two extant works, the *Confessio* and *Epistula ad Coroticum* have been published by J. D. Newport White, *Proceedings of the Royal Irish Academy*, 25 c (1904–5), pp. 201–326, cf. 542–52, with translation, notes, and indexes; also SPCK, *Texts for Students*, 4 (London, 1918); by L. Bieler, *Libri S. Patricii*, 2 vols., Dublin, 1952, translation *The Works of Saint Patrick* (Ancient Christian Writers, Catholic University of America, no. 17, Westminster, Maryland, and London, Longmans, 1953), with notes and indexes. Both translations require some caution, especially in the crucial passages. Both works are also included in Stokes's misnamed *Vita Tripartita* (Rolls Series, two volumes, with continuous pagination, 1887) which remains the only conveniently accessible corpus of Patrician Literature, here cited as *VT*. Bieler's *Codices Patriciani Latini* (1942), is a comprehensive catalogue of the manuscripts and editions thereof. The Brussels manuscript of Muirchu is published in *AB* 1 (1882), pp. 531 ff., the Novara manuscript in *Proceedings of the Royal Irish Academy*, 52 c (1948–50), pp. 179–220; Tirechan and the Additamenta thereto are also published, from the

Two of his own writings survive, a deeply moving revelation of his motives and ideals, of the men who helped and hindered him, of the circumstances in which he worked. Despite the clear witness of his own words, the interest of later Irish writers, ancient and modern, has bedevilled the nature and date of his mission; it is therefore imperative to examine closely what he wrote himself, before investigating what others wrote about him. His writings were not autobiographical, not arranged chronologically, but are tracts written for specific purposes; but when his scattered references to his own career are arranged in order of time, they constitute an outline autobiography.

He was[1] the son of a leading citizen of a British *civitas*, a substantial landowner, a town councillor, and also a priest, who bore the honourable and ancient Roman name of Calpurnius, perhaps Calpurnius Potitus.[2] When Patrick was sixteen he was captured by Irish raiders, and served six years as a slave before escaping by sea. A 'few years' later he returned to his parents in Britain, who begged him never to leave home again. But[3]

in the bosom of the night I saw a man named Victricius[4] coming as if

---

Armagh text, in *AB* 2 (1883), pp. 35 ff., 213 ff. With few exceptions, the Irish texts are derivatives, or expansions, or embellishments of these works. The chapter numeration of the *Confessio* and *Epistula* was introduced by White, that of Muirchu and Tirechan in *AB*. Neither is in *VT*.

[1] Chs. 1 ff. (*VT* 357 ff.).

[2] A *nomen* (family name) and *cognomen* (personal name). The old-fashioned common usage of the early empire survived in the fourth century especially among the curial classes. Later scribes, accustomed to one name for one man, tended to turn two names to two people and may have done so here; but since the family name passed from father to son, the grandfather, if not the father, will in any case have been properly Calpurnius Potitus.

[3] Ch. 23 (*VT* 364); chapter references are to the *Confessio*, unless otherwise stated.

[4] So the St. Vaast manuscript (Arras Bm 450), printed in *ASS*. Mart. 2, 530 ff. (ed. 2) where this passage is now mutilated. Of the other seven manuscripts, four read Victoricius, a name otherwise unknown, linguistically highly improbable, if not impossible. I have not been able to discover the readings of Bieler's manuscripts 2 and 8, nor to consult the critical apparatus of his text; White does not use them. On second-hand information they also read Victoricius. Otherwise only Armagh has the variant Victoricus, which has found its way into most printed versions. This is a genuine late Roman name, but almost exclusively African, whence come some 60 of the 66 instances in *CIL*. Victricius of Thérouanne (*BHL* 3224-9, cf. 6999 ff.) is an eighth-century invention; cf. Duchesne, *Fastes de la Gaule Anc.* 3, pp. 147 f. The Irish bishop Victoricus of Tirechan is in all probability a creature manufactured from *Confessio* 23. The St. Vaast form is therefore balanced against the Armagh spelling, and seems the better reading; as Grosjean observes (*AB* 63 (1945), p. 99 top) it is Victricius' 'image that would naturally appear in a dream' to Patrick; fancies bringing Victricius to preach to Roman army units raised centuries before in or near his diocese (Anscombe, *Eriu* vii (1914), pp. 13 ff.; cf. Simpson, *J.B.A.A.*, 3rd series,

from Ireland with innumerable letters. . . . as I read. . . I thought I heard the voice of those who were by the wood of Foclut near the western sea, crying out with one mouth, 'We beg thee, holy boy, to come and walk among us again'. . . . Thank God, the Lord vouchsafed their cry after many years.

In later life, he was continually guided by visions, in which the Holy Spirit determined his action:

I saw Him praying in me, and it was as though He was in my body. . . . I . . . pondered who it was that prayed in me. But, at the end. . . He spoke and said that He was the Spirit.[1]

He afterwards regretted that he 'did not quickly come to recognize the grace that was then in me . . . though I ought to have obeyed'.[2] What chiefly held him back for 'many years' was doubt about his own fitness, especially doubts about his weak Latin, due to his interrupted education, that put him at a disadvantage in contrast to his fellows, 'who seem wise and learned in the law and powerful with words and all else'.[3] Since he is comparing his own fitness for the episcopate with others, he is clearly thinking of other clerics.

Though he has much to say of the circumstances of his consecration, all that he hints of the years before is that he did not stay at home, and that at some time he came to know the 'saints of Gaul'.[4] When his appointment came, it was controversial. In accepting, he rejected his parents' plea to stay at home and accept public office[5] in his own state, and also unwillingly offended some of his 'seniors',[6] clearly ecclesiastical. There were

many who opposed my legation, saying behind my back 'Why does he risk himself among the enemy who know not God?' It was not from malice . . . but because of my rusticity.[7]

vii (1942), p. 51) have no relevance save that their absurdity tends to discredit what is otherwise the sounder reading. Victricius' name is similarly corrupted in the MSS. of Innocent *Ep.* 2, commonly spelt Victoricius.

[1] Ch. 24 (*VT* 364), reading 'erat' with the majority of manuscripts; the 'eram' of White and Bieler seems to me to make poor sense.

[2] Ch. 46 (*VT* 371).

[3] Ch. 13 (*VT* 361). Bieler's translation of the difficult 'dominicati rhetorici' as 'men of letters on their estates' is plainly impossible; the adjective from 'dominicum', estate, is well attested, and means attached to the estate, servile. Nor does the adjective mean 'lordly' (White); Christine Mohrmann's 'learned clergymen' (*The Latin of St. Patrick*, Dublin, 1961, p. 30), is much more attractive.

[4] Ch. 43 (*VT* 370).

[5] This is the proper meaning of 'munera multa', ch. 36 (*VT* 367). 'Gifts' is a possible alternative translation; but it seems a less likely inducement for an elderly father, himself holding public office, to hold out to his son, who must in any case soon expect his inheritance.

[6] Chs. 36–37 (*VT* 367). [7] Ch. 46 (*VT* 371).

Eventually, however, it was 'one of my dearest friends'[1] who pronounced the words 'You are fit to be given to the ranks of the episcopate.' The opposition of 'seniors', the discussion by 'many', the formal proposal for consecration, all imply a proposition put forward, debated, and decided in a competent assembly, a synod. Since his parents, his 'seniors', his 'dearest friend' were involved, it was a synod of British ecclesiastics, 'wise, learned in the law, powerful with words'. But it appointed Patrick as 'constituted bishop in Ireland';[2] yet the first bishop constituted to the Irish had been appointed by the Pope, and it was inconceivable that a later bishop should be consecrated without his approval; and papal initiative was to be expected. It is probable that, in the light of Palladius' limited success, the Pope judged it wise to secure the formal approval of the British episcopate, the more so since Patrick's appointment, unlike Palladius', was directed wholly towards the pagan Irish, with no sign of secondary direction towards the containment of British Pelagianism.

Patrick wrote his *Confessio* when he was aged about forty-five[3] or more, and had been in Ireland for some appreciable time. He had ordained a considerable number of priests, baptized very many, penetrated to areas[4] where no one had preached before, and induced 'sons and daughters of the underkings of the Irish'[5] to become monks and nuns, together with some slave girls; he had paid to lay rulers compensation to the value of at least fifteen men.

He must have received at least nominal licence and protection from either the king of Ireland or one or more provincial kings, for, though he risked death and suffered brief imprisonment, he makes it plain that in

[1] Ch. 32 (*VT* 366).
[2] *Ep.* ch. 1 (*VT* 375) 'Hiberione constitutum episcopum me esse fateor.' *Fateor* need bear no stronger emphasis than 'say', 'state as a fact'; White's 'confess' and Bieler's 'declare' seem over emphatic. *Constitutum* is by contrast the emphatic word, 'established', 'regularly appointed'. Hence the meaning is 'I am the consecrated bishop of (or in) Ireland' rather than 'a bishop (resident) in Ireland' (White, Bieler) which in normal English usage implies the existence of other bishops in Ireland, or even holders of Irish sees *in partibus*.
[3] Chs. 27 and 29 (*VT* 365). His sin was committed when he was barely fifteen, committed rather than confessed thirty years before he wrote.
[4] Ch. 51 (*VT* 372). The words imply previous missionaries. Further precision is unattainable; they could mean that he penetrated remoter districts, his predecessors only main centres; or that he worked in the north, others in the south.
[5] Ch. 41 (*VT* 369) 'Filii Scottorum et filiae regulorum monachi et virgines Christi esse videntur.' Bieler's translation here seems preferable to White's; the emendation 'sanctorum' for 'Scottorum' is unnecessary and improbable. The vows will have been personal, and need not imply monasteries; but the relative frequency of cells of virgins living in groups in the mid or late fifth century in later Irish tradition may derive from Patrick's converts. In Europe, the early church had also found that women found it more troublesome to live a life of dedicated chastity as individuals in society than men.

general he was allowed to go where he would, say what he liked, recruit whom he could.

He regarded himself as bishop in Ireland, and makes no mention of any other bishops; he could not have consecrated any himself without the co-operation of at least two other bishops, who must have come from outside, presumably Britain. Though an early story involves two British bishops in the consecration of one of his converts to the Isle of Man,[1] no comparable tale concerns any such consecration within Ireland.

It is unlikely that he received much co-operation from the British episcopate, for the *Confessio* was occasioned by the victory in Britain of those who opposed his mission. Some of his 'seniors' came to Ireland to call him to account for a boyhood sin,[2] evidently more of a pretext than the real basis of the attack. Guided by his inner voice, that must at times have irritated conventional ecclesiastics, he refused to heed them. But the 'dearest friend', who had once proposed his consecration, turned against him, and indicted[3] him at a meeting 'in Britain', where he was not present. Evidently he was summoned to Britain to defend his mission, for the *Confessio* explains his refusal to obey:

It would be possible for me to abandon them (my converts) and come to Britain. I should dearly love to visit my homeland and my parents; not only that, but also to go on to Gaul to visit the brethren and see the face of the saints of my Lord. God knows how I should love to. But I am bound by the Spirit and fear to lose the labour I have begun. It is not I, but Christ the Lord who ordered me to come, and to be with them for the rest of my life.[4]

The words formally reject the right of the British church to exercise jurisdiction over Ireland; the reminder that if he came to Britain he could also go to Gaul amounts to a gentle warning, for, though the bishops of Gaul had even less claim to legislate for Ireland, they were in a position to forward Patrick's case to Rome.

The *Confessio* names no persons and dates. But it depicts quite clearly the circumstances of the world in which it was written, in Britain as in Ireland. When he left Britain, his father was a decurion and he was him-

---

[1] Muirchu 22. Patrick set MacCuil adrift, his feet chained, in a coracle without rudder or oars, to take him to the land assigned to him by God. He landed on Evonia and was received by 'two holy bishops', Conindrus and Romulus (Rumilus), becoming their 'successor in the episcopate'. The story is already appreciably devolved; the drifting coracle is a popular dramatic theme in Celtic hagiography. The bishops have a British and a Roman name. Its probable origin is a consecration by Patrick and two British bishops.

[2] Chs. 27 ff. (*VT* 365). It seems probable that the incident was raked up in the service of a general attack on Patrick's work in Ireland.

[3] Ch. 32 (*VT* 366) 'pro me pulsaret'; 'put me to shame' (White); 'let me down' (Bieler). [4] Ch. 43 (*VT* 370).

self offered 'munera'. When he wrote, churchmen who were lawyers and rhetors by training were still an organized body, able to meet in synod, strong enough to claim superiority over Ireland and concerned to press their claim. This is an organized episcopate in a Roman land, still functioning in the manner of fifth-century Gaul and Britain. It is unlikely that the British church could have functioned in this way for any appreciable time after the outbreak of the Saxon revolt in the early 440s, next to impossible that what was left of it could even have bothered to assert such a claim after the disasters of the late 450s. The linguistic evidence agrees;[1] the words borrowed into Irish under the impetus of Patrick's mission are separated from those borrowed in the time of the monastic saints of the first half of the sixth century by a long interval, scarcely less than two or three generations. The Britain of Patrick's *Confessio* is a Roman Britain that ceased to exist in the middle of the fifth century.

The ancient literature about Patrick[2] requires exceptionally cool assessment, for the tradition of Patrick was eclipsed in Ireland by the monastic explosion of the sixth century, and was not widely revived until two hundred years after his death, at the time of the later stages of the Easter controversy. In the careful words of Kenney,[3] 'Patricius was not entirely forgotten, but ... his memory ... slipped into the background of old and far-off things.' The Easter controversy debated the external symbols of the date of Easter and the form of the tonsure, but it centred upon whether the Celtic churches should enter into full communion with the universal church of Latin Europe or remain in isolation. One aspect of this controversy was that Ireland lacked the hierarchical episcopal organization of the European church. The earliest surviving claim to such a hierarchy was advanced by Cogitosus,[4] whose life of

---

[1] Jackson, *LHEB* 125-48. The essence of the matter is that the main Irish borrowings from British Latin fall into two groups, trademarked the Cothriche and Pádraig groups from the form in which Patrick's name is spelt, separated from each other by a considerable interval of time. Jackson, MacNeill, and most scholars, assign the first group to Patrick and the early fifth century, the second group to the monastic saints of the mid sixth century, on the basis of the datable changes in British Latin. Binchy, however, has recently (*Studia Hibernica* 2 (1962), p. 166) made the acute observation that the earlier group has no word for bishop, though it has a word for priest; and therefore proposes to relegate it to the period before the first bishop, Palladius. There was, however, no need for a distinctive word so long as there was a single bishop; the name, Palladius or Patrick, was sufficient determinative. The point, however, serves to emphasize the evidence of the *Confessio* that until Patrick's death, or at least until his last years, he was sole bishop.   [2] Cf. p. 111, n. 3, above.

[3] J. F. Kenney, *The Sources for the Early History of Ireland*, vol. i, Ecclesiastical (all published, Columbia, 1929, cited hereunder as Kenney), p. 324.

[4] Prologue, Colgan, *ASH*, 518; *P.L.* 72. 775.

Bridget, probably written before 650, claimed for the Bishop of Kildare the title of 'Archbishop of the bishops of the Irish'. The claims of Kildare did not prevail; one hindrance was that monastic conservatism lasted longer and more strongly in the north, and the north was doubly indisposed to accept a southern primacy on a Roman model. One decisive change was the decision of Aed of Sletty,[1] one of the principal southern sees, to subordinate his church to Armagh. Armagh was believed to have been the principal church of Patrick, and Patrick was known to have been 'constituted bishop to the Irish', by an external episcopal authority, believed to be Rome. The assertion of Patrick's primacy both did away with innovation, in favour of an appeal to an accepted past fact of papal authority, and also gave the primacy of Ireland to the north. Aed's initiative was followed by the growth of the Patrician legend, whose essence was to claim for the paruchia of Patrick and Armagh all churches not contained within the paruchia of the greater monasteries, and some that those monasteries already claimed. The earliest and most influential of these works is Tirechan's Collections.

In considering the Patrician literature, it is therefore essential to distinguish the documents that show no trace of the claims of Armagh from those written in support of its claims. Only two such documents, free of Armagh influence, contain significant historical information ... a couple of entries in the Annals, and the biography of Patrick by Muirchu, son of Cogitosus. Several Annals record a 'Probatio Patricii'[2] by or in the time of Pope Leo the Great (440–61). The entry is the more significant because there is no attempt to explain its meaning; it plays no part whatever in the Patrician writers, though it is grist to their mill, and could not but have been heavily exploited by them if they had understood what it meant. Its origin is therefore old enough for its purport to have been forgotten by the latter part of the seventh century. The 'approval of Patrick' has, however, a clear meaning; it implies disapproval of his critics, by an authority superior to them. Patrick asserts himself that his principal critics were his 'seniors' in Britain; and the only authority capable of over-ruling them was the Pope. It is further known that Leo's principal ecclesiastical concern outside Italy, in Africa and Spain as in Gaul, was to assert the direct authority of Rome over individual bishops, to the detriment of metropolitans and synods; his policy committed him in advance to take Patrick's side in a dispute with

---

[1] *Tirechan Additamenta*, 16, *AB* 2 (1883), p. 231, *VT* 346. The notice was set down less than a hundred years after the event.

[2] Annals of *Inisfallen*, *Ulster*, and *Clonmacnoise* s.a. 440; the relevant section of *Tigernach* is waiting. The seventeenth-century annalists and Keating drop the entry.

the episcopate of Britain. Patrick himself, in dispute with the British bishops, cannot but have sought confirmation of his appointment independently of them, from Rome, and seems to hint at the possibility of such appeal in his reference to the brethren in Gaul. The travels of Germanus of Auxerre, who visited Britain and Italy, perhaps in 444-5,[1] provided a recorded occasion for the forwarding of an appeal; though there may well have been other, unrecorded, possible occasions. It is therefore highly probable that the sequel to the *Confessio* was a successful appeal for confirmation to Rome by Patrick, within the period 440-460, more happily in the 440s than the 450s.

The second relevant entry is the landing of Patrick in or about the year 432.[2] The year cannot be pressed over closely, for it rests on the plausible assumption that the mission of Palladius in 431 was of very short duration, and that Patrick followed immediately after his death; and the mention of Pope Celestine rather than of Xystus, who succeeded him in 432, need stem from no more than the knowledge that it was Celestine who consecrated Palladius. But it must be strongly emphasized that no ancient source whatsoever, whether written in the interest of Armagh or not, gives any authority for any other landing date than approximately 432.

Muirchu's biography,[3] commonly called Muirchu Book I, was written

[1] Cf. E. A. Thompson and P. Grosjean, *AB* 75 (1957), pp. 135 ff., 180 ff.; cf. *Antiquity* 30 (1956), p. 167.

[2] All Annals; cf. Muirchu, Prologue (*AB* p. 548), died 436 *a Passione*; ch. 7, arrived immediately after Palladius' short mission; Tirechan, ch. 2 (*AB* p. 36; *VT* 302), died 436 *a Passione*, after a mission of 31 to 34 years.

[3] The Book of Armagh transcribes Muirchu 'Book I', foll. 2^r to 7^r; at least one folio is wanting at the beginning, and the text begins in the middle of ch. 6; and transcribes separately fol. 20^{r-v}, the contents page, with a preface signed by Muirchu in his own name. The transcript of the text ends, at the bottom of 7^r, with the words 'finit primus incipit secundus liber'. Folio 7^v begins a second work with a contents table not ascribed to Muirchu, commonly described by modern writers as 'Muirchu Book II'. It is however simply the second book transcribed into the Armagh collection. The Brussels manuscript contains the full text of Muirchu 'Book I', but not the contents page and preface; it knows nothing of 'Muirchu Book II'; the Novara manuscript runs the two works together without contents pages or preface, and without ascription to any author. It must be emphasized that Armagh does not ascribe the second work to Muirchu; Brussels knew only the first; Novara thought both were one book. They may possibly be two works by the same author; but they are certainly not a single work divided into two books, as the modern descriptions easily lead the unwary to suppose. The second work is of an entirely different structure and character; it consists of a sentence on Patrick's prayers and a couple of anonymous unlocated miracles, followed by a 'de obitu et depositione Patricii' in ten chapters, while Muirchu's signed work is a 'Vita Patricii' properly so called, complete in itself. The second work is much more devolved; if it be by Muirchu, it bears the same relationship to the *Vita* as Sulpicius Severus' *Dialogi* to his *Vita Martini*, a later work following the success of the earlier.

at the instance of Aed of Sletty in the second half of the seventh century, perhaps about the 470s. It must be carefully distinguished from the complementary work that is commonly described as 'Muirchu Book II'. This work may or may not be a later product of the same author, but it is of a wholly different character, and is not ascribed to Muirchu in any ancient source. Muirchu begins and ends with a sober, scholarly, and accurate abstract of the biographical information contained in Patrick's surviving writings; in between he places an equally sober account of Patrick's life in Gaul, at Auxerre, under Amator(ex),[1] whom he did not know to be either Bishop of Auxerre or Germanus' predecessor, and under Germanus, an account which may well derive from lost writings of Patrick; and a collection of stories drawn from Irish tradition, cited on the authority of 'unreliable authors and fallible memory'. The study of Patrick's Latinity[2] tends to confirm the story of a prolonged stay in

[1] Muirchu 8 'declinaverunt iter ad . . . summum aepiscopum Amathoregem nomine in propinquo loco habitantem; ideoque sanctus Patricius . . . episcopalem gradum ab Amathorege sancto episcopo accepit' (Brussels manuscript; Armagh variants 'Amatho rege nomine', 'ab Matho rege'). The incident is placed after Palladius' death, on Patrick's departure from Auxerre for Britain. Amator was Germanus' predecessor at Auxerre, and died in 418. The obvious inference was long since drawn by Bury (*Life of St. Patrick*, pp. 347–9) and others; Muirchu added an oblique Irish case-ending -ig to Amator's name, and confused ordination as deacon with consecration as bishop, a mistake made easier since the Latin 'ordinavit' covers both modern terms.

[2] Patrick's Latin has been most recently discussed by Christine Mohrmann, *The Latin of St. Patrick* (Dublin, 1961). The facts are that we possess specimens of early to mid fifth-century Latin of Gaul, notably the Gallic (not Spanish) *Itinerarium Egeriae* (*P.L. Suppl.* i. 1047 ff.), probably written c. 414–17, cf. col. 1046, called in earlier editions the *Peregrinatio Aetheriae* or *Sylviae*, as well as numerous episcopal letters, etc.; and we also possess ample texts of early fifth-century British Latin, notably the various Pelagian British writers (cf. above, pp. 17–51) and Faustus of Riez, who had certainly left school before reaching Lérins about 426; though there is no positive indication of where he learnt his Latin, and well-to-do British adults certainly travelled in Europe, there are no grounds for supposing an education abroad for children, without evidence. The fact is that Patrick's Latin is much closer to that of Egeria than to any known British Latin. It is, of course, true that most writers, in Britain and Gaul, were better educated than Patrick and Egeria, and we have limited evidence for bad Latin in Britain or Europe; but it is rash to argue from the evidence we have not got, and that which we have links Patrick with Continental Latin. In particular, the argument of Binchy (*Studia Hibernica* 2 (1962), (here cited as *SH*), p. 88) that Patrick ought to have written better Latin if he had stayed any length of time at Auxerre rests on an unduly optimistic, unargued, estimate of the standards of Auxerre, and on an undue estimate of the amount of writing, and reading, that an ordinary cathedral cleric would be expected to undertake. It seems also to stem from the unspoken assumption, expressly formulated by R. P. C. Hanson, *St. Patrick* (Nottingham, 1966), that Britain was 'backward', 'unliterary', p. 14; such evidence as we have argues that a better Latin is to be expected from early fifth-century London or Cirencester than from Auxerre.

Gaul; though comparable texts are not numerous, as far as they go, Patrick's writing is very much closer to that of early fifth century Gaul than to that of Britain.

In Muirchu's account Patrick coasted Ireland to land in the centre of Ulaid territory in County Down. Apart from a dramatic visit to the highking (*imperator*) Laoghaire at Tara, and an expedition to found a church at Armagh, half an hour's walk from the ancient Ulaid capital of Emain Macha, long since absorbed in enemy territory, Patrick's activities are confined to Ulaid territory. Though Patrick's own account implies somewhat wider travels, Muirchu names no other places. Nor does it claim subordinate bishops; two later bishops, Fiacc of Sletty and Erc of Slane,[1] near Tara, are made his disciples, but Patrick is markedly not made to consecrate them. His only consecration, in which a muddled story involves two bishops with British and Roman names, is to the Isle of Man. Nor is there any sign in Muirchu that Armagh was his principal church; on the contrary, the neighbourhood of Downpatrick is his centre, Armagh not obviously introduced for any more cogent reason than the nostalgic patriotism of the Ulaid. Muirchu's account is wholly consistent with the *Confessio*; what it adds contains nothing improbable, save a wonder working virtue, that is noticeably less extravagant than that which Adomnan claims for Columba.

Muirchu's restraint is matched by the extravagance of Tirechan.[2] His Patrick consecrated 450 bishops, of whom about 50 are named;[3] his paruchia is 'the whole island and its inhabitants', including 'all the early churches of Ireland'.[4] Tirechan is good evidence for the seventh-

---

[1] Fiacc and Erc (Muirchu 16, 18) are both said to have been present at Patrick's encounter with Laoghaire at Tara, placed at his first Easter in Ireland. Fiacc 'qui postea mirabilis episcopus fuit, cuius reliquiae adorantur hi Sleibti' was an 'adoliscens poeta' with some substance and relevance to the story; 'Ercc filius Dego cuius nunc reliquiae adorantur in ... Slane' is not even said to have been a bishop, and is mentioned in a passing sentence. Both are named because of their seventh-century relics.

[2] Tirechan cites the oral evidence of Bishop Ultan, whose death the Annals place about 660; he wrote 'post mortalitates novissimos' (ch. 25), either the great plague of 664-8, or the cattle plague of 699-700 (MacNeill, *St. Patrick*, ed. Ryan (Dublin, 1964), pp. 127, 139). His first chapter uses Muirchu, or, less probably, Muirchu's sources, supplemented by Ultan. The whole of the rest of his claim concerns current Armagh claims, complementary to those made in the early eighth-century Book of the Angel (*VT* 352): *Book of Armagh*, foll. 20 ff.

[3] 450 Ch. 6 (*VT* 304; *AB* 37) 'de episcoporum numero quos ordinavit in Hibernia CCCCL; de prespiteris non possimus coordinare'. Forty-two bishops are named in ch. 6, three more in ch. 7, additional names in e.g. chs. 8, 16, 21, 22. The rest of the work enumerates the churches which Patrick 'plantavit', naming many of the bishops and priests installed, and of the lay princes who gave the sites.

[4] Ch. 18 (*VT* 311; *AB* 45) 'Omnia quae scripsi ... scitis quia in vestris regionibus gesta sunt. ... Cor autem meum cogitat in me de Patricii dilectione,

century topography of Ireland, and it is likely that he reproduces a number of genuine traditions of late fifth- and early sixth-century foundations, made before the mass monastic movement got under way. But his central theme is patent nonsense; Patrick certainly did not consecrate either 50 or 450 bishops, and while some of these early foundations may have derived directly or indirectly from his mission, many involve persons whose active life is ascribed to the very late fifth century or early sixth, in the Annals and Saints' Lives, whose own tradition knew nothing of Patrick. Tirechan connects them with Patrick because, at the time he wrote, their successors did not yet acknowledge the primacy of Patrick. His proclaimed bias and purpose, therefore, prohibits the use of any of his statements as evidence for the connexion of Patrick with any place or person not named in Muirchu. The statements of the numerous later Patrician writers who build upon him are even less admissible. Tirechan's method has some analogies with that of the compilers of the Book of Llandaff in Britain, in that both claim for their patrons the foundation of all early churches in the area of their later jurisdiction. But Tirechan lacks their relatively sound documentary basis, and it is not probable that any scholar would have paid serious attention to his claims, were it not for the abiding hold that the Patrician legend later took upon the church of Ireland.

The Armagh writers embroidered Patrick's dating. Muirchu, Tirechan's short biographical preface, and the Annals, bring him to Ireland about 432, and give his mission a duration of about thirty years, before his death in the early 460s. The addenda to 'Muirchu II' and the corresponding notices at the end of Tirechan give him the Mosaic age of 120 years,[1] sixty of them in Ireland.[2] This fancy, already developed by the late seventh or early eighth century, created endless confusion. Two

quia video dissertores et archiclocos et milites Hiberniae quod odio habent paruchiam Patricii, quia subtraxerunt ab eo quod ipsius erat . . . potest pene totam insolam sibi reddere in paruchiam quia Deus dedit illi totam insolam cum hominibus . . . ipsius sunt omnia primitivae ecclesiae Hiberniae.'

Tirechan here makes two statements; that Patrick 'planted' some 450 episcopal churches and many others served by presbyters; and that when he wrote many Irishmen did not believe that he was telling the truth. No one who considers his words is likely to accept the first statement, or to doubt the second. It is the modern history of Ireland that has prevented due consideration of these statements, and allowed his subsequent particular assertions to rank as serious historical evidence.

[1] 'Muirchu II' 6 (*VT* 296; *AB* 581); Tirechan 53 (*VT* 331; *AB* 67).

[2] Addenda to 'Muirchu II' ('Haec Constans in Gallia invenit') *VT* 300, *AB* *AB* 584, LXI years. Tirechan 53 (*VT* 331; *AB* 67), LXXII. In neither case do the sets of figures add up to the totals given; an instance of such figure corruption is elaborated by L. Bieler, *Proceedings of the Royal Irish Academy*, 52 c (1948–50), p. 215. The basic figure of sixty years before coming to Ireland is contained in

natural conclusions found their way into the Annals; 120 years were deducted from the death date[1] in the 460s to give a birth date about 340;[2] and thirty years were added to the death date in the 460s to give an alternative death date in the 490s. Then, faced with two death dates, the author of the penultimate note in Tirechan distinguished two Patricks, first and second, older and younger; and identified the first Patrick with Palladius;[3] though it must be noted that this author, the first contriver of two Patricks, makes his second Patrick the author of the *Confessio*, and brings him to Ireland about 432, relegating his first Patrick–Palladius to an unspecified earlier time.

Such confusions are the ordinary stuff of hagiography, that the modern student must unravel. They have, however, been recently revived in Ireland; though the arguments have evoked negligible support elsewhere, and most foreign scholars have abstained from involvement, they have created an atmosphere of uncertainty, and compel discussion. The thesis,[4] enunciated in 1942, is that Tirechan's two Patricks are fact, but that his dates must be changed, without ancient authority, to bring his second Patrick to Ireland about 460. The controversy has been surveyed, and the thesis maintained, in a monumental survey by Dr. Binchy,[5] which demolishes most of the arguments employed by both sides, but oddly falters when it passes from the criticism of modern scholars to criticism of the evidence.

The problem is set squarely in the context of modern Irish religious controversy, a natural reaction against pietist and interested distortions,

Muirchu 4 cf. 6, and Tirechan 1, deducing Patrick's age as thirty when he went to Auxerre, and adding that he stayed there thirty years or, 'as some say', forty.

[1] *Inisfallen* shows the origin of the confusion; the entry 'Quies Patricii hi x Kl April anno cccc xxxii a Passione Domini' (432 plus 34 from the Incarnation, or possibly 29 or 27 = 459/64) is placed at 496, with no entry 459/64. *Ulster, Four Masters, Chron. Scot.* give both dates, one *c.* 460, the other in the 490s; *Clonmacnoise* gives the late date only. The form of the *Inisfallen* entry makes it clear that *c.* 460 date was the earlier, later transposed.

[2] *Inisfallen*, para. 313, p. 40, immediately after the accession of Constantine's sons and the death of Paulus Thebaeus (340/1), just before Annus Mundi 5609 = ab Incarnatione 338; *Tigernach*, immediately after the death of Constantine II (340); *Chron. Scot.*, due to missing Kalends, dates to 353, dating Patrick's captivity at the age of sixteen to the reign of Eochaidh, given as *c.* 364–71, and is followed by *Clonmacnoise*, p. 63.

[3] Tirechan 56 (*VT* 332; *AB* 67). Grosjean's and Bieler's arguments that this passage derived from Bede, *H.E* 1. 13, has, I think, been disproved by Binchy *SH* 132.

[4] The thesis was enunciated in a lecture by T. F. O'Rahilly, *The Two Patricks* (Dublin, 1942); developed notably by James Carney, *Studies in Irish Literature and History* (Dublin, 1955), pp. 324–73; *The Problem of St. Patrick* (Dublin, 1961); and in a number of articles.

[5] D. A. Binchy, *Studia Hibernica* 2 (1962), pp. 7–173, cited as *SH*.

a protest against the Patrick who is seen as the object of the 'ceremonies ... or ... sermons' of the 'Catholic hierarchy' or as a 'primitive Protestant ... independent of Rome'.[1] Dissenters are anathematized under the threatening appellation of 'orthodox Mono-Patricians'.[2] Those who argue from the evidence are condemned for not basing themselves on their predecessors' premisses.[3] This eager involvement precludes the possibility of a dispassionate overall survey of the evidence and its origins, concentrates attention upon selected items,[4] and disregards[5] many of the relevant statements in the texts. Very much is made of the late death date assigned to Patrick, but the corresponding early birth date that explains it is altogether ignored. The whole of the earlier, unconfirmed, portions of the Annals have been rewritten[6] or written off,[7] with the exception of those dates which support the thesis. The quite different works of Tirechan and Muirchu[8] have been lumped together, as though they were of equal value, written for similar purposes in a similar manner. The linguistic evidence[9] has been by-passed or denied.

[1] *SH* 7 and 11.   [2] *SH passim*, e.g. 91 middle.
[3] e.g., *SH* 138 bottom.
[4] e.g. much is made of three Annals entries dating the death of Nathi to about 445; the reader is not informed that three other entries give a date about 428, and that alternative dates are a common feature of the Annals; or that the non-annalistic sources place Nathi before Laoghaire and Patrick.
[5] e.g. the Annals are impugned because they make several sons of Neill fight battles eighty years after their father's death; the extremely shaky evidence that makes these people sons of Neill is not considered, and is assumed to be fact. *Probatio Patricii*, Aed of Sletty, much of the *Confessio*, Tirechan's declaration of intent, and much else is not examined.
[6] e.g. Carney, *Studies*, pp. 324 ff.; *Problem*, pp. 1 ff.
[7] e.g. *SH* 71 'I do not believe that there is a single "genuine" entry throughout the whole of the fifth century.' But the late obit, emended to 485/500 (p. 114) is exempted, and dates in the first years of the sixth century are cited as fact (e.g., p. 29) without argument as to why the year 500 should mark a turning point in the credibility of the Annals; external confirmation is not earlier than the mid-century plague.
[8] e.g. *SH* 8; 68, etc. No external evidence makes the one more credible than the other. But they are wholly distinct in purpose and method, and cannot justifiably be lumped together. The essential difference is that Tirechan's account is impossible and demonstrably wrong; nothing in Muirchu is improbable, save the common conventions of hagiographic wonders, such as putting MacCuil in a drifting coracle (ch. 22, cf. p. 115, n. 1, above). Tirechan is to be rejected; Muirchu remains an open question.
[9] e.g. earlier loanwords assigned to Palladius (O'Rahilly, pp. 42 ff.), to pre-Palladian Christians (*SH* 165–6 cf. p. 363, n. 1), without evidence that they were numerous enough to change the vocabulary of the Irish language. The unwary reader might assume that the words are limited to a few ecclesiastical terms that might penetrate, as 'kuriakon' entered the Germanic languages, through a small Christian minority; but is not informed that they cover a wide range of material objects, *fenestra, puteus, pluma, fibula*, etc. (Jackson *LHEB* 126) implying a con-

More important, the Armagh propaganda has not been distinguished from texts not thereby contaminated; the nature of the Patrician literature, as partisan compilations of a much later age, has escaped investigation; and, despite occasional disclaimers,[1] there has been little serious dissection of the contemporary evidence of Patrick himself, but much overtrustful juggling with the contrivances of the eighth- and ninth-century sources. The sad limitations which restrict the vision of participants[2] in this overheated debate are nowhere plainer than in Binchy's presentation of the single solid argument that inclines him to accept a second Patrick and a late date.[3] 'Muirchu and Tirechan . . . were writing the life of Patrick; there was no reason whatever why they should . . . associate[4] him with persons who actually lived one or two

siderable Roman–British influence over a long period. Similarly, the solid arguments of Bieler and Mohrmann may be challenged, but are not set aside by guesses about the Latinity Patrick should have learnt at Auxerre (p. 88).

[1] "The only information about him (Patrick) which a historian can accept as reliable must be gleaned from the saint's own writings . . . the remaining sources . . . are all suspect' (*SH* 9); 'all the more reason . . . for studying every word of Patrick's . . . with the closest attention' (*SH* 40). But these unexceptionable precepts are not followed; in an article of 165 pages, few words of Patrick are studied, and the genesis of the suspect sources is not examined. Lack of such analysis begets, for instance, an imaginative excursus on the date of the destruction of Emain, ending with a disheartened Patrick traipsing across the Bann in the wake of a defeated Ulaid army (p. 154), built entirely upon the sources condemned in theory as suspect.

[2] Energy is diverted from source study to a gay arraignment of modern views, irrelevant until the sources have been probed. It is not encouraging to find Grosjean listed 'among the combatants', with an understandable wish expressed to 'be on his side' (*SH* 25–26). Historical insight is not easily gained by taking the side of combatants, and Grosjean steadfastly refused to do so.

[3] Binchy concludes (*SH* 172) with a proper 'protest' against 'opinions and speculations . . . paraded as historical facts' and claims to give a 'dusty answer', leaving the question open. But his answer is not 'dusty'; it fully endorses O'Rahilly's thesis of the two missionaries (e.g., pp. 136–7; 142–3), the important Patrick being the later (e.g., p. 114), having destroyed all arguments in its favour save one, association with later persons, that rests exclusively upon the most suspect of all the suspect sources condemned.

[4] O'Rahilly, pp. 75–76, and Carney, *Problem*, pp. 1 ff., list some scores of persons associated with Patrick whose deaths the Annals enter at dates up to 549. But, of those entered after 470, only Erc of Slane, 511/13, is associated with Patrick independently of Tirechan and Armagh. Muirchu (16) brings him to Tara at Patrick's first Easter, understood as about 433, implying that he lived to nearly a hundred. But even if Muirchu's tradition is genuine, his Irish tales are dateless, and the Tara encounter, if it were accepted as 'fact', might more happily relate to the Feast of Tara (Annals 454/7), which would allow Erc the more credible age of seventy-five. Moreover, Erc is brought to Tara because in Muirchu's day his relics were 'adored' at Slane, ten miles away. His alleged presence at Tara in 433 is a shaky foundation on which to build a late Patrick

generations later.'[1] It is not conceivable that so acute a scholar could have written these words[2] if he had been able to make plain to himself and his readers that no such associations are to be found in Muirchu; and that Tirechan, in whose writing they abound, expressly states that his purpose is to manufacture just such associations, in the face of Irishmen, who, he says, did not, in the seventh century, believe them to be true.

Nothing whatsoever of Tirechan, the Book of the Angel, the Tripartite Life and similar documents may reasonably be admitted as evidence for Patrick's work in Ireland; though persons named may be real, may in some cases and areas have known Patrick, these works can carry no weight, for their purpose was to invent connexion with Patrick. Their claims are no more acceptable than the archbishoprics of Conlaed or Dubricius. Annals dates, true or false, are scarcely relevant for they, too, lack confirmation or independent authority. The evidence for Patrick's date is restricted to his own writings; and to early traditions independent of Armagh, notably Muirchu and the 'Probatio Patricii' incident. These are plausible, possible, perhaps probable; if they are to be set aside, they need serious and exact discussion, which they have not received in the current controversy. They and the *Confessio* date Patrick to the mid-fifth century; when he wrote, he was in early middle age; he may have lived ten, twenty, possibly thirty years more. The Annals date for his death, about 461, about the middle of this time span, is possible, but wholly unconfirmed. He can hardly have outlived the 470s.

In the later fifth century, the church of lowland Britain altogether disappears from notice; the Saxon wars throttled the cities upon which it rested, and the economy that maintained their culture. Only in the extreme west, outside the war zone, are there faint memories of bishops. Dubricius[3] is held to have administered a large diocese west of the Severn, perhaps also on the opposite shore. His see must have been some substantial surviving *civitas*, Caerwent or possibly Gloucester. A still fainter tradition locates a somewhat earlier bishop, Doccus or Cyngar,[4]

---

theory; but it is the sole 'evidence' for late associations, unless Tirechan's 450 bishops and their accompanying princes be accorded the status of fact.

[1] *SH* 112.

[2] The pity is that the energy of so many brilliant and able scholars has been absorbed by internal polemic. If it had been able to concentrate on inquiry into the simple objective question of why the extant texts say what they do say, and whence they got their information, we should be a great deal clearer than we are about the problems of fifth-century Ireland.

[3] Dubricius is attested in the seventh century *vita Samsonis*; notices in the Book of Llandaff should not be here considered.

[4] *Vita* I, *NLA* 248 (XIVth century); *Vita* II, *J.T.S.* 20 (1918–19), pp. 97–108 (XIIth century), cf. 23 (1921–2), p. 15 and *AB* 42 (1924), pp. 100–20,

in Cornwall, Somerset, and Glamorgan; he was regarded as a monk and a teacher as well as bishop, said to have been of royal, conceivably imperial ancestry. British tradition sends him to Ireland in old age, and he is the only fifth-century British ecclesiastic remembered in Ireland, where he is said to have died in the 470s and perhaps to have fathered the sixth-century liturgy of Ireland.[1] Though the accounts of these men are feeble and uncertain, the obscurity is the result of a broken and devolved tradition; there is no sign that they or their connexions are the product of later ecclesiastical interest, such as that which prompted Tirechan.

Records are somewhat stronger in Ireland, but in the north they rarely reach beyond the name of a place and person. The Annals acknowledge bishops at Armagh and in four other sees that surround Armagh, covering Ulster, Connacht, and Meath.[2] Besides them, the names of

where Grosjean's discussion is marred by the use of documents in the Iolo manuscripts and Myvyrian Archaeology. Summaries in Doble 4. 105 (= 12, 1927) and *LBS* 2. 248. Death, *c.* 473 (Doccus), Annals of Clonmacnoise and Ulster.

'Cungarus apud Angligenas vocabitur, Doccuinus . . . apud Britannigenas', *Vita* I; eponym of Congresbury in Somerset, the two Llandoughs in Glamorgan, St. Kew in Cornwall (*Vita Samsonis*, cf. LBS and Doble). He is 'consobrinus senex' of Kebi (*Vita Kebi* 9 and 11) descended from Gerontius and Constantine Corneu (genealogies Bonedd y Saint 26–27, *Vita Kebi* 1) (Kengar). The whole of this tradition has reached a degree of baffling devolution beyond what is normal even in late British lives: *Vita* II makes him son of 'Constantinopolitanus imperator'; this extraordinary statement, without parallel in Celtic lives, forms no integral part of the story, and is not impressed to the credit of the saint or his church. It is, therefore, more probably a textual corruption than an invention; 'Constantinus imperator' is the likely original. Its foundation may be the Constantine Corneu of the genealogies, emended by a copyist who assumed that Constantine the Great was intended and corrected the error. But it is to be noted that Doccus was of an age to be son, grandson, or nephew of Constantine III, whose known son Constans was, on the testimony of Orosius, one of the earliest British monks. The *Vita Kebi* takes him to Ireland and to Enda in Aran.

[1] *Catalogus ordinum Sanctorum* (*CS* col. 161; Haddan and Stubbs, *Councils*, 2, p. 292; *AB* 73 (1955), p. 206 ff., 289 ff.) section 2, 'Hii (the second order of sixth century saints) ritum celebrandi missam acceperunt . . . a sancto David et sancto Gilda et a sancto Doco'. Irish hagiographers easily confused Doccus and Cadoc. Doccus who taught Cainnech of Achad Bo (*VSH*, ch. 3 and 5), who lived *c.* 516–99, was certainly Cadoc, Bishop Doccus who died *c.* 470 equally certainly Docco. It is not clear which saint the Catalogue intended, or indeed whether it was concerned to distinguish them. That David, Gildas, Doccus are the only fifth- and sixth-century British saints whose obits the Annals note, and the British tradition of his visit to Enda, speak for the earlier saint; that he is named third in the Catalogue and spelt with one 'c' speaks for Cadoc. But Cadoc is not known to Irish hagiography, outside the lives of Cainnech and Finnian of Clonard.

[2] Mel of Ardagh (487); Bronn of Cuill Irra, near Sligo (511); MacCartni of Cloghar, west of Armagh (505); Erc of Slane, north of Dublin (511). Mel has a British name and is expressly called British in e.g. the *Vitae Brigidae* TT 527, 546, 567–8, etc.

half a dozen other ecclesiastics[1] are remembered, and biographies survive of two more, neither of them Irish. Mocteus of Louth[2] is said to have been a Briton who came to Ireland as a child, and was remembered as an outstanding teacher, and as an authority for annalistic entries. His life sends him to be consecrated bishop in Rome, but the Annals, quoting what they believed to be his own words, call him a priest and disciple of Patrick, and are followed by Adomnan. Boecius of Monsterbuite[3] bore a Roman name, perhaps Roman–British, and came from Italy to Pictland, and, quite exceptionally, is assigned no named Irish ancestors. Pictish records[4] independently remember the conversion of their king in his time, but do not name him; and his migration to Ireland followed the Pictish mission, whose base can hardly have been other than Whithorn. At Armagh, the virgin Darerca[5] was trained in the south, styled 'daughter of Mocteus'; she took the name Mo-Nenn, reminiscent of Whithorn and Nennius, and received a considerable cult in England. Even at the end of the century, Eugenius of Ardstraw[6] and Tigernach of Clones[7] are both described as Leinstermen trained at Whithorn and sent thence to evangelize still pagan Irish. Those accounts which have survived heavily emphasize missionaries sent from Britain, in particular from Whithorn, independently of Patrick. It is very

---

[1] Cianan of Duleek (490); MoChoe of Nendrum (498); MacCaille of Croghar (490); MacCuilin of Lusk (495); MacNissi of Condere (509); Cerpan of Tara (503).

[2] *Vita, CS* col. 903; *Vita Ibari AB* 77 (1959), p. 439, ch. 5. Only the Calendars and the *Four Masters* call him Bishop; *Tigernach, Ulster, Clonmacnoise* and *Chron. Scot.* cite the incipit of a lost letter ascribed to him, 'Mocteus peccator prespiter, sancti Patricii discipulus; in Domino salutem'. The letter or the Annal was probably known to Adomnan (Prologue, 3a) who calls him 'proselytus Brito homo sanctus sancti Patricii episcopi discipulus Maucteus', who prophesied Columba's birth (522); the *Vita* reports the prophecy. The Annals cite him as a written authority for an event of *c.* 474, and date his own death *c.* 534. If the immigrant priest Maucteus in Louth accepted the episcopal authority of Patrick's northern successors a generation after his death, in preference to that of southern bishops, he was entitled to call himself Patrick's disciple, without implying personal acquaintance.

[3] *VSH* 1. 87; Annals 519/23.

[4] Nectan Morbet in the king lists (Skene, *Chronicles of the Picts and Scots*, pp. 8 ff., 28 ff., 148 ff., cf. pp. 171, 201, 284, 289) said to have reigned *c.* 461–85 (for twenty four years, from four years after the death of Drust, son of Erp, Clonmacnoise *c.* 457) is the only ruler before Columba's time (*c.* 565) regarded as Christian by the Picts; they make him take refuge with Bridget (Annals *c.* 454–525), while in exile. These statements would place Boecius' arrival about 475/80. Plummer's ingenious emendation of the monastery of Tilianus in Italia to that of Teiliavus in Wallia (*VSH* xxxv), therefore, presents a chronological difficulty, since Teilo's foundation did not begin till half a century later.

[5] *CS*, col. 165; Annals 517/19.
[6] *CS*, col. 915; Annals 549.   [7] *CS*, col. 211; *VSH* 2. 262; Annals 548.

possible that the four bishops whose lives are unrecorded may have been the heirs of Patrick's mission; Mocteus' odd epithet, 'disciple of Patrick', may rest on a belief that he accepted the authority of Patrician clergy. The word does not, of course, imply that he knew Patrick personally, though chronologically he might have done so in childhood.

The record of southern Ireland is very different. The great saint of northern Leinster was Bridget of Kildare,[1] with her attendant bishop Conlaed. Muirchu is the authority for the existence of Fiacc of Sletty,[2] a disciple of Patrick, in southern Leinster. Southern tradition, however, remembers Bishop Ibar of Wexford,[3] associated with the Munster bishops Ailbe,[4] Declan,[5] and Ciaran of Saigir.[6] The four were held to have been earlier than Patrick, credited with life-spans up to 300 years, and independent of him; and to have been consecrated in Rome by Hilarius (461–8),[7] almost the only pope[8] named in Irish hagiography. With them was Enda,[9] a chieftain's son educated at Whithorn, and a person named 'Pubeus'.[10] The wholly independent British life of Cybi also

[1] *TT* 515 ff.; *CS*, col. 1; Annals 525.
[2] Muirchu 18 and many Patrician sources; no Annals date.
[3] *AB* 77 (1959), p. 426; frequently mentioned in the life of his nephew Abban, *CS*, col. 505; *VSH* 1. 3; Annals 501.
[4] *CS*, col. 235; *VSH* 1. 46; cf. *Vita David*, *VSB* 150; Annals 517 (535; 544).
[5] *VSH* 2. 32; *Irish Texts Society*, xvi (Dublin, 1914); no Annals date.
[6] *CS*, col. 805; *VSH* 1. 217; *ASH* 458; *AB* 59 (1941), 217; no Annals date.
[7] 'summus pontifex', 'pontifex Romanus', 'summus pontifex qui tunc abbas Romae dicitur', *Vita Endei* 20–21; 'Bishop Hilary in Rome', *Vitae Albei, Declani*; glossed as 'Hilarius, Pictavensis episcopus (presul)' *Vita Kebi* 3. 4. The 'summus pontifex' is not named in *Vita Ciaran* 3, but in *Vita Declani* 12, cf. 18, Ciaran is said to have been consecrated jointly with Ailbe, Declan, and Ibar.

The *Vita Albei* names, or describes, the Pope in the time of Hilary as 'Clemens'. The term 'Pope Hilary' is avoided for scholarly reasons; these saints were held to have been consecrated before Celestine consecrated Patrick; though named popes are rare in hagiography, they are plentiful in the Annals, and a glance at the Annals would have shown that Celestine preceded Hilary. Since these saints were credited with an age of 300 years, Clemens (died *c.* 95) is not a bad guess for the pope of their youth.

[8] Plummer, *VSH* cxxiii, notes 'an almost complete ignorance of any individual Popes' in Irish Saints' Lives; 'Celestine is known because he . . . sent Palladius and was said to have sent Patrick . . . Gregory the Great occurs fairly frequently', doing duty for nameless popes at any period; and 'a non-existent Clement occurs in . . . Ailbe, a John (V or . . . VI) in . . . Flannan' (early seventh century, *CS*, col. 643). To whom should be added Hilarius (specifically pope in *Vita Endei*), and Pelagius (I) in Finnian of Moville (Fridian), *Vita* II, 2, Colgan, *ASH* 638. The extreme rarity of named popes emphasizes the coincidence that these four lives, British and Irish, have hit upon the name of a pope who coincides with the dates furnished by the Annals and their own internal content.

[9] *VSH* 2. 60; Colgan, *ASH* 704. No Annals date.
[10] Pubeus with Enda at Rome and in Aran, *Vita Endei* 20–23; with Enda in Aran, *Vita I Brendani Clonfert* (*VSH* 1. 98) 71. Senior to Enda, and 'auctoritate

has him consecrated by Hilarius, and sends him to Ireland with his aged relative Doccus to join Enda; it is not impossible that 'Pubeus' is identical with Cybi (Kebius). Later, in the Irish version, a dispute arose over Pubeus' authority over Enda's monastery; a delegation, which included Erlatheus (Bishop of Armagh *c.* 468–81) referred the dispute to the pope, who ruled in Enda's favour. In the British version, Cybi was driven from Ireland by the machinations of a wicked priest 'Fintam'. These saints are said to have been natives of their area; but are given an alien upbringing. Ailbe had British teachers, Ibar was a pupil of Mocteus the Briton, Enda a student of Whithorn. Ciaran had to go abroad to find Christian teachers, and only Declan found an Irish master.

It is an odd tale, circumstantial, unrelated to the problems, interests, preconceptions of any later age, corresponding to the actual problems of Rome and Ireland in the later fifth century, told in complementary Irish and British versions. Rome had established a see, and sent two successive bishops, each on his own, unable to consecrate others. Patrick died about the time of Hilary's pontificate, whether or not the Annals date is valid. The pope had to consolidate organizationally what had been achieved. The Patrician north acquired four sees, in addition to Armagh; the consecration of two additional bishops, the minimum necessary to permit further consecrations in Ireland, might have been the work of Leo, after the date of the *Confessio*, or of his successor on Patrick's death. There is no evidence beyond the later Irish belief that they existed in the latter part of the century. In the south, where, as far as we know, Patrick had little or no influence, there is a quite different tradition. Patrick's pupil Fiacc was not remembered. What was believed was that Pope Hilary established four new sees at one time, and that with them was associated the only known British bishop of that generation, who was credited for a while with some kind of superior authority, from which the Irish soon won papal exemption. This is what the Lives say. It has no external

---

dignior', the 'principatus' of Aran was disputed between him and Enda, and referred by an embassy of Finnianus iunior, MacCrichi and Erlatheus to the pope, who decided for Enda, *Vita Endei* 23. That Enda offered primacy to Pubeus, who declined it, is plainly a polite retouching of the hagiographer. In the *Vita Kebi*, Kebi came to Ireland and to the isle of Aruin, with his 'consobrinus senex Kengar', and built a monastery; Crubthir Fintam quarrelled with him, and Enda pacified them, but Fintam's enmity persisted, and an angel bade Kebi leave for Meath, where he founded MoChop. The names are strikingly similar for two persons in dispute in Aran in the late fifth century (Kebi is so dated by King Ethelic, uncle of Cadoc and Petroc in other stories, as well as by the Irish date given to Cyngar-Docco). It is possible that an Irish scholar, who knew that Ciaran and Cothriche were rendered in British Perran and Patrick, mistook Kebius for an Irish form that should properly be Pebius, Pubeus in British or Latin.

confirmation, and cannot pass as fact; but it is reasonable, not impossible, and is most unlike a later invention. In contrasting this plausible essence with the pitifully broken versions of the lives whence it must be extracted, it is well to consider how other, better documented stories would appear if their texts had suffered as crippling a deformation; if the Life of Wilfred survived only in a form like that of Cybi, we should have a story of a wandering ecclesiastic, uncertainly located at Ripon or Hexham, pursued by the malicious magic of wicked priests and kings, preposterously accorded in late tradition the title of Archbishop, bestowed by a muddled pope named Agilbert rather than Agatho, perhaps transformed to Leo or Gregory.

When these southern tales assert in words an origin independent of Patrick, they doubtless contain an element of regional patriotism. The circumstantial detail of Hilary, and of Cybi and Docco, is less easily so explained. More impressive is their unconscious emphasis on an outlook totally opposed to that of Patrick. Enda asked king Angus of Munster (died 491)[1] for the island of Aran. The king demurred, on the ground that 'Saint Patrick told me to offer to God only good fertile lands... near to my royal city'. It is unlikely, though just possible, that Angus ever met Patrick, but the concepts are historical enough. Patrick was trained in the church of the late Roman empire, where the cure of the priest necessarily coincided with the unit of secular government, in Europe and Britain the *civitas*, in Ireland the province, kingdom, and tuath. Though the dedicated life assumed with a monastic vow was a high ideal, particularly to be enjoined upon ordained clergy, the business of the bishop and priest was to attend to the spiritual needs of a secular community, to stand beside the lay ruler and guide him to Christian ways. The ideal of Enda was to withdraw from civil society to establish direct communion with God as far away as possible from the habitat of men and the politics of princes.

This was the original concept of monasticism, developed in the mass migration to the deserts of Egypt, Cappadocia, and the Levant in the fourth century. As yet, it had found little echo in the west. Egyptian monasticism had at first seemed another nasty oriental excess; and in the fourth century western monks were individual *sancti*, living ascetic lives in their own houses. First Eusebius of Vercelli, then Ambrose of Milan, Martin of Tours, Amator, and Germanus of Auxerre encouraged their cathedral clergy to take monastic vows, living dedicated lives in the sight of their congregations, and established schools around their monastic clergy. After the fall of Rome, Honoratus founded a monastic

---

[1] *Vita Endei* 13.

island community in Lérins, of high-powered intellectuals, whose achievement was to reform the church by inducing churches to elect monastic reformers as their Bishops. The segregated community was introduced by John Cassian at Marseilles, and Cassian[1] was disappointed at the feeble response of the Latins to the concept and spirit of Egyptian monasticism. A few communities initiated in the turmoil of fifth-century Gaul appeared more as retreats from a disordered world than as zealous pioneers of a new way of life. The few fifth-century foundations of Britain of which anything is remembered, St. Kew, Llaniltut, Caldey, were likewise centres of comfortable gentlemanly life. In Gaul and Britain, these few quiet houses were easily absorbed into the structure of a hierarchical church, existing on the licence of the Bishop. Western monasticism was a faint ripple of the edges of a distant movement, its force already spent; in the words of Montalembert,[2] the historian of early western monks, it was, by the end of the fifth century, 'torpid and sterile', suffering 'a sort of eclipse'.

This was the European experience behind Celtic monasticism. Its first origins are diverse. Patrick states that many of his converts took monastic vows, and speaks more often of women than of men. Several communities headed by Irish women are recorded in the later fifth century; the virgin Faencha, who is held to have converted Enda not long after 450, will have been a contemporary of Patrick; Darerca, and whatever lies behind the later legend of Bridget, were not many decades later. But the future lay with communities of men. Well before the end of the century, perhaps by the end of the 460's, nine or ten bishops continued the work of Palladius and Patrick, with the approval of Rome. But the monastic impetus came from outside. Enda was regarded as the earliest of the monastic founders, teacher of Finnian of Clonard and other later leaders;[3] and the chronological indications concealed in the writings of hagiographers who cared little for chronology, place his settlement on Aran, away from the society of men, not much after 470. He was trained in Britain; he visited Rome, and appeared under the aegis of Doccus, who in Britain is the earliest ecclesiastic credited with the foundation of such segregated monasteries, and in Ireland is held to have been the first inspirer of the later monastic order. Not many decades later came Mocteus the Briton, and the several monastic emissaries from Whithorn to northern Ireland. In Europe and in

[1] Cassian, *Inst.* x. 23.
[2] *Les Moines en Occident* (Paris, 1863), 1, 288; English edition (Edinburgh, 1861), i. 514.
[3] It is probable that by Finianus senex (chs. 32, 33) Enda's biographer understood Finian of Clonard. The *Vita Finiani, CS*, col. 189, does not know this tradition, but has Finian baptized by Abban, nephew of Ibar.

Britain, the archetype of vigorous monasticism was Martin, and in Ireland the name of Martin held pride of place in the calendars until he was superseded in later centuries by Patrick.

But monasteries were yet few. They received a certain impetus from Ireland; Senan, Breaca, Ia (St. Ives), Fingar, and others[1] appear in Cornwall as disciples of Ciaran of Saigir, changed in British mouths to Perran, but they were also enemy aliens, resisted as invaders. Probably early in the sixth century, the children of Brychan are represented as carrying to south Wales and Cornwall an equally alien blend of armed lay immigrants and monks. The ferocious Cairnech,[2] identified with Carantoc, was held to have used Cardiganshire as a base for militant intervention in the high politics of secular Ireland; in the same area the gentler Brioc,[3] given a life span of about 460–550, began his work towards the end of the century, though his numerous foundations in Cornwall and Brittany were not established until his old age.

These are shadowy insubstantial tales. Firmer tradition begins with the school of Iltut[4] in Glamorgan. He and his school are described in the earliest of all Celtic saints' lives, that of Samson, written in the early seventh century on the basis of a written contemporary account. He is depicted as a cultured Roman gentleman of the old school, perhaps a generation younger than Docco, living a monastic life on his hereditary estate, much in the continental tradition of Paulinus of Nola or Turcius Apronianus in the early fifth century; and maintaining a school not significantly different from those described by the writers of early fifth-century Britain.

His establishment still bears his name, and has been excavated.[5] The discoveries do not conflict with the written account; the mansion, the largest Roman house yet found in Wales, was in large part long decayed in the fifth century; one wing survived at least as long as Roman objects

---

[1] *s.v.* Senan (*Vita CS* 21) was 'comes semper et socius' of Ciaran.

[2] Todd, *Irish Version of Nennius* (Dublin, 1848), pp. 178 ff. (Book of Ballymote, with translation); Stokes in *Revue Celtique* 23 (1902), pp. 195 ff., summarized O'Donovan, *Four Masters*, 1, p. 173, n. (Yellow Book of Lecan, with translation), cf. *Vita Carannog, VSB* 142; *Martyrology of Oengus*, ed. Stokes (London, 1905), p. 132. Whether or not the identification is valid, he is represented as the backer of King Muirchetach, victor at Ocha, dated to the 480s, exiled, king of Ireland 508–33.   [3] *AB* 2 (1883), pp. 2 ff.

[4] Iltut is recorded in the lives of Samson (p. 348, n. 3 above), and Paul Aurelian *AB* 1 (1882), pp. 209 ff. = *Revue Celtique* 5 (1881–3), pp. 413 ff. His own life (*VSB* 194) is exceptionally devolved.

[5] *Archaeologia Cambrensis* 102 (1953), p. 89, cf. 43 (1888), p. 413: *Bulletin of the Board of Celtic Studies*, 13 (1949), p. 163; *Cardiff Natural History Society Report and Transactions*, 20 (1888), p. 49. Nash-Williams's doubts of the veracity of his predecessors do not seem justified, though their amateur phrenology does not command confidence.

stayed in use, and numerous post-Roman Christian graves were dug into the buried ruins of the rest of the house. A mile from the mansion, the church is rich in royal and monastic tombstones of the eighth and later centuries.[1] Nor was Iltut's the only school; tradition knew another at Caerwent,[2] and St. David's and St. Teilo's teacher Paulinus[3] is probably to be identified with Paulinus 'cultor pientissimi aequi' buried beneath a tombstone engraved in hexameters in Carmarthenshire, perhaps also with Cybi's pupil Paulinus.

Change came suddenly. Monasticism grew in the space of a few years from the eccentricity of a few marginal holy men to a mass movement. It had three main starting points; Samson and Paul Aurelian are attested as pupils of Iltut in early texts that cannot be set aside, Gildas[4] and Leonore[5] in later lives; David[6] of Demetia, south-west Wales, was a pupil of the Irish Ailbe as well as of Paulinus, and is so remembered in both Ireland and Britain; Cadoc,[7] Arthmael,[8] and others were held to have studied at the Caerwent schools. Iltut's pupils have the best and earliest documentations. Samson was five when he entered the school and stayed till he was old enough to be ordained by Bishop Dubricius. His youthful asceticism seemed excessive to Iltut and his fellows, and he was granted a transfer to Piro's newly founded retreat on Caldey island. But his single-minded purpose was not mellowed; he refused to 'return to Egypt' to visit his dying father, until Piro rebuked his inhumanity and ordered him as a priest to administer the last sacrament. On the way, he encountered a demented old woman in a forest, who died when he cursed her. His father recovered, and his family renounced the world, except for a pleasure-loving sister, then a child, whom he excommunicated for her sins. Back at Caldey, Dubricius held an inquiry into the old woman's death, and acquitted him; when Piro, 'saint and a gentleman' (*egregio viro ac sancto presbitero*) died through stumbling into

---

[1] The dating of the inscriptions in *Early Christian Monuments of Wales* (cited as *ECMW*) 220 and 223 seems over late. The names of the kings of Morgannwg are well known and outweigh arguments from typology; no King Iuthehal is recorded later than the eighth century, and both stones should be assigned to Ris, son of Iuthael, father of Houelt (*Liber Landav* 212, etc.) and of Artmail (Harleian genealogies 29).   [2] *Vitae Cadoci, Beuno, Tathei*, etc. (*VSB*).

[3] *ECMW* 139; *Vita Kebi* 5, cf. Mostyn MS. 110, p. 189, cited *LBS* 4, 104, note 2; cf. also Teilo's teacher, *Liber Landav* 99; David's teacher, *Vita David* (*VSB*) 10; he may be Paulennanus, whose relics were preserved with Gurthiern's; *Cartulaire de Quimperlé*, ed. Maître and Berthou (Paris and Rennes, 1904), p. 46, cf. note.

[4] *BHL* 3542, sup.; Williams, *Gildas*, 2, pp. 322 ff.; *Vita Pauli Aureliani*, 3, etc.   [5] *BHL* 4880–1.

[6] *VSB*; *BHL* 2107 ff.; *Buched Dewi*, in *Elucidarium*, ed. Morris-Jones and Rhŷs (Oxford, 1894), pp. 105–18.   [7] *VSB* 24 ff.; *AB* 60 (1942), pp. 45 ff.

[8] Le Grand 522; *ASS* 3, 298–9; *Vita Cadoci* 20; *BHL* 678–9.

the well after drinking too much wine at dinner, Samson succeeded as abbot. He soon left, for the monks resented his abstemious example, and he found their life too easy. He accompanied some Irish monks returning home from Italy, where they had doubtless encountered stories of St. Benedict and his contemporaries; and from Ireland moved to a cave on the Severn shore. A 'synod' constrained him to leave his cell to become an abbot, soon after a bishop, on the initiative of Dubricius. But he soon abandoned his see, and sought admission to one of Docco's foundations at St. Kew in Cornwall. The abbot found his proposal not 'conveniens', since he was one of the 'meliores', whose strictness would be unacceptable to monks who had somewhat 'lapsed from our former institutes'. Samson, 'stupefactus', moved to a nearby cell, whence he was evicted by Petroc,[1] an associate of Cadoc who had spent some time in Ireland. Leaving a dedication at Castle Dore by Fowey, he passed on to Dol in Brittany, where he emerged some years later as the principal bishop of the British immigrants. He was perhaps the only one to have been consecrated canonically.

His contemporary, Paul Aurelian, sought the desert at the age of sixteen. Disturbed by like pressures, he refused to serve as bishop to the people of King Marcus, 'quem alio nomine Quonomorium vocant', and passed on to Brittany, where he founded a large number of monasteries, in Iltut's name or his own, headed by St. Pol-de-Léon. King Mark acquired an accidental prominence in several different contexts. Many Breton Lives describe the career of the 'iudex externus' Conomorus[2] who mastered Brittany and their princely patrons; Gregory of Tours relates how he overplayed his hand and was killed by the king of the Franks in December 560. His name, Cunomorus, is still legible on the memorial stone of his son Drustanus by Castle Dore, which excavation

---

[1] *AB* 74 (1956), p. 137; Leland, *SB* 61; *BHL* 6639–40.
[2] 'Regis Marci . . . quem alio nomine Quonomorium vocant', *Vita Pauli Aureliani*, 8; Cunomorus, Conmor, etc., *Vitae Samsonis, Leonori, Melori, Machuti* (Malo), *Goueznou, Huerve, Arthmael, Teilo, Tudwal, Gildae*, etc. Conomoris, Chonoober, Greg. Tur. *H.F.* 4. 4; 4. 20. 'Drustanus hic iacit Cunomori filius', *CIIC* 487, emended *Journal of the Royal Institution of Cornwall*, N.S. i (1951), p. 117; excavations, ibid. Legend, cf. Béroul, especially lines 1155, 2359, 2438, 2453, 2792–6, and Gerbert de Monteuil's continuation of Perceval, especially lines 3642, 3880, equating 'la ville . . . du roi Marc' with 'la grant chité Lancien'. Castle Dore, in the parish of St. Samson, lay in the Domesday manor of Lantyen. This is one of the rare instances where it is possible to set side by side the evidence of a continental contemporary; of hagiography in all stages from the near contemporary to the very devolved; of developed medieval legend; of excavation; of epigraphy; and of local tradition, that has long made Castle Dore the fortress of king Mark. The detail variations in concept and treatment of the story constitute one of the few pieces of hard evidence on how these diverse sources relate to fact.

has shown to be a royal residence of the sixth century. Under the name of Mark, and turned to the uncle instead of the father of Tristan, he lives in romantic legend, whose earliest versions accurately remember the location of his principal residence near Fowey.

Cunomorus' short-lived hegemony of Brittany also provides a cardinal dating point for the movement of the saints. Very many among those who emigrated to Brittany, including Samson, Paul Aurelian, Brioc, are said to have gone to Paris[1] in face of his encroachments, seeking Frankish aid on behalf of their patrons, and to have returned on his defeat. The minutes of a Church Council[2] held in Paris about 557 include the signatures of two British bishops; one is Samson; the other is Kentigern,[3] the only monastic pioneer of northern Britain, who signed as bishop of Senlis near Paris. His late and very devolved life unwittingly retells a misunderstood incident from his Gallic episcopate held in exile.

Another central date is the incidence of the Justinian plague,[4] with its Irish and British sequel, the Yellow Plague. Procopius and Gregory of Tours trace its spread from Egypt in 541/2 to central and southern Gaul in 544/5. Native annals place its ravages in Britain and Ireland in the years 546/50. The plague not only confirms the dating of the Annals; it dates many men not therein named. On its outbreak Teilo crossed from Wales to Brittany, where it was less severe, while the aged Brioc hastened home in the opposite direction to comfort his countrymen. The Breton lives name very many lay and monastic immigrants, a majority of whom arrived in the time of king Childebert, who became sovereign of Brittany in 528, and had arrived before the outbreak of the plague. The worst ravages of the plague were in Ireland, where also there is strongest evidence, both from texts and from excavation, of sea-borne imports from the plague-ridden areas of Gaul. It forms a caesura in the expansion of Irish monasticism. It killed Finnian of Clonard,[5] teacher of the Irish saints, said to have been baptized by Abban, and also an associate of David and Cadoc. Clonard does not appear to have been

---

[1] Tudwal (*BHL* 8350 ff.) was accompanied by Albinus of Angers (*Vita* III. 8, cf. I. 3; II. 4) who died not later than 558 (Venantius Fortunatus, *MGH Scr. Ant.* 4. 27 B, a contemporary gives him an episcopate of twenty years and six months; he was already a bishop in 538, Mansi, ix. 9; he died on 1 March; cf. Duchesne, *Fastes de la Gaule Ancienne*, 2. 357).

[2] Mansi, ix. 743; cf. above, p. 92, n. 114.

[3] *BHL* 4645 ff., cf. preceding note.

[4] For the date cf. above, p. 58 and p. 86, nn. 25–27; for the nature of the plague, cf. Sir William MacArthur, *Irish Historical Studies*, 6 (1949), pp. 169 ff.; but cf. Creighton, *History of Epidemics in Great Britain*, i, p. 8, who cites (p. 3) Siebel, *Die grosse Pest zur Zeit Justinians* (Dillingen, 1857) for collected references; and A. H. M. Jones, *The Later Roman Empire*, pp. 287–8 and n. 43.

[5] *CS*, col. 189; *ASH* 393; Annals 549.

long founded; Ciaran the Wheelwright's son,[1] one of its earliest monks, had already left to found Clonmacnoise shortly before his death in the plague at the age of thirty-three. Another of Finnian's pupils, who survived the plague, was Columba,[2] born about 522. A third was Columba of Terryglas,[3] who had also founded his own monastery, and had visited the continent, and preached to pagan Saxons in England,[4] before he died of the plague. Though there is no certainty, Clonard would appear to have been established about ten to fifteen years before Finnian's death, near to 550.

Gildas[5] implies a somewhat similar date for the flowering of the movement in Britain. He wrote not many years before 540, and at the time he wrote the monks whom he admired were still few. It is doubtful if he could have so written after the movement was strong enough to impel Cunomorus, by no means an *avant-garde* pioneer of monasticism, to seek the hermit Paul Aurelian for bishop, and strong enough for those who sought a bishop in the Severn region to extract the unwilling Samson from his cell. These events may well have occurred soon after Gildas wrote, for his book constituted a manifesto of the growing movement, and made him its counsellor and leader. He is mentioned more often than any other individual in the lives of other saints, as the wise senior who advised or blessed younger men; in Irish tradition he was in old age invited[6] to advise the monasteries on the aftermath of the Columba controversy. A number of his rulings are extant, and one is cited by Columban under his name in the 590s. He denounced the society

---

[1] *CS*, col. 155; *VSH* 1, 200; Annals 549.

[2] *BHL* 1884 ff., especially 1886, 'auctore Adomnano', ed. Reeves (Dublin, 1857); also Pinkerton, *Lives of the Scottish Saints* (London, 1789), republished ed. Metcalfe (Paisley, 1889), 1. 73 (1. 51 = *BHL* 1884), and A. O. and M. O. Anderson (London, 1961). The Lives are collected in Colgan *TT*.

[3] *CS*, col. 445; *BHL* 1897; Annals 549. [4] Ch. 10.

[5] Date: see above, p. 58 and p. 86, n. 30. On fewness of monks, see 'nostro quoque ordine', ch. 65; 'quorum vitam ... cunctis mundi opibus praefero, cuiusque me ... particıpem opto et sitio', ch. 65. The 'boni' are 'paucius et valde paucis', ch. 26; 'illi pauci', ch. 50; he ends the *de Excidio* with a prayer for 'paucissimos bonos pastores', ch. 110.

[6] 'Cumque ... paenitentiam ... Columba quaereret ... Seniores Hiberniae miserunt per nuncios fideles epistolam ad S. Gildam de genere Saxonum ut charitatem mutuam nutrirent. Cumque ... epistolam a S. Columba scriptam in manibus teneret, statim illam osculatus est, dicens "Homo qui scripsit hanc Spiritu Sancto plenus est." Et ait unus de nunciis ... "A synodo Hiberniae reprehenditur..." ... S. Gildas respondit "O quam stultum est genus vestrum!"' Colgan *TT* 463, citing Ussher, *de Primordiis Ecclesiarum Brittanicarum*, p. 902. 'Navigatio Gildae in Hibernia', *Annales Cambriae*, MS. B, a. 565. Columban (*MGH. Epp.* iii. 158–9) cites one of his rulings, possibly his extant *Ep.* iv, as addressed to a Finnian. David and Gildas are the only British sixth-century saints whose obits the Irish Annals record.

which Samson, Paul Aurelian, and their fellows wished to abjure; it is probable that its publication gave strength and solidarity to feelings previously inchoate and inarticulate.

The dates of Samson's career point to the same conclusion. He was an old man at his death; but probably not exceptionally old, for the lives commonly stress or date the extreme age of octogenarians. He died not many years after Cunomorus, somewhere in the 560s, and is likely to have been born somewhere in the 490s. He did not leave Llantwit till after his ordination, scarcely younger than twenty-five, sometime not far from 520. He then spent some years at Caldey, some in Ireland, some in his Severn hermitage before he was sought out as bishop. These imprecise hints would place his consecration in the 530s. It is probable that the wide popular appeal of monasticism, both in Ireland and in Britain, began soon after 535 and accelerated over the next ten or twelve years, until the onset of the plague.

After the plague, the growth of the movement is well dated in Ireland, less well in Britain. It probably made its first impact in north Wales, in Gwynedd,[1] about 550, in central Wales, north Cardigan, and Merioneth[2] not much later; but in Powys[3] the monastic saints who were regarded as the founders are held to have worked early in the next century. In northern Britain Kentigern[4] was not believed to have established himself until the 570s. In south Wales, the movement speedily divided into two radically opposed tendencies. David Aquaticus, the teetotaller, is said to have been born thirty years after Patrick's *discessio*, which was probably understood to mean that he was born in the 490s. In his youth he was a pupil of Ailbe, whose death the Irish Annals put at 517. His stringent rule, forbidding the acquisition of landed property, the use of animals in agriculture or the consumption of meat, is set down with approbation by his eleventh-century biographer from his old

---

[1] Daniel's (*LBS* 4. 387, from Peniarth MS. 225,155, dated 1602, lectiones from a *Vita*). Bangor on Menai was the Great Bangor, evidently founded before Congall's Irish Bangor (Annals, c. 568), perhaps not until the death of Maelgwn. The assumption in lectio 4 that Daniel followed an earlier 'bishop of Bangor' is a late fancy. Though Daniel came from near Menevia, no tradition makes him a disciple of David, and the story that he was there endowed with estates animals and slaves conflicts with the David tradition.

[2] The principal saints of the region were the followers of Cadvan, who included Paternus of Llanbadarn near Aberystwyth. Their tradition has almost wholly disintegrated; its single substantial element is that these saints came from Brittany, not South Wales, and their impetus, therefore, probably dates after the initial monastic penetration of Brittany; they might date as early as the plague, hardly earlier.

[3] Notably Beuno (*VSB* 16 (Welsh); translation *Archaeologia Cambrensis*, 85 (1930), pp. 315 ff.) and Tyssilio, cf. *LBS* 4, 296 ff.

[4] *BHL* 4645 ff.; *LBS* 2, 231.

worm-eaten sources; Gildas,[1] in the later sixth century, attacks it violently, but cites the same peculiar phrases. Since Gildas does not name David, it is not conceivable that the later biographer copied his abuse, turning it to praise, and the rule must rank as, in the main, a genuine sixth-century text. David's rival was Cadoc, grandson of Brychan, the founder of Brecon, and son of Gwynnlliw, ruler of eastern Glamorgan. His florid, rewritten life makes him deal with Maelgwn (died 547) and his son Rhun, and the charter tradition of his monastery prolongs his life into the 570s. The life, though padded with medieval pietism, contains elements that have no place in medieval interest. Unlike any other British saint, he is made to inherit and retain his father's secular principality,[2] held simultaneously with his abbacy, and to maintain a hundred men-at-arms.[3] Unlike David, he is given many rich estates.[4] Both lives recount the story of a synod[5] convened at Llandewi Brefi by David, in Cadoc's absence abroad, where David accused his critics of Pelagianism, and won majority support. Cadoc's biographer records his hero's blinding anger, that raged until an angel commanded forgiveness. A large part of Gildas' monastic rulings are taken up with defending a moderately comfortable gentlemanly monastic life, in accord with the practice of Cadoc and Iltut, against the plebeian excesses of David, which seemed to him subversive of social order.

But monasticism was by its nature subversive. Its extent in Britain can only be estimated from the place names it fixed upon the map. Its inspiration, constantly stressed in the saints' lives, is the literature of the Egyptian Fathers, particularly as described by St. Jerome. Jerome's account of the Pachomian organization[6] describes a *populus*, divided into a number of *tribus*, each consisting of a number of *domus*. The terms are Jerome's Latin equivalents for Greek originals. The British substituted *plebs* for *populus*. In Welsh the word *plwyf* means parish; in Brittany, as

[1] *Epp.* II to IV, Williams, pp. 258 ff.; cf. p. 102, n. 4 above.
[2] 'Abbas enim erat et princeps super Gunliauc post genitorem' (Lifris 18 = Caradoc 16); 'utrumque tenens regimen et abbaciam Nantcarbanice callis' (*vita Gwynnliw*, VSB 7); 'regimine concesso et commendatio sancto Cadoco suo filio ad regendum' (*vita Gwynnliw*, 4). The statements are as emphatic as they are unique, paralleled only later in Munster.
[3] *Vita* 18; I know no parallel to this statement. This force was stationed in the Iron Age hill fort above the church, *Vita* 9.   [4] e.g. *Vita* 9, cf. 18.
[5] *Vita David* (Ricemarchus) 49 ff.; *Vita Cadoci* (Lifris) 13 and 17.
[6] *In Regulam S. Pachomii Praef.* 2 'Ita ut in una domo XL vel amplius fratres habitent qui obediant Praeposito; sintque pro numero fratrum XXX vel XL domus in uno monasterio, et ternae vel quaternae domus in unam tribum foederantur' (P.L. 23. 66 = 50. 275–6); ch. 16 'vocatur autem una tribus, habens III vel IV domos, pro numero et frequentia monasterii; quas nos familias, vel populos unius gentis possumus appellare' (P.L. 23. 69–70). Cf. Bede, *H.E.* 2. 2 on Bangor-on-Dee.

Plou-, *Pleu-*, and the like, it names the chief town of an early settlement area, and it occurs occasionally in Cornwall. Throughout Wales, Cornwall, and Brittany a collection of houses, a town or village, is termed a *tref*,[1] or *tribus*. The term, applied to the lay settlements that accompanied the monasteries, is older than the ninth century, when Wrmonoc[2] described *Plebs Telmedovia* (Ploudalmezeau) as comprising a number of *tribus*, one of which was a former *fundus* called the *Villa Petri*, renamed Lampaul. This *tribus* had precise territorial bounds, which the monks marked out. Since the life elsewhere cites sixth-century spellings from its original, and since it was in the sixth century that the political geography of the region was shaped, Wrmonoc is probably accurate in ascribing the use of these terms to Paul's original settlement. No such terminology was employed in Roman administration, to which *fundus* and *pagus* belong, nor is there any trace of them in the considerable record of Roman toponomy in Britain or Gaul.

The normal word for the monastery itself was a *Llan* (Irish *Cluain*, Latin *Claustra*, English *enclosure*), though smaller cells bore the name *Loq* (*locus*, (burial) place). In Wales, Cornwall, and Brittany there are many hundreds of *Llan*. Many bear the names of persons whose approximate date is known; the vast majority of these belong to the sixth century, a few to the early seventh, a minute minority to a later date. Beside them are thousands of *trefydd*; though *tref* remained in use for new settlements till modern times, producing *entrepreneur* names like Treherbert and Treharris in the mining valleys, the majority of *trefydd* also hark back to the sixth century. The quantity of these names is enormous in relation to the population, though they are noticeably less frequent in north Wales, where the monastic movement was later and weaker, than in the south. They represent the sudden withdrawal of a considerable part of the population from the civil communities to which they had belonged, a loss of manpower and rents to landowners, a loss of tribute and military strength to princes. The impact on Irish society was comparable, and explains the frequent opposition of chiefs to the *turba monachorum*, whom they attacked as *seductores* of their manpower. The migration of lay cultivators to new homes and new lands under the protection of the monasteries was, however, more than a simple transfer of people and of their allegiances; it is accompanied by numerous references to the clearing of woodland and scrub, to drainage and flood prevention by dykes, in order to open new lands to agriculture,

---

[1] There is no reason to regard the relatively infrequent Irish *treabh* (tribe; house) as anything other than a borrowing of British *tref*.

[2] The 'Common Celtic' **trebos* lacks substance. *Vita Pauli Aureliani* 12 cf. 19. Childebert assigned to the saint 100 of the *tribus* in the *pagi* of Achm and Léon.

and in Ireland by the spread of fields enclosed by walls and hedges into what had formerly been open plain, by the gradual increase of calculation of social status by the ownership of land as well as of cattle.

There is comparatively little sign of the expansion of British monasticism at home after the middle of the sixth century, though there was a little expansion abroad. A British recluse named John[1] encouraged the Frankish queen Radegund to establish her monastery at Poitiers; when Columban arrived in the Vosges at the end of the century, he was rescued from starvation by the good offices of an abbot, Carantocus,[2] already there established; and in the next generation the British Winnoc[3] evangelized the Flanders littoral. There are a few other names; but their impact was relatively feeble, and neither Carantocus nor his fellows inspired Gaul as Columban did. At home, the abbots of the major endowed monasteries made their peace with lay society, and served as bishops of their respective kings, or else supplied monks to act as bishops, on the principle of one bishop–abbot and major house for each territorial state. But in Ireland the monastic impetus revived with ever renewed vigour. The years that followed the plague produced more and greater monastic leaders than those before; but, great as they were, they were overshadowed by the mighty genius of Columba.

Columba was a prince of the royal family of Tara, a potential heir to the throne, who would almost certainly have become high king[4] of Ireland if he had not been tonsured. His birth reinforced his limitless energy, and men flocked to join the houses he established, whose number tradition pushes to about forty in Ireland alone. But his birth and strong purpose brought problems. When Finnian of Moville brought a gospel book from Italy, perhaps a Vulgate text, Columba copied it without permission: prosecuted before King Diarmit, of a collateral and rival branch of the royal house, he made a passionate

---

[1] *BHL* 7049 ch. 4; cf. Greg. Tur. *de Gloria Confessorum* 23.

[2] Jonas, *Vita Columbani*, i. 7. The name is British.   [3] *BHL* 8952 ff.

[4] There is a recent tendency to assert, but not to demonstrate, that the term 'high king' is anachronistic. The essential evidence is that Adomnan 1. 36 (36. b) calls the mid sixth-century Diarmit 'totius Scotiae regnator', and Muirchu (9) calls the mid fifth-century Laoghaire 'imperator barbarorum regnans in Temoria, quae erat caput Scotorum . . . filius Neill, origo stirpis regiae huius pene insolae'. They are both using the idiom of the later seventh century, but were well informed; Adomnan's grandfather was second cousin to the reigning 'regnator', and Muirchu uses the past tense for the primacy of Tara. There is no evidence to suggest any sharp increase in the status of Tara or its monarchs between the time of Laoghaire or of Diarmit and of Muirchu and Adomnan; on the contrary, the texts concur in depicting a central monarchy whose authority waxed when it coordinated overseas military expeditions in the fourth century, and waned in the fifth and sixth when fighting was virtually confined to domestic wars.

attack on the law of copyright but lost his case. Worse followed. The king of Connacht's son, a hostage at the high king's court, guilty of manslaughter, fled to him for protection; Diarmit violated his sanctuary and executed him. Columba raised the armies of his own clan and of the boy's father, and appeared with them at the disastrous battle of Cuildremhne, when three thousand lives were lost, and Finnian prayed against him for Diarmit.[1] The excess of ecclesiastical violence had plenty of precedents, but its scale outraged the monasteries of Ireland. At the synod of Telltown Columba was excommunicated; at the instance of Brendan of Birr, and, in one version, of Gildas,[2] the sentence was commuted to one of exile and he departed to Iona.

The full story is coherently related only in late sources. But its elements are present in Adomnan's well-informed life; Adomnan connects his emigration with the battle, relates the synod and the excommunication and the intervention of Brendan.[3] He suppresses the charges, glossed as 'certain light and pardonable offences'. But he also explains his own concept of what did and did not constitute offence, for he praises Columba[4] because 'the power of his prayers obtained from God the victory of some kings in the terrible clash of war and the defeat of others'. This 'virtue' is precisely the offence for which Columba is said to have been excommunicated. The story tends to be avoided[5] by many ancient and modern writers, *auribus piis offensus*; and the greatness of Columba is thereby degraded to the level of a painted saint and trite wonderworker. For the consequence transformed Europe. With his grim experience behind him, Columba in exile imposed by precept and example a doctrine of non-violence in word and deed that commanded respect for centuries in many lands. After converting the king of the northern Picts, the moral authority of his advice prevailed with their king, the king of the Irish colonists in Argyll, and with the king of the British of the Clyde; as long as he lived, these three neighbouring kings refrained from fighting each other, and the ultimate downfall of the colonist dynasty was attributed in later ages to wilful disregard of his

---

[1] The principal sources are assembled and discussed by Reeves (*Adomnan*, pp. 247 ff.) who notes that Adomnan makes the battle 'a kind of Hegira in the Saint's life', and comments that 'his participation in these evils could not be denied'. It must be observed, however, that Columba's involvement in two later battles, asserted by O'Donnell and Keating in the sixteenth and seventeenth centuries, is not known to the hagiographers, annalists, or Adomnan, or to any source earlier than the late preface to the Altus Prosator hymn.

[2] p. 383, n. 6.   [3] Adomnan 3. 3 (105 b).   [4] Ibid. 1. 1 (8a).

[5] e.g. Anderson, *Adomnan*, 73–74, without mention of Reeves; cf. Binchy, *Ériu*, 18 (1958), p. 123 'the accounts of his various grievances against Diarmait can be dismissed as later fables ... we are quite safe in discounting the legend that his exile was imposed as a penance for the bloodshed he had caused'.

injunction not to make war on neighbours. The strong gentle piety that he imprinted on his monks, illustrated in the innumerable tales set down by Adomnan, established a code of respect for the dignity and equality of men, of restraint from anger, abuse, and complaint, that long outlived him. It was this quality in his successors that attracted and inspired the Northumbrian Angles, and through them the rest of England; so that when the English abandoned the Irish Easter and tonsure, they also rejected the authoritarian prelatism of Wilfred and kept their Ionian simplicity and Columban monastic basis.

His powerful example spread back to Ireland, which he many times visited; and through the Irish and the English spread abroad. For his emigration was but one instance of the astonishing, restless movement of Irish monks. Many set out for the first time on a deliberate search for new lands across the western ocean.[1] Though their quest failed, it opened men's horizons. Most of their travel sagas survive only as jejune fables, but a few contain a startling realism. Brendan of Clonfert[2] is said to have sailed westward from Iceland for several weeks, passing through a great foggy darkness to reach far beyond it to a fair and fertile shore; after marching for a fortnight up a river to its watershed, he met a splendid chief who told him that the Lord had vouchsafed him to behold the land of promise, but not to people it; for it was reserved for the habitation of Irishmen many centuries hence when there should be a great persecution of the faithful in Ireland. The medieval manuscripts rest on an original not later than the ninth century, though the prophecy is more appropriate to the nineteenth. Quite irrespective of whether or not these tales build upon a basis of real voyages, the imaginative concept of a habitable land to be found across the Atlantic injected a new adventurous aspiration into the thinking of northern Europe.

Migration to Europe brought more immediate achievement than

[1] The tradition of Atlantic exploration begins with the stories of Ailbe and Ibar at the end of the fifth century; much of the Irish literature consists of bald epitomes of giant wonders, that plainly bored their editors as much as their readers; but the major Latin texts, concerning notably Brendan and Malo, with Adomnan's tales of Cormac, deserve attention.

[2] e.g. *Vita prima*, *VSH* 1. 98 ff., especially chs. 13 and 65, two versions of the same tale with varying detail; in 13, the 'caligo' is defined as 'nebulae', with visibility scarcely as far as the bows and stern of the vessel. Warned by the virgin Ita that he would never find the promised land in the 'skins of dead animals,' he went to Connacht to find suitable timber, where enthusiastic 'artifices et fabri' gave their services free, on condition that he signed them on as crew; and the expedition set off with the blessing of Enda and Pupeus (ch. 71). The Brendan story is not arranged in sequence of time, and it is one of the few that, on the surface, appears to violate chronology, by bringing its hero into contact with persons, who lived well before him; the reason is that it is a collection of travellers' tales grouped together under Brendan's name.

ocean voyages. When Columban strode into the court of a Merovingian king at the turn of the century and denounced his lechery, or earnestly pleaded with another king to resign his crown and assume the higher glory of a tonsure, kings might laugh at him, threaten him, or exile him; but lesser men applauded the bold expression of words they dared not utter. No man had shown such confident disregard of earthly dignity since Martin reproached Valentinian and Maximus to their faces. A generation later, large numbers of monks from Ireland, and from the Anglo-Irish church of England, poured into Europe, bringing with them their scholarship and the splendid art they had developed at home. The combination of Irish enthusiasm, of English organizing ability, and of Columba's stern simplicity was irresistible. An English bishop, with a staff of English and Irish monks, evangelized and monasticized Germany; thence the more adventurous Irish penetrated to the Slavs, the Magyars, and ultimately the Ukraine. The schools of Charlemagne were organized by Englishmen, largely staffed by Irishmen; numerous native Franks, many of them of royal or noble birth, joined the houses founded by the Irish and the English, and established others on their model. As experience taught that the unlicensed enthusiasm which created monasteries might easily beget abuses in the second or third generation, abbots increasingly adopted a settled moderate rule, grounded on those ascribed to Columban and to Benedict of Nursia, to form the basis of what was later termed the Benedictine Order.

This was the first eruption in Latin Europe of monastic enthusiasm on a scale comparable with the eastern Mediterranean. Its origins were numerous and diverse; but they were not of equal importance. The houses founded before the middle of the sixth century were few in number, restricted in their scope, limited in their influence. The great majority of the monasteries north of the Alps came into being directly or indirectly through the energy of the English, Irish, and British; those that owe their being to Benedict or his disciples, or to native Italian, Frankish, or other influences independent of the impetus from the British Isles, are few. Though the fact of this insular impact on the continent is well enough known, the nature of the influences it brought to bear on the practices and ideas of Christendom may easily escape observation. For the incursion is taken for granted. It appears as an adventitious intervention arriving fully fashioned, unexplained, and scarcely needing explanation, as much an act of God as an earthquake or a Mongol invasion. Its peculiar contribution cannot be understood and evaluated without some grasp of its formative experience in its homeland. In view of the apparent uncertainty of the sources, it has been dangerously easy to abandon them to a few specialists, who are encouraged to play jigsaw puzzles with the names and dates, leaving alone the substance of the history they concern, and to begin the story of European monasticism with the reforms of Cluny.

Yet, the uncertainties are less than they sometimes seem. Apart from the recent Patrician controversy in Ireland, the outline of dates and the sequence of main events here set down constitute a framework whose rough and ready validity is not likely to be widely contested. Despite their formidable technical difficulties, the study of the sources is possible, and offers a rich reward. They have not yet been the object of much serious investigation, beyond the preliminary level of textual criticism, authorship, date. Their content and the story they tell awaits inquiry. That story traces the rise of a mass monastic movement, engendered from a variety of smaller beginnings, in south Wales and Ireland, in the 530s; of its subsequent sweep through Ireland to Iona, Northumbria, and the rest of England, thence converging from these several centres to Europe in the seventh and eighth centuries. At each stage in its growth, this movement was moulded by the specific circumstances of the society in which it grew; and its development changed those circumstances. Its influence upon the politics and theology, the literature and learning of Europe is great enough to warrant thorough and careful study. Celtic monasticism, and with it the secular history of early Britain and Ireland which gave it birth, is not an amiable recondite sideline, to be left to those whose temperament disposes them to browse upon the margins of history. It is an element of high importance in the main stream of European ecclesiastical history and theology, in an age when ecclesiastical history and theology were themselves of more than usual moment.

THE DATE OF SAINT ALBAN*

Saint Alban and his church are unfortunately undervalued, even in St Albans. The common belief, echoed, for example, in the St Alban Guide of 1957, makes him a 'Roman soldier', beheaded 'early in the fourth century', and therefore 'Britain's first martyr'. But the earliest records make him much more than the first martyr of Britain; he lived and died a hundred years earlier, and in his own day he was a much more important person than a 'soldier'. The common belief rests upon the account given by the Venerable Bede; but the earlier records, identified and published by Professor Meyer of Göttingen in 1904,[1] are the sources that Bede used, and show how the date was misplaced. They survive in three dreadfully corrupt manuscripts of the eighth and ninth centuries, illiterate copies of an original set down not far from the year A.D. 500. The manuscripts are preserved at Turin and Paris, with an abbreviated excerpt preserved in manuscripts of Autun, London, and Einsiedeln. The Turin manuscript records Alban's death in the time of the emperor Severus, at the beginning of the third century. The Paris manuscript and the Excerpts leave out the emperor's name, perhaps because their scribes took it as an adjective, severe. Gildas,[2] writing in Britain about the year 540, had a version which named no emperor, and 'supposed' (*ut conicimus*) that Alban and other martyrs suffered under Diocletian in the early fourth century; Bede,[3] writing nearly two hundred years later, left out the word 'suppose'. It is not surprising that the modern local tradition in St Albans is content with Bede, for the Proceedings of the Royal Academy of Sciences of Göttingen are not easily available, even to those who know German, and the texts there published have occasioned only one important article in English;[4] and the ecclesiastical historians who there discussed the texts were not fully alive to the historical allusions to the politics of Severus' reign. It is therefore the duty of those who are privileged to have easy access to these documents to explain what they say, and offer an opinion on how far they may be believed.

First, there is negative evidence; whenever Saint Alban was martyred, it was not in the great persecution of Diocletian that began in 303. There were then four emperors, two senior *Augusti* and two junior *Caesares*; Diocletian Augustus and his Caesar Galerius ruled the East, and in the West Maximian Augustus ruled Italy and Africa, Constantius Caesar the Gauls (Spain, Gaul and Britain). Constantius had married a Christian wife Helena, by whom he was father of Constantine; and contemporaries categorically assert that there was no persecution in his dominions. Lactantius, writing in Latin,[5] says that 'In order that he should not seem to be at odds with his senior colleagues, he permitted the destruction of meeting places, that

---

* Reprinted (and re-set) from *Hertfordshire Archaeology* 1 (1968) 1–8, by kind permission of the publisher.

is of buildings that could be restored, but kept unharmed the true temple of God, that is in men'; Eusebius,[6] writing in the Greek East, goes even further: 'He stood apart from the war against us, and protected the pious who were under him from harm and insult, and did not pull down the houses of the churches or devise any other evil against us.' Lactantius goes on to say that 'the three wild beasts raged throughout the world, from the east to the west, except in the Gauls.' It is probable that Eusebius exaggerated, and that at least some churches were destroyed; but certain that persons were not condemned;[7] a few years earlier, when Maximian administered Spain and Gaul, there was certainly one prosecution in Spain, perhaps others in eastern Gaul, but they do not concern us, for Maximian did not govern Britain.

Second, it is necessary to explain the character of the form of literature known as Hagiography, or Lives of the Saints. From the fifth century onwards, such lives increasingly became the most widespread and popular form of cheap literature, catering for as wide a range of taste as the modern paperback, from serious history and biography to romance, wonder, crime, sex, and horror. Very often those who had known a saint or martyr wrote his biography soon after his death, or even before, and occasionally our surviving manuscripts are a more or less accurate copy of the original, though even then, in an age of credulity, quite ordinary experiences are not infrequently romanticised into improbable miracles. But usually our manuscripts are much later versions; the original has been copied and recopied half a dozen times, each new author embellishing his story with edifying and dramatic additions, leaving out detail of the names of persons and places that no longer interest later ages, importing good stories filched from the lives of other saints, and often making a sad hash of abridging accounts he does not understand.

The Turin manuscript is very far from being an original; written in Gaul, it consists of three main parts, a narrative full of muddles, using a dialogue between Alban and the court lifted from other Gallic lives; a vivid description of the ground upon which modern St Albans now stands, discussed below, which seems to me to have been copied from a much earlier original, probably of the fourth century; and a short account of Saint Germanus' visit, taken from the life of the saint, written by the priest Constantius of Arles about 470. The essentials of the manuscript are excerpted below.

The first two paragraphs concern Gaul and are here omitted.

3. Then the emperor Severus went to Britain . . . When it became clear that there were very many Christians there, with his customary fury he ordered them all to be put to the sword.
4. Saint Alban received a fugitive cleric and
5. put on his garment and his *caracalla* that he was wearing and delivered himself up to be killed in his stead, although, according to ancient tradition, he was still a pagan, and was immediately delivered up to the evil Caesar Severus.
6. . . . he prayed . . .
7. . . . the wicked Caesar ordered his tribunal to be made ready . . .
8-13. Dialogue, in which Alban refuses Caesar's command to sacrifice, and is condemned.
14. When he was led like a lamb to the sacrifice, [he came to a river] whose rapid stream divided the wall from the arena where he was to be executed . . . By which crossing he saw on the further bank a great crowd of people of both sexes and all ages and conditions who had undoubtedly been sum-

THE DATE OF SAINT ALBAN

moned by divine prompting to attend the martyr. [The crowd was so numerous] that they could hardly get across the bridge by evening, and the judge was left in the city without attendants. So he [i.e. Saint Alban] betook himself to the stream he had to pass to reach the place of martyrdom, and turned his eyes to heaven. Thereupon the river yielded to his footsteps and provided a dry bed.

15. When he came to the place appointed for his death, the executioner ran [towards him] with his sword drawn, begging that he, who was to have killed the martyr, should himself be punished in his stead, and threw away his sword and fell at Saint Alban's feet, urging him to pray to the Lord for him.

16. As the sword lay on the ground among the other executioners, who hesitated, the holy martyr and the crowds climbed the hill, which rose with inexpressible beauty for 500 paces from the arena. It was clothed and coloured with various kinds of flowers, with nothing difficult or steep or sharp about it, its sides in all directions smoothed by nature like a level surface. It had undoubtedly been made ready long since for the martyr; before it was consecrated with sacred blood, its natural beauty had made it like a shrine [*sacrum*].

17. At the top of the hill Saint Alban asked for a drink of water; immediately and incredibly a perpetual spring sprang up at the martyr's feet . . . when its task was done, it returned to nature.

18. . . . the executioner's eyes . . . fell out on the ground.

19. . . . the executioner who had refused to kill the saint of God . . . was himself killed.

20. Then the evil Caesar, aghast at such wonders, ordered the persecution to end, without the orders of the emperors, setting down in his report that the religion actually prospered from the slaughter of the saints, which they had intended to be the means of its abolition.

21. When Saint Germanus, Bishop of Auxerre, came to his basilica . . . he ordered his tomb to be opened, and the limbs of saints brought from various countries, whom heaven held in equal honour, to be deposited therein.

22. Saint Germanus seized a mass of dust from the place where the martyr's blood had been shed, with a devotion that was indeed violent. But it was a pious sacrilege . . . By the preaching of Saint Germanus and the power of Saint Alban the crowd was converted, under the aegis of the Lord, to whom is honour and glory for ever and ever. The date was 22 June, thanks be to God for ever. Amen.[8]

The Paris manuscript and the Excerpts are essentially similar; they leave out the name of the emperor, substitute *iudex* (judge) for 'Caesar', and make fewer grammatical mistakes than the Turin text; the well-known text of Bede is a transcript of the Paris version, with verbal changes, designed to improve its style and grammar. The Turin version, or its original, is his source and theirs. Much is to be learnt from it.

First, the date. Severus was in Britain from the summer of 208 till his death in February 211; he was accompanied by his wife and his two sons, Antoninus Augustus and Geta Caesar. The terms Augustus and Caesar were in process of development; throughout the Roman empire, the terms 'Augustus', 'Caesar', 'Princeps' were interchangeable words meaning emperor, with subtle differentiation in their usage, rather as today the terms 'the King', 'His Majesty', 'the Monarch' are used in different contexts of the same ruler. But comparatively recently, from the middle of the second century, an additional usage had come into being: the son of the reigning emperor, natural or adoptive, from time to time received the title Caesar, without becoming Augustus or Princeps; and might later be proclaimed joint Augustus with his father. At this date there had been Caesars who were not Augusti on three occasions: from 137 to 161, from 166 to 177, and again from 198 to 209. Paragraph 20 supplies a close date; Mayer[9] was puzzled by the impossible conception that the Caesar should call off the persecution without the emperor's orders (*iniussu etiam principum*), and in desperation wondered if his sixth-century author might not be thinking of the four Merovingian brothers who in his time ruled Gaul and might act without one another's orders. It is in general an impossible concept; but it fits one known year in Roman history, and one only. During the summer of 209, Severus and Antoninus went beyond the northern frontier to campaign against the Caledonians, and left Geta Caesar behind in the province of Britain, in charge of the civilian administration.[10] By autumn they had returned, and Geta was proclaimed Augustus in September or October. The Caesar who acted *iniussu principum* was Geta, and Saint Alban's martyrdom dates to 22 June 209.

The date is to be accepted because the compiler of the Turin Life took over a quite extraordinary phrase that had no meaning for him and puzzled his readers from Bede (who left out the words *iniussu principum*) to Meyer; but which nevertheless has a meaning at this date. The compiler, or one of his predecessors, also muddled another detail of early third-century history which he did not understand. Antoninus ostentatiously wore a kind of greatcoat, called 'caracalla', popular among the soldiers of the Rhine army; and was therefore nicknamed 'Caracalla' by his enemies and by posterity. The word 'Caracalla' creeps awkwardly into the text; Turin says that when Saint Alban received the priest he put on 'his garment and his caracalla' (*ipsius [h]abitu ipsiusque caracalla*); Paris, the Excerpts, and Bede read *ipsius habitu, id est caracalla* (his garment, that is to say his caracalla); but two lines below, Turin reads *statimque Severo impiisimo Cesari oblatus est* (he was immediately delivered to the evil Caesar Severus). It is likely than an earlier version of the text had carried a marginal note *et Caracalla* against the name of Severus, and that a later copyist, who knew that *caracalla* was a greatcoat, but did not know that it was the name of an emperor, inserted it into his text in the wrong place. The mistake had a long later history; for in later versions of the line, when the word 'caracalla' had passed from the Latin language, the copyists replaced it with the then current word, 'amphibalon', a winter cloak or overcoat. Later still, when the meaning of this word too had been forgotten, it was turned from the garment of Saint Alban's 'teacher' to his name, and the fugitive priest became 'Saint Amphibalus'. In the late twelfth century, Abbot Simon excavated the bones of a pagan Saxon warrior of the sixth or seventh century from a barrow at Redbourn, whom a divine vision proclaimed to be Amphibalus,[11] and 'Saint Overcoat' continued to work prodigious miracles for over three centuries, until Henry VIII's reformers scattered his bones. But the mistake, preserving the fact that the original Alban story associated Caracalla with Severus in Britain, is additional evidence that the lost original harks back to a very early time, when the names of third-century emperors were known to readers and authors, and the brief authority of the Caesar Geta still remembered.

The trial scenes of paragraphs 6 to 13 were borrowed from Gallic lives of other saints, and the miracles of paragraphs 17 to 18 are also standard wonders, repeated in very many lives of saints. But the short introductory chapters 3 to 5, and 20, the conclusion, are plainly an abridgement of a fuller original, that was well informed, and much earlier than the date, after about 500, when the Turin version was compiled. Between them lies the much fuller account of the martyrdom, paragraphs 14 to 16. Its detail and local knowledge suggest a separate and earlier account.

Two circumstances seem to me to fix the composition of the original of the martyrdom account to the fourth century. A river divided the wall from the amphitheatre; though the date of the construction of the wall of Verulamium is still unsettled, it is, on present evidence, unlikely to have existed as early as 209. Though a recognisable Antonine bank may have fronted the Ver, it is not probable, though just possible, that such a bank would have been termed a *murus*. The tale is likely to have been composed by someone who knew an account, quite possibly verbal, of Saint Alban's route, but described it in terms of the features visible at the time he wrote. The spread of Christianity in Britain, discussed below, makes it rather unlikely that there would have been a market for a written and published account earlier than the middle decades of the fourth century.

The account of the execution in paragraph 14 suggests a date before which the passage was written. The author describes the place of execution as naturally fit for a shrine, *sacrum*. Such shrines were commonly erected over the graves of martyrs, and Gildas says that there were plenty of them in Britain still to be seen in the sixth century.[12] But if the shrine had been replaced by a church at the time when the account was written, it is most unlikely that the author would have refrained from saying so, in some such phrase as 'where his church now stands'. The probable date of the building of a church above the grave can be fairly closely fixed. According to the Turin version of Constantius' life of Germanus, it was there by the time of Germanus' visit in 429; and, even without that testimony, it is highly improbable that a shrine that seemed so important to Germanus should be without a church at so late a date. One record suggests a probable date. About 396 Bishop Victricius of Rouen[13] visited Britain; 'Holy and venerable martyrs', he wrote, 'my worthy fellow Bishops called me over to [help] make peace ... it was your concerns that detained me ... your salutary commands and the Lord Jesus' that I carried out to the best of my ability. I filled the sensible with love of peace, taught the teachable, overbore the ignorant, and attacked the unwilling.' Victricius was a controversial character, well known as the devoted pupil of Saint Martin of Tours; he was a fervent advocate of the widespread cult of the martyrs, newly developed by Ambrose of Milan, to whom he wrote his letter; like Martin, he pursued the novelty of preaching to ignorant rustics, not merely townsmen and gentlefolk, and carried Martin's teaching further by being the first-known bishop to preach to western barbarians; and, like Martin, he was a pioneer of the monastery, at this date rare in northern Europe beyond his own work and Martin's. His interests were known to the bishops who invited him over to settle disputes; since it was he whom they invited, the disputes are likely to have centred upon the innovations that he championed – relics, monks, and the evangelisation of peasants and barbarians. He claims success; and in the decade after his visit comes the first solid evidence in Britain of the causes that he championed; the first-known British monks, the Caesar Constans, Pelagius, Faustus, perhaps Coelestius, the Sicilian Briton,[14] and his associates, Antiochus and others unnamed; Bede says that St Martin's in Canterbury was built and named after Martin (hardly before 398) 'while the Romans yet ruled Britain' (probably meaning before 410), and Whithorn in Galloway, built among rustic barbarians, to whom Victricius alone had previously preached, bears Martin's name, and is said to have been completed in 398, a date not in conflict with the structure of the church. These considerations make the years 396-8 a probable, though not a certain, occasion for the construction of a monastic church upon the site of the shrine of St Alban; and therefore argue that the probable date of the compilation of the description of the martyrdom lies between *c*.340 and *c*.395.

Excavation at St Albans, and the written record of Christian Gaul, enable us to form some tenuous idea of the Christian public for whom the account was composed. The origins of Christianity in Gaul were first collated by Bishop Gregory of Tours in the later sixth century;[15] his fullest account naturally concerns his own city, a provincial metropolis whose importance is comparable with that of Verulamium. A shadowy bishop is 'said to have been' active in Tours with 'a few converts' from 250 to 300. Then the episcopate ceased until 338, when Litorius was consecrated. He held office for thirty-three years, and in the course of his episcopate 'he built the first church in Tours, when the Christians became numerous; at first, he had used a senator's house as a church.' He was buried in the 'church that bears his name'; then Saint Martin, his successor, 'built a church in honour of the holy apostles Peter and Paul', and when he died, his successor Briccius 'built a church above the body of St Martin'; it sufficed for a hundred years, until the 'Church that Briccius built over Martin' was pulled down, to be replaced by a 'much larger one', which, for the first time, bore the simple title 'Saint Martin's church'.

Two things stand out from this account; first, the earlier, fourth-century custom was to name a church after its founder or inspirer, Litorius' church; though it was not of course 'dedicated' to him. From the beginning of the fifth century, it became increasingly common to name churches in honour of the apostles or distant saints, and there is a reluctance to name churches from living or recently dead founders. Litorius' church continued to bear his name, but the basilica of Liberius, his contemporary in Rome, was in the 430s renamed in honour of Saint Mary, Santa Maria Maggiore, and the 'church built over Martin' was not replaced by a Church of Martin till nearly a century after his death. Just as the churches of Canterbury and Whithorn could not have been called 'St Martin's' much before 400 or much after 600, so the Verulamium church could have borne the name of the long-dead Alban from the beginning.

Second, the church building at Tours matched the known spread of Christianity in the West. At the accession of Constantine in 312, Christians were numerous in the East, few in the Latin West; it was after the reforms of Martin, Ambrose, and Damascus that in the generation between 370 and 400 'the whole world went Christian', in the words of the contemporary Rufinus. The first church in Tours was built somewhere about 350; within about thirty years it proved too small, but the two churches by and above Martin in the years about 400 sufficed for nearly a century. The rate of growth among Christians in Verulamium is not likely to have been greater than in the metropolitan city of Tours. As in Tours, three possible sites for churches come into consideration. A small, oblong fourth-century building with an apse just outside the London gate is of a plan that is commonly that of a church; its site and size are appropriate to a small community, just able to afford a building after, as at Tours, having previously met in a private house. A larger building, excavated by Wheeler, within the walls, north-west of the London gate, that might possibly be a church, would correspond in size, date, and site to the church Martin dedicated in Tours to Peter and Paul, the monastic site on the hilltop 'built above Saint Alban', to the church built above Martin. As three churches satisfied the needs of Tours for a century, three churches would suffice for the remaining life of Roman Verulamium. These considerations do not of course prove that these particular buildings are churches; they do argue that if these buildings are not churches, then similar buildings that are churches, of much the same size and siting, ought to be somewhere in Verulamium awaiting discovery.

THE DATE OF SAINT ALBAN

The description of the martyrdom is of considerable topograhical interest. The eloquent description of the hill reads like the work of an eye-witness; it is most unlike the invention of a hagiographer; and it is an exact description of the hill on which the Abbey now stands. It is further relevant that just enough Roman cremation burials have been discovered in the immediate neighbourhood of the Abbey[16] to show that the hill-top was the site of a cemetery in the first to third centuries A.D.; though inhumation burials have not yet been discovered to show that it continued in use as a cemetery in the fourth century, when inhumation replaced cremation. Saint Alban crossed the river by a bridge hard by the amphitheatre at a point 500 paces from the hill-top and site of the shrine; a circle of 500 paces, half a Roman mile, in radius with its centre on the Abbey, cuts the Ver in two places, by St Michael's Ford and much farther downstream. It is therefore likely that the site of the as yet undiscovered amphitheatre lies close to the ford, opposite the town, somewhere not far from the west end of Bridge Street.

Something of the status of Saint Alban may be inferred from the martyrdom account. The story that he went first to the amphitheatre, where he should have been executed, in the presence of great crowds, but was subsequently taken to a cemetery and there beheaded and buried, corresponds to what we know of other Christian trials. In the first two centuries A.D., when only a minority of free-born provincials were Roman citizens, non-Romans were commonly sentenced to fight beasts or gladiators in the arena, while Roman citizens were beheaded. In 112 Trajan instructed Pliny to deal with non-Romans on the spot, but send the Romans to Rome for trial. Sixty years later, when both Romans and Christians were more numerous, trials in Rome were no longer practicable. In the trials at Lugudunum in 177,[17] the governor wrote for instructions to the emperor Marcus, then campaigning on the Danube, and was told that Attalus and other Roman citizens should be beheaded, non-Romans sent to the amphitheatre. But the governor did not discover that Attalus was a Roman citizen until after he had been sent to the arena, and paraded round with a derisory placard round his neck. The account of Saint Alban reads very much as though he was first taken to face the swords of gladiators in the amphitheatre, and only then discovered, by the officials in charge of the games, to be a Roman; for it was they rather than the court who would get into trouble for killing a Roman in a wrongful manner. Appearance at the amphitheatre is also a more probable explanation of large crowds trying to get across the bridge than divine inspiration; it is likely that 22 June would have been a holiday on which games were commonly to be expected in Verulamium. It is therefore likely that Alban was a Roman citizen, at that date a rank confined to a minority of the notables of the major cities of Britain; in the dialogue of the trial, the wicked Caesar calls him a young man on the threshold of his career, and offers him a career in the public service and a noble wife if he will renounce Christianity; but these remarks belong to a section built upon the repertoire of the story-teller, not to the sections which carry conviction as his early sources.

Date and rank make Saint Alban more than 'Britain's first martyr'. Christianity was in his day a religion almost exclusive to the eastern provinces and to poorer people; the first western Christians are his contemporaries. Even in Rome, all known Christians, including bishops, were Greek-speaking until Victor, under Severus. Victor was an African, and his contemporary Tertullian, the first Latin Christian writer, was also African, as was the first Latin martyr, Namphamo, executed in 180. The martyrs of Lugudunum may very well have included some Latins, but their leaders, Pothinus and Irenaeus, were Greeks, and many of their fellows, all whose nationality we can determine, were Easterners, like Attalus; Christianity flourished there among a community of alien merchants and financiers, and the persecution aroused against them will have contained an element of xenophobia. There will of course have been other unrecorded martyrs, and some few Christian individuals; Tertullian, writing within a year or two of Saint Alban's execution, boasts of the provinces where Christianity has penetrated[18] and includes 'various Gallic peoples and the parts of Britain the Romans have not reached'. His odd wording implies that he had something to go on, even if it were no more than a single Christian; but some Christians in the parts the Romans ruled are probable. Saint Alban was probably not the only Christian in Britain, but he is the earliest authentic martyr of Latin Europe whom we know.

His church can claim as high an antiquity among its fellows. It was probably founded c.398 as a monastic church, at a time when monastic communities were extremely rare; if the date is right, it is earlier than Lerins, Marseilles, Auxerre. Its only predecessors known to me in Latin Europe, apart from small communities in private houses in Italian towns, are Martin's successive *monasteria* at Liguge near Poitiers and at Marmoutiers near Tours. St Albans is still an Abbey, though the monastic community died in the reformation. It is not merely an Abbey, but the oldest surviving monastic church in Latin Europe, surpassed in antiquity only by Mount Athos and a few other sites in the eastern Mediterranean. The importance of Saint Alban and his church are to be seen in relation to other saints and other churches; their pre-eminence is disguised in Bede's account, based on sources which had lost their dates; the chance preservation of the Turin manuscript, and the evidences of date that its compiler uncomprehendingly and unwittingly preserved, establish their priority, at least until some other chance discovery indicates a still earlier martyr and earlier monastery. Given what we know of the slow spread of Christianity in the West during the fourth century, it is not very likely that such discoveries will be made.

APPENDIX

3. Eo tempore Severus imperator ad Brittaniam dirigit regionem ... Et ubi praeclaruit, quod multitudo Christianorum ibidem essent, secundum sue rabiei morem gladio universos ferire praecepit.
4. Clericum persecutores fugientem hospicio suo sanctus Albanus recepit.
5. ipsiusque habitu ipsiusque caracalla, qua vestibatur, indutus, pro eodem se obtulit feriendum, sed, quantum antiquitas tradidit, adhuc paganus: statimque Severo impiisimo Cesari oblatus est.
6. ... orabat ...
7. ... tribunal sibi impiissimus Caesar parare praecepit ...
14. Cumque ad victimam sicut agnus duceretur, * quo murus et arena, ubi feriendus erat, meatu rapidissimo dividebatur ... * quo transducto ulteriore ripa vidit ingentem multitudinem hominum utriusque sexus condicionis et aetatis, qui sine dubio divinitatis instinctu ad obsequium martyris vocabantur, ut intra vesperam transire ponte vix possent. Denique iudex sine obsequio in civitate substiterat. Confert se ad torrentem, cui diu erat ad martyrium pervenire, et dirigente ad caelum lumina, ilico siccato alveo suis cessit unda vestigiis.
15. Cum ad locum destinatum morti venisset, occurrit stricto gladio carnifex, precans qui martyrem percussurus erat pro martyre se puniri; proiectoque gladio ad sancti Albani pedes advolvitur, et, ut pro eodem oraret dominum, deprecatur ...
16. Verum dum iacente ferro esset inter carnifices iusta cunctatio, montem cum

THE DATE OF SAINT ALBAN

turbis sanctus martyr ascendit, qui oportune editus gracia ineffabili quingentis fere passibus ab arena situs est, variis floribus picturatus atque vestitus; in quo nihil arduum nihil preceps nihil abruptum; quem lateribus longe lateque deductum a facie aequoris natura conplanat; quem haut dubie martyri praeparatum iam prius, quam sacro consacraretur cruore, sacro similem fecerat pulchritudo.

17. In cuius vertice sanctus Albanus aquam sibi dari rogavit; statimque incredi[ib]ili * coeto ante martyris pedes fons perennis exortus est ... qui denique ministerio persoluto ... reversus est ad naturam.
18. ... carnifici illi curvato ad terram lumina ... conciderunt ...
19. ... carnifex ille qui sanctum dei ferire noluit ... ipse percussus est ...
20. Tunc impiisimus Caesar, exanimis tanta novitate perculsus, iniussu etiam principum iubet de persecutione cessare, referens gaudere potius religionem caede sanctorum, per quam eandem opinabantur aboleri.
21. * Ad cuius basilicam cum sanctus Germanus Antesioderensis episcopus ... revelatoque sepulcro iubet [ut] membra sanctorum ex diversis regionibus collecta, quos pares merito receperat caelum, sepulchri unius retineret ospicium.
22. ... de loco illo, ubi martyris sanguis effluxerat, massam pulveris sanctus Germanus rapuit violenta quidem devotione, sed pio sacrilegio ... per sancti Germani episcopi praedicationem et virtutibus sancti Albani turba conversa est, prestante domino nostro, cui est honor et gloria in secula seculorum. Acta sunt X kl. Iulius, Deo gracias semper, Amen.

The language of the Turin manuscript is excessively corrupt. The text above is Meyer's edition, which removes the worst confusions and restores some grammatical cohesion. Meyer printed the uncorrected text of the manuscript on pp. 35-46.

NOTES

1. *Abhandlungen der königlichen Gesellschaft der Wissenschaften zu Göttingen*, Phil.Hist. Klasse, N.F., VIII, 1 (1904), 3-81.
2. *de Excidio Britanniae*, 10-11.
3. *Hist. Eccl.*, 1, 7.
4. W. Levison, *Antiquity*, 15 (1941), 337 ff.
5. *de Mortibus Persecutorum*, 15, 7 and cf. 16, 1; cf. also *Optatus*, 1, 22.
6. *Hist. Eccl.*, 8, 13; cf. *vita Constantini*, 1, 16.
7. Cf. A. H. M. Jones, *Later Roman Empire*, p. 72.
8. *Abhandlungen ... Göttingen*, pp. 48-62, Turin version. See Appendix for text.
9. Pp. 20-1.
10. Herodian, 3, 14, 9.
11. *Roger of Wendover, and related Chronicles*, A.D. 1178; cf. A. Meaney, *Gazetteer of Anglo-Saxon Burial Sites*, p. 104.
12. Ch. 10.
13. Migne, *Patr. Lat.*, 20, 443.
14. Cf. pp. 17–51, above.
15. *Hist. Franc.*, 10, 31.
16. *St Albans Transactions*, 1893/4, 62.
17. Eusebius, *Hist. Eccl.*, 5, 1.
18. *adversus Iudaeos*, 7.

Christianity in Britain, 300–700: The Literary Evidence*

The trouble with the literary evidence for fifth- and sixth-century Britain is that there is a vast amount of it, and that it is difficult to know what to make of it. The easiest way to deal with it is to say that half of it is worthless rubbish: what you choose to accept gives you a short cut to a quick answer, and you have a foolproof excuse for ignoring awkward bits that do not fit, or for explaining them away.

Put so simply, this sounds like a crude and silly approach that any serious historian will naturally and easily avoid; but it is not easy to avoid if you treat these texts as you might treat the evidence for better documented periods, if you aim at achieving a simple clear cut distinction between the reliable and the unreliable, between fact and fancy. Such simplicity is risky at the best, dangerous with these difficult texts. The historian does well to bear in mind the dictum of the late Professor J. B. S. Haldane, challenging the alleged exactitude of the physical sciences, that 'a fact is a theory in which no one has made a large hole for a long time.' The historian's problem was expressed neatly by Professor Ludwig Bieler in a recent article: 'according to a widely accepted view, it is the historian's task to find out "what has actually happened". This, I believe, is impossible. The historian cannot do more than collect, assess and interpret evidence.'[1]

This does not mean that we must wail our sirens in a fog of uncertainty. Though nothing is perfectly certain, we can distinguish the probable from the possible and the unlikely, isolate the extremes of the virtually certain and virtually impossible, and weigh the degrees of probability in between. Our texts have been collected; most of them are printed somewhere in some form. Our main problem is assessment, and here our first concern must be to detect and recognize the bias and purpose of each source before we attempt interpretation. Every text has bias and purpose. All great historians, from Thucydides, Tacitus and Bede to Gibbon, have preached their own beliefs; they are great because they recognize their purpose and make it plain to their readers, and because they found their argument on a careful assessment of their own sources, distinguishing between knowledge and report. If we reject their conclusions, we do so on the basis of their own evidence, interpreting it differently. We need a sharper criticism of more pedestrian writers, ancient or modern, who are less aware of their own bias, who are content to endorse a conclusion because it is

* Reprinted from *Christianity in Britain, 300–700*, edd. M. W. Barley & R. P. C. Hanson (Leicester, 1968), pp. 55–73, by kind permission of Leicester University Press.

'generally accepted' or 'universally agreed,' and we must be especially wary of the man who claims to set down objective truth free from bias, for the closer he comes to his ideal, the more he is enslaved to the passing prejudice of his own day, uncritically reading present assumptions into the experience of the past.

We are all products of the world we live in, and we cannot hope to escape from its present assumptions. We can try to recognize them, to criticize them, to discount what is not valid for the past. But our world and our experience changes, so that each generation requires a new interpretation of the past. The historians of stable Victorian England could afford to deplore the bellicosity of Greek city states, to bewail the blind decadence of the later Roman Empire; the modern veteran of two world wars has less authority to condemn past follies, but is better equipped to understand them. That is why assessment and interpretation go hand in hand. Each new acceptable interpretation of a period establishes a working hypothesis, that demands and prompts fresh assessment of old evidence, and that assessment modifies or overturns the accepted interpretation.

I have set down elsewhere[2] my present interpretation of the sources for the history of the British Isles in the fifth and sixth centuries, and must summarize it before venturing assessment. We have good contemporary evidence for the beginning and the end of the period. In 400 A.D. the British Isles were divided between the civilized Roman diocese and the barbarians beyond its frontiers, Picts and Scots. Romans and barbarians were a world apart, alien and hostile in speech, culture and interest, in government and in religion. By the seventh century, the whole of the British islands were split into a multitude of small kingdoms, speaking four main tongues, Irish, Welsh and Pictish native and long established, English foreign and recent. But they were comparable kingdoms, sharing a common homebred religion, analogous political institutions, a similar rural economy. There were great differences between the speakers of one language and another, between the individual kingdoms; but these internal differences were much less than those which distinguished seventh-century Britain from its own past, and from contemporary Europe.

At the top of society, the influence of the past was least apparent; unlike Europe, there was little continuity of urban political institutions or of the ownership of large rural estates. But at the bottom, there was less change; unlike Europe, the bulk of the population still spoke essentially the same languages as their ancestors in the Roman and pre-Roman past, and still observed much customary ancient law. Whereas in Europe barbarians settled within Roman society with comparatively little native resistance, to fuse into the society conventionally termed feudal, in Britain 200 years of war left the Germanic immigrants little influenced by native Roman civilization, the natives almost totally unaffected by Germanic custom. The impact of Merovingian Europe and of papal Christianity bore down upon diverse traditions whose interaction at home was more recent in time, and quite different in kind.

Late Roman Britain and the Britain of Bede are relatively easy to comprehend, because they are amply depicted in contemporary records, and because they were relatively stable. The centuries between changed rapidly, and the changes are ill-described. They were initiated by an administrative decision of the year 410. Hitherto the bulk of the day-to-day civil administration of Roman Britain had been the responsibility of the council and magistrates of a dozen or more *civitates*, internally self-governing, and equivalent smaller communities. Defence, finance and the coordination of the *civitates* had been the responsibility of a dozen senior officers, and some scores of lesser officials, appointed by the imperial government in Italy. In 410 the imperial government declined to make further appointments to these posts, or to continue responsibility for defence, finance or any other aspect of central administration. These responsibilities were thrust upon the common council of the British states, hitherto an advisory body and a means of pressure, not a decision-making authority. Now, it had to replace the central functions of the imperial rulers, to make the appointments they had made, to take charge of finance and defence. The ruin of Roman Britain in the next two centuries was in a general sense a by-product of the fall of western Rome; in detail, it stemmed from the failure of the states of Britain to agree upon a central government whose authority all could and would respect.

There is neither evidence nor likelihood that anything else changed in 410 beyond the change in the central administration. There is no evidence for any evacuation of troops or withdrawal of 'Romans'; for all freeborn inhabitants of the diocese had long been Romans, as fully Roman as Spaniards, Italians or Syrians, as Roman as their descendants are today English or British. What army there was remained; nothing suggests that existing posts were abolished or new ones created in or about 410. What changed was the authority that appointed their holders.

There is a little general evidence for the outline of what happened. Procopius,[3] well informed, but writing a century or more later far away in Constantinople, says that the island was governed by 'tyrants'; that is, by local emperors, replacing the authority that the emperor in Italy had abdicated. Various sources indicate who one or two of them were.[4] One text[5] suggests the obvious, that at least at first the British named their own consuls. The British were compelled, as one contemporary observed,[6] to live 'independently,' no longer subject to laws enacted by the emperors in Italy, and the increasing weakness of the emperors soon put much of Gaul in the same position.[7] But the same contemporary noted that British were outstandingly and surprisingly successful in repelling their external enemies.

This success means that at least for a short time the British reached some kind of agreement; for victories cannot be won without soldiers, and soldiers cannot fight unless civilians provide the money for their pay, food, weapons. In Britain in 410, political power lay in essentially the same kind of hands as in the rest of the empire, in the *potentiores*, landed nobility who dominated the *civitates* and the council, and *viri militares*, senior army officers whose power lay in the willingness of their troops to obey their orders. No government could hope to achieve lasting stability without overwhelming support among one of these elements, or the support of considerable sections of both. In Europe, there was commonly a clear cut difference between the outlook of the military and the civilian leaders, but it was rarely that all army officers embraced one side in any given conflict, all civilian noblemen the other; most governments, legitimate or otherwise, rested upon varying combinations of some military and some civil support. Though those that fell were commonly defeated in battle, they retained until defeat the support of soldiers prepared to fight for them and civilians prepared to finance and administer them; they fell because the combination behind their enemies proved stronger.

The little evidence we have suggests that the political conditions of Britain did not differ. One text[8] appears to describe the replacement of one government of *potentiores* by another of different views but similar social composition about 410-11, and implies that at that date neither had elevated an emperor. To survive, the new government must have earned at least passive acceptance by at least one of the main military authorities; the proper institutions of government are headed by an emperor, a *praefectus praetorio*, by definition and tradition civilian, and a *magister militum*, by definition an army officer. The emperor might be either a civilian or a soldier. Some ten or fifteen years later, political authority is said to have been vested in a *superbus tyrannus* named Vortigern and his council; the term *tyrannus* is most commonly and properly applied to an emperor, but does not exclude the possibility that Vortigern was the all-powerful prefect of a military emperor. We do not know and shall not know what titles he or others used, though we do know the range of titles that it was open to him to employ. We are told that he was subject to the same pressures as continental emperors; he employed Saxon, English, *foederati* to repel the Picts; their job done, a decisive section of the *potentiores* refused to continue to finance them or him; and in conflict with the *potentiores* he was driven to hire still larger numbers of *foederati*, who took pains to augment their numbers on their own initiative, until they were strong enough to attack and defeat both parties among their Roman British employers.

The outline of subsequent history is set down by Gildas, writing a century or slightly less after the rebellion; and continued by other writers, British and English. The first Saxon revolt was followed by a long period of war, in which the British were ultimately victorious. For several generations, up till Gildas' day, native British authority prevailed, with the English confined to specified areas, whose limits the archaeological evidence is able to determine. Later, a second Saxon revolt overthrew British authority in the greater part of what is now England in a single generation, annexed, colonized, and changed the language of the rest more slowly over a period of several centuries.

There is just enough evidence to indicate the approximate dates of the main events which divide these centuries into distinct periods. A contemporary

CHRISTIANITY: THE LITERARY EVIDENCE

Gallic Chronicle baldly notes the Saxon subjugation of Britain in 441 or 442, and evidently means the first Saxon revolt. It therefore implies that the federate settlements began a decade or more earlier, somewhere about the 420s; and the evidence of many thousands of excavated graves agrees that the main body of federate Anglo-Saxon cemeteries begins somewhere about the 420s, though a small proportion of the grave goods was then anything up to a generation old; while the literary and archaeological evidence argues that the main fabric of Roman British civilization endured and prospered for a generation after 410, until at least the early 440s. The narrative of the wars of Vortigern preserved by Nennius ends with a massacre of the 300 *seniores*, the principal citizens of the civilian *civitates*, followed by a mass emigration to Gaul of their surviving fellow citizens, and by the initiation of a guerila resistance among the remainder under Ambrosius Aurelianus. Ample contemporary continental evidence witnesses the arrival in Gaul of a large number of immigrants from Britain in or just before 460. The resistance initiated by Ambrosius triumphed at the siege of Mount Badon, something over a generation before Gildas wrote, about or just before 540, and Badon is therefore to be dated about or a little before 500, somewhere in the 490s. Neither English nor British tradition knows anything of war between the two peoples in the early sixth century, but both concur in recording the outbreak of the second Saxon revolt, on a small local scale immediately after the Justinian plague about 550, attaining its decisive victories twenty years later, and permanently securing the future England in the years 570–600. The main periods are therefore: I, the continuation of Roman Britain under its own emperors for a generation, from 410 to about 440; II, the British-Saxon wars between about 440 and about 495, in two stages, (a) the initial success of the first Saxon revolt from about 440 to about 457 and (b) the increasingly successful war of resistance by the British between about 460 and about 495; III, the period of British dominance after the wars, from about 495 to about 570; and IV, the success of the second Saxon revolt, in the years 570 to 600.

The key dates in this broad outline are reasonably secure, for they rest upon contemporary and continental evidence. Anything beyond the broad outline requires close assessment of the individual native sources that concern each period. Those that concern the first period, the early fifth century, are extensive and informative; one of the ironies of Roman Britain is that until the very end it remains voiceless and anonymous, for no single native literary work is known, but that the surviving works of early fifth-century British writers, most of them composed after the end of Roman rule, fill a fair sized bookcase. These works are Christian and controversial; most of them were written by Britons abroad, and most of them are Pelagian. Their assessment means that they must be seen in the context of Latin Christianity, and of the impact of British thinking thereon.

The main stages in Latin Christian evolution during the fourth century are fully recorded. In 311 Christianity suddenly, and somewhat prematurely, became the religion of the government. It had grown first and strongest among the cities of the eastern Greek-speaking provinces, and preserved a strong radical element, exalting the virtues of the poor against the evil of riches; so strong that even in the fifth century, St Augustine had to still the doubts of the last of the pagan aristocrats of Rome, that Christian doctrine threatened the rights of property. Though his argument was and is persuasive, radicalism persisted. By 311 Christianity had grown powerful in the west in Africa and Italy, and had made a considerable impact in Spain and the Rhineland; but in the rest of Gaul and in Britain it remained weak. In the whole of the provinces of Lugdunensis and Aquitania, barely half a dozen sees are known to have existed before Constantine; in a provincial capital of the importance of Tours, the first effective bishop took office in 340, and the Christians were few enough to assemble in a private house, neither rich enough nor numerous enough to afford a church building until about 350, and the see of Orleans was no earlier, that of Angers still later. Throughout the Gallic provinces, Christianity came in as the religion of the government and its officials, strong where they were numerous, weak where they were few; and earned affection or distrust as a government religion. On the one hand, the politically ambitious speedily learnt the practical advantages of conformity with Christian ritual and idiom, and bishops suddenly promoted from the status of persecuted sectaries to that of influential government advisers delighted in the triumph of the church; but other Christians distrusted the influx of time-serving converts, and feared the government's authority over the church, while the bulk of the population of rural Gaul paid little regard to a new government religion confined to the towns.

The sordid wrangles of the Arian controversy at first evoked contempt and disgust among non-Christians. But their outcome demonstrated that in Gaul very small conventicles of plebeian subjects were prepared to risk exile, imprisonment and even life for the sake of beliefs dearly held, and that their perseverance was able to defy government with success. The dispute spurred the Christians to reform; the majesty of Pope Damasus, the stern sincerity of Ambrose of Milan, the simple piety of Martin of Tours revealed the Christian church as an effective champion of human rights, able to restrain and defeat the arbitrary violence of emperors and their officers, while the vigorous promotion of the cult of martyrs made the veneration of men who died resisting unjust rulers a major part of Christian worship. Martin and his pupils began to extend Christianity to peasants and border barbarians, and in the last years of the century, immediately before the break between Britain and Rome, the whole western world became Christian in a generation. Conversion to Christianity did not of course mean that the converts ceased to be pagans; though church fathers might thunder the wishful belief that 'the same mouth cannot utter the praises of Christ and of Jupiter,' the poems of Ausonius, writing hymns to Christ and Jupiter with equal delight in language, proved them wrong; as did the ordinary laity, whose persistent practice of attending mass on Sunday mornings and sacrificing to their Lares in the afternoon long earned censure from church councils.

The triumph of Christianity was immediately followed by the capture of Rome in 410, and the first barbarian federate settlements in Gaul in 418. Disaster forced men to think afresh, and new thought begot controversy, in which British writers were prominent. In the interests of building a disciplined monolithic Christian church able to survive the disintegration of lay society, Augustine of Hippo elaborated the theology centred upon the original sin inherited by all men from Adam, only to be redeemed by the sacramental grace of God. Men trained in the older humanist values of Latin Christianity were deeply offended, and found their spokesman in Pelagius, a monastic Briton then regarded as the most polished writer in Rome. Augustine's views made little headway until after the fall of Rome shocked men's thinking, and then not through the normal processes of a church council or the approval of the Pope, but by a secular edict for the arrest of Pelagius and his colleagues issued by the civil government over the head of Pope Zosimus, who still refused to condemn Pelagius. The government enforced conformity in the Mediterranean, but its writ had ceased to run in Britain, and was already weak in northern Gaul. There, the author of the Chronography of 452 could remark, with casual detachment, that 418 was said to be the year in which Augustine 'invented the heresy of predestination.' In Britain, Pelagian thinking was and remained orthodox, Augustinianism a foreign heresy imposed by a lay government that had no authority in Britain, though its universal acceptance in the Mediterranean made it a foreign ideology of considerable weight.

Pelagianism produced a radical wing of its own, a group of young British writers, the most prominent of whom is termed the 'Sicilian Briton'[9] because he wrote in Sicily in and shortly after 411. His socialist concepts are more advanced than any other of the recorded radical thinking of antiquity; to him 'mankind is divided into three classes, the rich, the poor and those who have enough,' and its problems are to be solved by taking from the rich their excess and giving it to the poor, so that everyone has enough and class distinctions are abolished. But he does not, like most early Christian egalitarians, stop at a single redistribution of wealth; he also aims to end the causes of class difference, with the argument 'Abolish the rich, and you thereby automatically abolish the poor; for the few rich are the cause of the many poor.' The slogan 'Abolish the rich,' *Tolle divitem*, has a rhythm that a formidable crowd might shout; Augustine exploited his outspokenness to the full, and tried without success to make Pelagius responsible for his extreme views; but there is no doubt that the voicing of such views will have helped to induce the government to back Augustine's demands. There is of course no evidence to show whether or not such views were widespread in Britain; but more than a century later, the writings of one of his close associates were cited by Gildas with approval, as the work of 'one of us.' At least that tract had been read and recopied in Britain for four generations, surviving the storms of the Saxon wars; and the thinking of Gildas and of later British and Irish Christian writers shows a total unawareness of the controversy, with the occasional utterance of sentiments that would have angered conscious Augustinians.

These are polemical theologians; though they and others wrote mostly abroad, they were reared in Britain, and their similes and analogies reflect a good deal of the social, political and educational practice and assumptions of early fifth-century Britain. They admired the monastic way of life, preached by Martin's pupil Victricius in Britain about 396. Victricius also zealously propagated the cult of martyrs, champions of conscience against unjust authority. Gildas[10] attests the rapid spread and long persistence of the martyr cult in Britain: 'the splendid lamps of holy martyrs, whose shrines would have inspired divine love in the minds of pilgrims, had not many of them been torn from us for our sins by the miserable partition with the barbarians' (*lugubri divortio barbarorum*). He names two shrines that remained, and the concept took sufficient root for the name 'martyrium' to spread widely, surviving to this day in south Wales as 'Merthyr', though it is unlikely that the *martyria* made any significant impact before 400 A.D., probable that their spread belongs in the decades thereafter. St Patrick's account of his early life and of the British ecclesiastics, whose authority he rejected not far from 440, as well as Constantius' description of Germanus' visits, based on tales told him by the bishop's companions, attest the continuance of the vigorous intellectual and political life, the rich and sophisticated culture of Roman Britain into the 440s. Thereafter, evidence ends.

The sources for the next century are much more difficult to evaluate. There was little continuing written tradition, and virtually no records were preserved; what we have was set down by men who had little understanding of the vanished past they described. Their distorted statements often appear to conflict with one another and with common sense, and it is essential to get our priorities right in assessing them. It is rarely helpful to ask directly of any writer or statement the simple question, do we believe it? Our belief or disbelief has little more value than the statement itself. What we have to recognize is that there is a reason for every statement; it may be that it is true, that its author is a congenital liar, ignorant, ill-informed, or the like; but the first priority is to pinpoint the origin and purpose of the statement as far as we are able, to relate it to the author's bias and circumstances; thereafter to place it in the context of the time to which it relates.

The second priority is to understand the knowledge of the author's first readers. All our sources are either contemporary with the events they describe; or written within living memory; or set down later. A contemporary may misrepresent an event, or invent an obscure incident outside his readers' knowledge, but he cannot foist upon them an important public event which they well know did not happen. So it is with living memory. In ours or any other society, we add to our own experience what our fathers have told us of theirs, but we rarely know our grandfathers well enough to learn more from them than odd disjointed

CHRISTIANITY: THE LITERARY EVIDENCE

incidents of the distant past. The experience of each of us is much alike. My father's stories of his own life give me some understanding of who Gladstone and Asquith were and when they lived. As a child I was taken to gape at the empress Eugenie, and told something of her life, so that I know that the Franco–Prussian war was about a hundred years ago. My father knew an old lady who had danced in Brussels on the eve of Waterloo, so that I know that Wellington beat Napoleon well over a century ago, and would not confuse the two Napoleons. But that is the limit of living memory; it tells me nothing of the French Revolution, let alone of Cromwell and the English revolution. Its furthest limits lie between a 100 and 150 years back, at most a century before my own birth. Behind it lie a jumble of names of people, events and places, ill-related to one another or to time. They derive not from living memory, but from a historical tradition, that may be oral, or may be written, but is still out of living experience. If our historical record was entirely oral, if we lacked history books and records, a writer or a lecturer might describe how Marlborough beat Gustavus Adolphus at Minden, or explain the Martello towers of the south coast as defences erected against the Spanish Armada, without meeting protest or denial; but if he congratulated his readers on our freedom from war in our generation, or praised the long unbroken democratic tradition of modern Germany, he would be treated as a humorist or a lunatic. So it is with Gildas. He may talk nonsense about Magnus Maximus or the date of the Roman walls in innocence, for these lay outside living memory in 540; but when he complains[11] that the generation which won the war at Badon has died out, so that the country is now run by a generation ignorant of past troubles, that has only known our present security (*illis decedentibus cum successisset aetas tempestatis illius nescia et praesentis tamen serenitatis experta*) he cannot be wrong, because his readers knew, just as modern readers' knowledge prevents us from contrasting the serenity of our own day with the ghastly anarchy of Victorian England. So it is when he says that the Britain of his day is governed by impotent *rectores* and overmighty *duces*, who assume the style of *reges*, by duly consecrated bishops and ordained priests, that the island is partitioned but has been at peace for more than a generation. The assessment of Gildas must concentrate upon what he says of his own day and of the recent past; it must respect his account of Vortigern, a century earlier; but it need not regard his guesses about the more remote past, nor about the relative date and meaning that he gives to a single document incorporated into the early part of his narrative.

It is therefore obvious that the date of a writer is of supreme importance if he is contemporary with the event, or writes within living memory, but is of little moment if he writes later. If a text describing sixth-century events is shown to be of the seventh century, then its early date commands high respect; if its date be later, it matters little whether it belongs to the ninth century or the seventeenth; what matters then is the historical tradition upon which it relies, and this tradition varies with circumstance, not necessarily with time. Thus, Baldwin's life of Samson, written six or seven centuries after the event, is much closer to its near contemporary original than is the eighth-century life of Germanus used by Nennius, three or four hundred years nearer to its original in time. These self-evident priorities in assessment need emphasis, for the cult of the *codex vetustior* has done much to muddle modern studies of these centuries.

Apart from Gildas, the principal written sources for fifth- and sixth-century Britain are the documents collected under the name of Nennius, the Welsh Poems, the Saints' Lives, the Annals, and the Genealogies. Each have their own rules. The purpose of genealogies is to connect living persons with persons at least believed to have been mighty in the past; the two ends are likely to be a great deal more substantial than the links in the middle. National customs vary the method of distortion; since descent through the female was acceptable in Wales, the commonest contrivance of Welsh genealogists is to concoct a marriage between a man and a woman who may have lived centuries apart, so that the two lines connected have greater validity than the marriage. Irish and English custom did not acknowledge descent through the woman, so their genealogists contrive ancestry by allotting an improbable excess of sons to a long dead hero like Ida or Niall; and both not infrequently tack a pedigree whose origin they do not know on to a father of several sons, so that the younger among a group of sons are always suspect if their relationship is not attested outside the genealogical tradition.

Annalists, usually monastic, command a higher respect, for their deliberate distortion is commonly confined to entries enhancing their own house, order, or patron. They require however a more patient critical analysis, for their early form is commonly a relative order, to which later hands have added absolute dates; sometimes an extant text is itself a conflation of two or more earlier annals, and its author slots his sources together in the wrong places. These however are the routine problems of textual criticism, arduous, but in themselves easier to sort out than conscious manipulation.

Nennius' documents each require separate study; some are contemporary or near contemporary, others within living memory, others later. Some have been closely studied; Kenneth Jackson[12] has established the early date of some northern documents, within living memory of their later entries; the Kentish Chronicle is a rational narrative out of keeping with known British writing significantly later than the sixth century, with a close knowledge of the British toponomy of Kent; the list of Arthurian battles reads like an epitome of a lost poem. On the other hand, the stories of Ambrose and Vortigern draw upon the story teller rather upon historical record, and are of more interest to students of literature than of history; the accounts of Patrick and of Germanus rest on devolved, perhaps even vernacular, saints' lives, and other sections are transcriptions and epitomes of Irish legend. The essential fact is that Nennius in himself is no authority, and has no entity, and the differences between the manuscripts is of marginal importance; some of his texts have high historical value, some negligible, and the whole collection is in urgent need of close study.

Historical study of the Welsh poems has begun, but only begun; and is unlikely to be as thorough as the texts deserve until the critical discussions, at present only published in modern Welsh, are translated for the attention of a wider range of scholars. Sir Ifor Williams' conclusion that the core of the *Gododdin* was composed very soon after the campaign it describes is not likely to be overset; but since a large number of verses concern heroes who lived a generation before or after that campaign, the study of the poem's growth during the seventh century, the detection and explanation of the added stanzas, invites further study. So do the later poems; a few lie so close in content and concept to events much earlier than their present form that they may be modernizations of earlier poems, or even of translations from British, while many preserve twisted allusive fragments taken from older traditions and from poems not preserved. The essence of the matter is that the older poems, preserved entire, are versions of works first composed in honour of living men, or of their immediate ancestors, and that many of the later poems make use of similar lost originals. The poet's bias is to honour his patron for the virtues that the patron esteemed; like all government propaganda, it is excellent evidence for the aims and intentions of government, and is necessarily concerned with the misrepresentation of actual events.

I have discussed elsewhere[13] the Saints' Lives, the bulkiest group of documents, and the main conclusions must here be summarized. In general, most extant lives rest ultimately upon an original composed either just before the saint's death, or soon after. But unlike most other sources, they were popular literature, widely read for centuries; they were therefore altered more often, and more drastically, than other sources, in order to bring them into line with changing taste. The nature of the changes is therefore fairly uniform, and adequate texts survive to show what kind of changes were commonly introduced at what period. The grammar of the critical evaluation of these texts is not hard to discover; it has however as yet been little employed, and most lives lack detailed study. Reeves' critical edition of Adamnan's Columba, published 110 years ago, remains a model of the type and scale of treatment which each life deserves, and which no other has yet received. Later editions of the same life, and most studies of other lives, compare with it as a first year undergraduate's essay compares with a doctoral thesis.

The evidence upon which assessment of the normal behaviour of the hagiographer rests consists of a relatively small number of key texts. A few surviving texts are contemporary with the events they describe, or were written within living memory, among them the pioneer works of Athanasius, Jerome and Severus, Jonas' Columban, Adamnan's Columba, the first life of Samson. A number of later lives, as Wrmonoc's Paul Aurelian and Wrdisten's Winwaloe, reproduce the orthography of primitive Welsh or even British names of people and places that are certainly not the product of scholarly archaism; others, like

Richemarcus' David or Jocelyn's Kentigern, are conflations of earlier lost versions of diverse date, and occasionally incorporate an incident or cite a document written down in or near the saint's lifetime. More important is the study of the evolution of those few lives which exist in successive versions, notably the lives of Samson; unfortunately many later versions remain unpublished, disregarded as epitomes or devolved accounts that add nothing of value to the biography of the saint concerned.

The detectable changes in such successive versions are few and simple. If the cleric commissioned to copy or edit an old life had a sense of purpose or a delight in literary achievement, he tended to insert names and incidents that honoured his hero or his monastery and to suppress what he considered uninteresting or unedifying. Fortunately, the majority of such clerics had less ambition, and were content to transcribe what they found mechanically into the normal language of their own day, omitting or awkwardly adapting only the most grossly offensive incidents, retaining a great many names of people and places, that can have held little interest for their readers, often epitomizing the story to the point of obscurity, sometimes expanding it or replacing it with an edifying homily annexed from one of the fathers of the church, or with a colourful miracle borrowed from the lives of other saints or from the repertoire of the story teller. The result is that a few great names appear in many lives out of due time and place, Patrick, Germanus, Martin, Arthur and the like; otherwise, names are taken over from version to version, or else omitted; they are not inserted unless they give honour to the saint or the monastery. When Glastonbury tradition brings Patrick, Gildas, or Joseph of Arimathea to Glastonbury, it is to be discounted; but when Bangor tradition places Daniel's first monastery at Pembroke, with no kind of reference to David, it serves no Bangor interest. When the Irish life of Abban sends its hero to the pagan English king at Abbandune (Abingdon) in the late fifth century, it claims Abingdon for its own on the strength of a similarity of name, and raises suspicion; but when Columba Terryglass is made to visit an unnamed English kingdom where cremation is practised in the mid-sixth-century, no monastic interest is served, and the passing reference to cremation, not exploited to the saint's credit, argues a near contemporary source, for cremation at that date was rare and remote from Ireland. The life of Berachus is mainly concerned with a juridically interesting law suit with a *magus* over title to land; the numerous monks and kings named were contemporaries with one another, but two nuns who lived long after are imported as witnesses; they play no further part, but are involved because their houses were neighbours, with a potential interest in the property concerned. Likewise, the unedifying incident discreditable to the hero, often adapted or omitted in later versions, belongs to the near contemporary account; but the miracle attending the saint's illegitimate birth is usually imported for the gratification of the reader, and his royal parents are almost always suspect or demonstrable inventions; for, since a few saints were of royal or noble origin, royal rank became a fashionable prerequisite of very many biographers, and inspired in Welsh an elaborate tract on the genealogies of the saints. Though there is very rarely reason to credit the saint's paternity, the majority of the royal pedigrees to which they are attached are valid, an important contribution to the corpus of genealogies.

The enormous mass of trite miracles sometimes discourages the unwary modern reader. The miracles themselves are commonly of more interest to the student of literary tradition than to the historian; but the persons and the circumstances involved are of great interest, for a very high proportion of the people occur also in genealogies, annals and other sources, and very rarely occur in the lives at a discordant date; while the attendant circumstances commonly find their parallels in legal and social tracts, sometimes in archaeology. The miracles are there because the authors and the readers automatically assumed that a supernatural was more probable than a natural explanation for many ordinary phenomena; and because the credit of the saint rested on the quantity and quality of his miracles. Saints appeared as powerful protectors in an age when mere men seemed impotent, and their divine *virtus* is manifest from the earliest known lives. Jerome's Paul, Severus' Martin relate quantities of miracles for which the modern critic may easily discern more human explanations: the source of one of the more striking Irish water-working wonders is the *Dialogues* of Gregory the Great, who heard the story 'the day before yesterday,' soon after the event; no account could be more contemporary, and, though the human explanation is plain to the reader, embellished later versions of such tales turn wonder to absurdity. The commonest miracle is the resurrection of the dead, and in late versions few saints are worth venerating unless they can resurrect more corpses than Christ. The stories are of two main kinds, revival from a faint or coma, or the personified consolation. Earlier versions make plain that the invalid 'is not dead but sleepeth,' but repetition swells the wonder until the decapitated hero picks up his severed head and replaces it on his shoulders, and delivers a homily lifted from Gregory the Great. Usually he dies again soon after, occasionally he enjoys long life. In the consolation miracle, the saint's comforting assurance, usually addressed to bereaved parents, is personified by reviving the dead child to let him explain in person the delights of heaven, and to end with a plea to be permitted to return thereto, a plea that is soon granted with a speedy second death. Later lives are often swollen, their deleted incidents replaced, with stock miracles that reappear again and again; the future saint who in boyhood carried live coals in his apron without burning it, to relight his master's fire, a tale harking back to an age when fire lighting was difficult, occurs in something over 70 lives. The broken cup miraculously mended, the gifts given away and miraculously replaced, the ring swallowed by a fish caught by a fisherman, the bull that gave milk and many other stories occur with varying frequency, in lives early and late, of good bad and indifferent validity, and neither the nature nor the quantity of the miracles has any bearing on the historicity or otherwise of the persons, places, and events narrated in the life. These events however are of outstanding importance for political and social history.

Various groups of lives share important differences from each other. In general, British lives are varied, often extant in extremely devolved versions, so far removed from the originals that the remnant of historical information is extremely small, so corrupt in detail that it is hard to extract from the surrounding banal marvels. Many lives are products of the eleventh and twelfth centuries, edited from decayed manuscripts, difficult to trace, hard to decipher and unedifying in content, that had mouldered for centuries when no one wanted to read a life of the saint concerned; some, however, were preserved within the sacred covers of a gospel book, and with them are preserved, as at Llancarfan and Llandav, records of charter grants made to the monastery and rated as least as valuable as the life, of high importance for the modern historian. The Irish lives are however much more homogenous. They are preserved in two main medieval collections, conforming to a standard pattern of a *Liber miraculorum* set between an account of the saint's youth and of his old age. Exceedingly few earlier texts survive, but the main corpus is much less devolved than most of the British lives, and is much richer in the recorded names of people places and events. In Ireland, the Latin lives are supplemented by a large number of vernacular lives, most of them so contaminated by the story teller that little can be extracted from them beyond a very few names of persons and places; by contrast, Welsh vernacular lives are fewer in number, and less notably devolved from the Latin originals. A comparison of the two traditions prompts comparisons between the intellectual life of the two countries between the eighth and the twelfth centuries.

The saints' lives, the genealogies, and the annals constitute an interlocking corpus of information; the same persons, the same events the same relationships, the same evolution in political government and in economy occurs in each. Though it is plainly unwise to study them in isolation, it is as yet difficult to study them together, for the necessary works of reference are lacking. No dictionary of persons exists for either country, and Hogan's *Onomasticon*, a comprehensive dictionary of Irish place names, is nearly 60 years old, requires replacements by a modern edition with more exact references, and needs to be matched with a corresponding geographical dictionary of early British place names. Until these elementary tools of study exist, critical editions of individual texts is a labour too daunting to be undertaken with serious success. Though at present essential initial problems of person, place and time claim highest priority, the ancient laws of Wales and of Ireland, whose only comprehensive publication is also a hundred years old, and rests on imperfect texts, need re-editing with ample commentaries, that their information may be related to that contained in the saints' lives and other sources.

These heavy labours are unlikely to be undertaken until their value is more widely appreciated than at present. Their greatest single importance lies in their account of the Irish and Welsh ecclesiastical reforms of the sixth century; and the purpose and nature of these reforms cannot be understood without a clearer grasp of the political society whence they sprang and wherein they grew. Kathleen Hughes' recent work has made clear the existence and extent of the episcopalian diocesan church, with its married clergy, but its relations with the monastic reformers is still imperfectly understood. The episcopate of Patrick was followed by the creation of ten or twelve late fifth-century sees, but attempts to establish a metropolitan hierarchy, under the leadership of Armagh or Saul, of Kildare, or of British bishops, wholly failed. Rapidly the concept grew, with the wide spread of the new religion, that each small state, each *tuath*, should have its own bishop. The British church evolved towards the same principle from a different starting point; a normal diocesan organization based on towns, under the metropolitan authority of the bishops of provincial capitals, emerged while Roman Britain endured. Its ideas survived, but not its roots, for the towns withered; only Bishop Dubricius, of Caerwent, of Gloucester or perhaps of Ariconium, has left a mark on later record. Elsewhere, the all powerful *duces* left over by the fifth-century wars turned their commands into *de facto* independent states, divided them into still smaller units among their sons, some of whom reunited their father's dominions by the slaughter of brothers and uncles on a Merovingian scale. Each king sought his own bishop, so that diocesan boundaries change with each political change, and without an independent ecclesiastic hierarchy the bishops of the small kingdoms became the creatures of the kings; and the kings became bloodier and more oppressive, freed from even the limited moral authority that the church of Europe was able to bring to bear upon its lay governments. This was the situation that Gildas' tract described and denounced.

The cure came from the monks. Hitherto, Latin monasticism had been confined to the individual monastic dedication of wealthy citizens, housing a few poorer fellows in their great houses; to the cathedral monasteries designed to impose monastic discipline on ordained and trained diocesan clergy; to one or two seminaries devoted to the training of a scholarly and ascetic elite who might fill the bishoprics and provide the theologians of Gaul; and to a few quieter retreats for men of substance anxious to escape the chaos of Roman collapse. Martin, the cathedral monasteries, and a few noblemen like Iltut in Wales, and later Cassiodorus in Italy, kept schools, but the mass migration to the desert of the Egyptian and Cappadocian monks found no parallel in the west until the publication of Gildas' book. That book gave a voice to the reformers, taught them cohesion and confidence, so that when a generation of young ascetics, headed by a number of Iltut's pupils, pioneered a personal escape from the corruptions of their society into the uninhabited wastes of southwestern Britain and of Brittany, they were immediately followed by a mass of converts to monasticism, and also by lay emigrants, as eager to escape the oppression of the *duces*. Within a decade, the movement grew to massive proportions. In

Wales, several hundred *Llans* and the bulk of ubiquitous early *Tre-* names attest a very large movement of men from their former homes to new settlements, whose security was protected by religious respect for the abbot. Others moved to Cornwall and Devon, more still to Gaul; there emigrants of the late 450s, and perhaps survivors of Magnus Maximus' army before them in 388, had established homes within the northern Gallic states from Belgium to Brest. In Normandy and eastward their numbers were few enough for them to be absorbed among the native population, but the lay and monastic migration of the mid sixth century to Armorica, northwestern Gaul, reinforcing the earlier settlers, was large enough to displace the name and speech of the previous inhabitants, and to turn the peninsula into lesser Britain, Brittany. The emigrants opened new lands; but their withdrawal from their own homes deprived the kings of taxpaying subjects and infantry soldiers. The bishops of the weakened kings disappeared, and in the course of time the British monastic reformers were able to establish the general principle that the abbots of half a dozen principal monasteries were simultaneously bishops of larger kingdoms, and maintained their dioceses intact, whatever the shifts in political frontiers.

Monastic reform grew to a mass movement at almost the same time in Ireland; and there too Irish tradition acknowledged Gildas as its inspiration, its theoretician, and its spiritual guide. The multiplicity of local bishops prevented a simple identification of greater abbots with the bishoprics of large states, though a few greater abbots became the spiritual guides of some of the greater kings. Instead, an increasing number of the local bishops were drawn from the ranks of the monks. In both countries, kings stood in awe of great abbots; in Brittany and Cornwall, King Mark, also called Cunomorus, faced powerful opposition among the monks, whose pressure at the court of Paris contributed to his downfall and death at the hands of Clothaire in December 560. His son Tristan, turned in story to his romantic nephew, succeeded him in Cornwall, but has left no trace in Brittany. In Ireland, a bitter struggle broke the rising power of the central monarchy, complicated by the accidental circumstance that the greatest of the monastic leaders of the second generation, Columba, was also an heir to the throne and a potent force in lay politics. Columba's energetic combination of his lay military strength and his ecclesiastical authority culminated in a major battle of unparalleled ferocity, and occasioned his migration to Iona, on the borders of the heathen Picts, whom he speedily converted, and of the Irish Scot colonists in Pictland. Bishops were yet few among either people, and as their number increased they were regularly taken from the monks of Iona. The sovereign authority of abbot Columba over his monks made the creation of a diocesan hierarchy unnecessary, and produced the form of organization that puzzled Bede, that an abbot who was but a priest should be master of bishops who knew no metropolitan.

In Britain, Cadoc is said to have exercised the double authority that Columba did not attain, ruling as king and abbot over much of southeast Wales; and when

CHRISTIANITY: THE LITERARY EVIDENCE

a different dynasty succeeded, its monastic bishop was strong enough to exile kings who murdered their rivals. But in Britain the monastic movement split into two wings, aristocratic abbots in the tradition of Cadoc and Gildas, hostile to ascetic extremism, dominant in the former villa lands of Monmouth and Glamorgan, and determined plebeian ascetics headed by David, strong in the southwest and in the uplands of Brecon, where men were poorer and Irish settlers more numerous. Similar divisions were reproduced in Ireland, but in Ireland they engendered an extraordinary and enduring blend of scholarship and piety, initiative and authority, ideally adapted to the aspirations of the rural kingdoms of the English and of barbarian Germany. When the death of Edwin and of Aethelbert ended the authority of Augustine's Roman mission outside Kent, Irish monks converted the bulk of the English, in the north, the midlands, and the south, and though the English early accepted the organizational supremacy and hierarchical structure of the church of Rome, they kept a church rooted on monasteries of Irish inspiration. Irish energy and English discipline proved an ideal combination; in the seventh century Irish and English monks found a massive and widespread response in eastern Gaul and northern Italy, far exceeding that which peninsular Italy accorded to Benedict and Cassiodorus, and carried Christianity, in monastic form, to the heathen Germans beyond the Rhine, to some of the Slav peoples. Their numerous seventh- and eighth-century foundations within the frontiers of the former empire formed the basis of the future Benedictine order.

This is the story of the saints' lives. Its impact upon England and Europe is well known, less intelligible than it should be because the genesis of the movement in Ireland and Wales is less observed, its nature still very inadequately studied. This is the importance which justifies and indeed demands the laborious compilation of the necessary works of reference, the meticulous critical examination of the saints' lives and related sources, which alone can explain the birth and early growth of mass monasticism in Europe.

At present, the contribution of archaeology to our understanding of fifth- and sixth-century Britain is comparatively slight; the great quantity of grave goods interred with pagan English bodies serves to delimit the advance of the English in space and time, but, with little historical context behind it, reveals less than it might of the evolution of their society. The archaeology of the British, who used no grave goods, is very much harder to understand, but the advances of the last few years have been relatively great, and promise rapidly expanding knowledge. Growing archaeological knowledge will greatly enrich, deepen and enliven the story that the texts can tell; but until the overdue parallel work is put into their study, the archaeology will be lamed. The state of the texts is comparable with that of the Greek and Roman writers in the early sixteenth century; a very large number of texts have been printed, even though many of them can only be found in a few large or specialized libraries. They still await the thorough systematic commentaries that Stephanus, Gronovius, Valesius,

Godefridus and their many colleagues supplied to classical texts in the late sixteenth and seventeenth centuries, themselves the inescapable prelude to the synthetic researches of a Gibbon, a Grote, or a Mommsen, on which modern learning builds. When printing was young and the tools of scholarship primitive, the literature of a thousand years of classical civilization required several centuries of protracted study before we could reach our present level of understanding. The literature of two or three centuries of the British Isles, vastly less in size, undertaken with modern equipment and modern understanding, will be the work of as many decades. Able scholars are to hand, and the relatively small sums needed will not be wanting once the full value of the study is widely understood.

The value of the study of these centuries lies in their unique contribution to the future of Europe. The different history of Britain, where alone among the peoples of western Rome the natives for a period contained the Germanic invaders, produced a society where native and newcomer did not fuse, whose evolution provides a laboratory control upon the validity of our judgements upon European feudalism, distinguishes that which arises from the nature of subsistence rural economy from that which may be attributed to the laws and institutions of Rome or of the Germans; while in the British Isles, the survival of the old languages preserved something of the poor man's culture of the Roman and pre-Roman period, and in Ireland alone preserves the literature of an iron age barbarian society virtually unaffected by civilised Roman thought. The peculiarities of British history produced vernacular literature several centuries earlier than in Europe, and also begot much earlier a consciousness of national identity, rooted on a common language, and overriding the political frontiers of small states. The formative centuries between 400 and 600 are neither Roman, nor yet medieval. They constitute a period in their own right, whose changing institutions, economy and ideas merit study on their own, independently of our ideas about Europe in their day, or to the compartments and labels used to classify and identify them. These centuries produced two major contributions to the thought and practice of medieval Europe. The monastic impulse that began in south Wales under the impact of Gildas' book, that spread to Ireland, thence to northern England and to Gaul and central Europe, is the principal point of origin of the monasteries of medieval Europe. It was the product of the three generations in which the British mastered their country, keeping the Saxons of the east under control. The military victory and political failure of the British became the hope of Europe. From among the many possible heroic tales that might have served their purpose, much of Europe selected the splendid failure of king Arthur as the pattern of a golden age of good government, using sovereign power to protect the weak and right injustice. That men might comfort their misfortunes with empty dreams of the great king's return is of lesser moment; but their assertion of their ideal, their belief that it had in the past existed, and would and could come again, urged chivalrous restraint upon the crude

CHRISTIANITY: THE LITERARY EVIDENCE

authority of arbitrary governments, and gave courage to their subjects to struggle for a just and free society of peace and ease. The concepts formed in and about the centuries that Arthur spans inspired the egalitarianism of the monks. They also fired laymen, and especially in England and France contributed to the early stages of independent thinking that emboldened subjects to rebel. The strength of the Arthurian legend is that it is rooted in factual history, whose meaning and moral survives where the detail is lost. That is why the centuries that produced Arthur and the monks deserve and demand a long overdue study.

Notes

1. *Irish Ecclesiastical Record*, 5th series, 107 (1967) 2.
2. See above, pp. 53–93.
3. *De bello Vandalico*, 1, 1.
4. The parents of Ambrosius Aurelianus, *purpura induti*, Gildas, 25 (40, 13); his father was probably the elder Ambrosius, Vortigern's rival. On Vortigern's status, see pp. 158–9. Welsh texts apply the term *imperator* to Arthur. The term remained in use in Britain. Though it is never applied to any European ruler except a Roman emperor, it was used of English supreme kings by Adomnán, Boniface and occasionally in charters, and twice of Irish high kings. The usage, peculiar to the British Isles, suggests that it had been regarded by the British of the fifth and sixth centuries as the proper term for a ruler of the whole island.
5. The Sicilian Briton, *Ep.* 2, 7: *PL* Sup. 1. 1380.
6. Zosimus, 6, 5.
7. Both the Germanic kingdoms and the territories of Aegidius became in fact independent principalities.
8. *De Vita Christiana*, *PL* 40. 1031=50.383; cf. pp. 23–6, above.
9. Migne, *PL* Sup 1. 1687ff; 1375ff; cf. pp. 18–32, 34–41, above.
10. 10 (31, 17, 18).
11. 26 (41, 1ff.).
12. *Celt and Saxon*, ed. N. K. Chadwick (Cambridge, 1963) 20–62.
13. See above, pp. 95–144.

STUDIES IN THE EARLY BRITISH CHURCH:

A REVIEW*

STUDIES IN THE EARLY BRITISH CHURCH. Edited by Nora K. Chadwick. Cambridge University Press, 1958. Pp. 375.

It is not lack of record that makes the Dark Ages dark; on the contrary, the light of reason is obscured by a towering range of doubtful documents, that we can neither explore nor avoid until their fantastic outline has been accurately mapped. They are hard to understand, because we are used to a Roman tradition of straightforward narrative and description, transcribed by clerks trained to copy what they found; but we are faced with authors whose aim was to compose an elegant and useful tale, set down from diverse sources that they usually despised as old-fashioned, barbaric, and unedifying. We have to try and sort out these varied originals, and detect what was added, altered, or left out; and the modern rational historian is only just beginning to learn how to deal with fundamentally irrational sources. It used to be legitimate, and indeed fashionable, to dismiss almost the whole of most documents as worthless late invention, and accept or reject 'plausible' bits and pieces of the rest. But the obstinate evidence of archaic spellings, of verified events and circumstance long forgotten when the authors wrote now enjoins greater caution; the Chadwicks and their associates are the pioneers of serious study, and their latest volume follows the laborious but unavoidable track to real understanding, the relentless worrying of the sources with little immediate reward for strenuous effort.

Mrs. Chadwick's patient introduction states its purpose; the historian's function is to perceive 'the significance of interlocking and interrelated evidence . . . drawn from widely divergent disciplines'; but 'before a survey or narrative can properly be made of the period as a whole, it is essential to have before us studies by a number of individuals . . . whose discipline and technique . . . differ widely'. The six contributions are source studies, of interest to the laymen and value to the specialist, not least when their detail provokes controversy and disagreement.

* Reprinted from the *Welsh History Review* 1 (1960–3) 229–32, by kind permission of the editor, Professor Ralph A. Griffiths.

In the first, Mrs. Chadwick fixes the outline of the early ninth-century historical, or antiquarian, revival, whence originated many of the lost sources of later authors, and in the second establishes a compelling picture of the aim and achievement of the late eleventh-century *clas* of Llanbadarn, a centre of scholarship for nearly four hundred years. Kathleen Hughes follows with a similarly practical study of the Irish scriptoria, and another of the setting and purpose of the principal manuscript collection of Welsh saints' *Lives*, which achieved the 'preservation, though abbreviated, enfeebled and but half-understood, of the traditions of the Celtic Church in the west'. Kenneth Jackson exploits the firm ground of philology, that he has himself reclaimed from shifting uncertainty, to deduce the chain of sources behind the extant *Lives* of Kentigern, two lost eleventh-century lives, resting on the lost compositions of the ninth-century historians.

These five articles are permanent gains, establishing secure reference points to which a multitude of other documents and stories may be related, however much one may dispute particular interpretations or ommissions in each article. It is therefore a pity that their authority should shelter Christopher Brooke's article on 'The Archbishops of St. David's, Llandaff, and Caerleon-on-Usk'. Brief, easily worded, well constructed, its much simpler assertions make a stronger and more abiding impact on the reader than the painstaking complexity of his colleagues' enquiry; for whereas they are all concerned with tracing the evolution of tradition from the sixth to the twelfth century, he is confined to his own twelfth century. The opening sentence, 'The one thing which all the prelates incorporated in my title had in common was that they never existed', is forceful, but misleading; for it implies that these places made in common similar claims to metropolitan status, based on the use or abuse of ancient tradition. But the diligent reader soon observes that the archbishopric of Caerleon is a pretty fancy of Geoffrey's, not asserted by any local clerics at any time; that Llandaff never claimed metropolitan status, but that the prelates of St. David's were in fact styled archbishop, though not 'first . . . in the late eleventh century', but in the ninth (Asser, not cited). This conflation of unlike stories is, however, confined to the headline and opening; the body of the article develops into an attack on the *Book of Llandaff* whose 'nucleus . . . consists of the Lives of . . . the first three archbishops of Llandaff, Dubricius, Teilo, and Oudoceus', together with charters which are 'a classic statement of the principles of fake diplomatic', since they 'never vary in form', and their witness lists are 'certainly faked' by a 'forger' who deduced from genealogies 'which bishop should be associated with which king'. 'The whole of the book was undoubtedly composed by a single author' in the 'second quarter of the twelfth century'. The reader might pardonably assume that Llandaff, like St. David's, claimed metropolitan status, and wrote the book to prove it. He needs warning, unless he has studied the book himself.

The date is reached by dismissing E. D. Jones's careful analysis, whose conclusions do not fit the thesis, with the unargued footnote phrase, 'I think a more general view would be' that Mr. Jones is wrong . . . but Professor Morgan Watkin (*National Library of Wales Journal*, May 1960) has since transformed the argument. As for the alleged archbishops, Teilo and Oudoceus are so styled only in the titles of their *Lives*, nowhere in the text. Oudoceus and his successors are called bishop on many hundreds of occasions, never archbishop; Dubricius and Teilo are mentioned in some three hundred notices, styled archbishop in but eight of them, with the see localized at Llandaff only in three parenthetic insertions; no claim to metropolitan jurisdiction is asserted anywhere in the text. Three half-hearted interpolations and two titles claiming an honorific precedence six hundred years before are all that Llandaff can set against two centuries of determined effort to establish an actual contemporary archbishopric at St. David's.

Llandaff's concern was not with status, but with property. The new-style cathedral see claimed ownership of church lands all over the diocese, and in transcribing their title deeds substituted its own name, normally, but not always, for the name of the original grantee. It was a natural and old-established practice; one of the parallel grants of Llancarfan (whose alleged 'substantial authenticity', in contrast to the 'forgeries' of Llandaff, seems somewhat naïve) preserves the name of the older foundation whose lands it absorbed, Llandough; and Llandaff, annexing this one grant (but not the rest, as Brooke maintains, curiously citing the authority of Canon Doble rather than of the the documents themselves), leaves out both Llancarfan and Llandough. The formulae of rights claimed are, of course, expressed in contemporary language in both collections, but otherwise the grants are anything but uniform. Seventh-century prices are expressed as single objects—a chased swordhilt, a 'best horse', etc.; in the eighth century they are calculated according to a uniform standard of value, the cow, but from the ninth century onward in gold and silver. Early kings consult *cum senioribus Guent et Ercig*, but later kings have *comites*; early bishops are styled *episcopus*, later ones *pontifex* or *praesul*; orthography varies from Iudhail to Ithel, etc. Of the 'elaborate witness lists . . . skilfully and plausibly devised', most of the later kings and some of the bishops are named at the right times in both Welsh and Anglo-Saxon contemporary notices, while half a dozen earlier rulers are found in the

Cambrian Annals and contemporary inscriptions. But kings and bishops are a tiny fraction of the 1,200 witnesses, who sign over the centuries, father succeeding son, each only in his own ancestral area, without serious chronological inconsistency. So large and cohesive a list has not been 'certainly faked' by any known forger.

There is room for argument about the interpretation of these and similar facts; understanding is not advanced by ignoring them. The 'charters' are a not very skilful attempt to scrape together a sufficient title to threatened estates; they were inadequate to their purpose, for the margins are full of notes put in by an irritated user who wished the Book were the bold forgery Brooke would make it. 'Note what robbers the bishops of St. David and Hereford are!'; 'Therefore Oudoceus was an archbishop'; 'Note that this proves that Llandaff used to be chief of all the churches of South Wales'; 'Reverend Bishop . . . I hope you recover all properties unjustly alienated', and many like comments, are proof enough that the compiler had failed to forge the clear authority his chapter needed.

It is distasteful to have to deal at length with the one bad article in a good book. It is necessary, not only because the quality of its company may blind the reader to its limitations, but because it is the only article which is not about the early British Church and which makes no attempt to trace the sources of the compiler. To colour a medieval picture, it appropriates a valuable record of the early Church, and does so well enough to persuade all but the few who know that record. The purposes to which the volume is dedicated are not thus well served. The Llandaff Book is a potentially important source for the centuries between the Romans and the Normans; but it will remain unusable until its matter and method have been thoroughly sifted. That arduous and meritorious labour needs to be encouraged, not to be lightly laughed away.

GILDAS*

Gildas wrote his main work, the 'Ruin of Britain',[1] about A.D. 540 or just before, when he was forty-three years old.[2] It is a fierce denunciation of the rulers and churchmen of his day, prefaced by a brief explanation of how these evils came to be. This preface is the only surviving narrative history of fifth-century Britain.[3] But it was not written as history. Gildas names in the fifth century only one person, one place, and one date, which he misplaced.[4] Just enough is known to make his narrative intelligible, two key dates from contemporary Europe, and isolated detail from other sources, chief among them a collection of historical texts assembled about A.D. 800, known by the name of *Historia Brittonum*, 'History of the Britons'.[5]

At the beginning of the fifth century Britain had been a Roman province for nearly 400 years, and for 200 years all freeborn Britons had been Roman citizens; there was no more contrast between 'native' and 'Roman' than there is to-day between 'Yorkshireman' and 'Englishman'. Society was dominated by a landed nobility, whose splendid country mansions, abundant in the southern lowlands, were built and furnished on a scale not matched again until the 18th century. The rents which sustained them were drawn from a vigorous agriculture and industry, whose output was distributed along an intricate road-system. But in the highland-regions of the South-west, of Wales and the North, there was little comparable prosperity; poorer farmers supported no wealthy gentry. Beyond the frontier, northern border-kingdoms were still uneasy allies of Roman authority, and beyond the Clyde and Forth lived the hostile barbarian Picts, ready allies of the *Scotti*, the late Roman name for the inhabitants of Ireland,[6] who raided when they could and had established a number of colonies on the western coasts of Britain.

This sophisticated civilisation was destroyed long before Gildas was born. When he wrote, its realities were fast fading from men's memories; to Gildas, Romans were again foreigners, their empire a thing of the past.[7] The Roman empire of the West was mortally wounded in 410, when the western Goths took Rome, although its ghost survived for two generations. The Goths obtained the right to settle in Roman territory under their own laws and rulers, with the status of federate allies, in 418. They were the first, but others soon followed, and when Gildas was young the Western Empire was divided between four Germanic kingdoms, in France, Spain, Italy and North Africa. Roman and German fused; German kings inherited the centralised authoritarian rule of Rome and preserved the property and power of landlords.

The British differed. In 410 the emperor in Italy instructed them to provide their own defence and government. At first they were outstandingly successful and kept their society undamaged for a generation. A strong sovereign emerged in the 420s and survived for some thirty years. Later writers knew him by the name Vortigern, which, if literally translated, means 'superior ruler'; Gildas' word-play describes him as *superbus tyrannus*, proud tyrant.[8] Invasion from Ireland and beyond the Forth, which had harassed previous Roman governments for centuries, was permanently ended;[9] but to curb it he settled German federates.[10] Romans, British and Irish called them Saxons, but in Britain they called themselves English; the two words mean the same people, in different languages.[11]

In or about 441 the English rebelled.[12] Gildas condenses nearly twenty years' fighting, which ended with the destruction of a large part of the nobility of Britain and the emigration of many of the survivors.[13] The migration, to northern and central Gaul, was dated by contemporary Continentals to 460, or a year or two before.[14] At home, renewed resistance was begun under the leadership of Ambrosius Aurelianus[15] and continued, traditionally under the leadership of Arthur,[16] for over thirty years until 'the final victory of our fatherland',[17] after the decisive battle at Badon Hill, probably near Bath, in the 490s.[18]

Gildas asserted that the victors maintained orderly government for a generation, but that in recent years power had passed to regional war-lords, whose mutual violence overrode law and convention and corrupted the Church. But the British had won the war. The English were beaten, though not expelled, and were confined to partitioned reservations, chiefly in the east.[19] Yet victory had come too late, at the cost of almost everything which the victors had striven to protect. Although Britain was 'calm' and 'secure', freed from 'external wars', Roman civilisation was destroyed. Industry and market-agriculture perished as roads became unsafe; towns which lost their supplies became 'ruinous and unkempt'; country-mansions not built for defence were abandoned to wind and rain. After more than fifty years of war, peace could not revive a dead society. The skills of the builder, the potter, the tool-maker and other crafts were buried with old men who had trained no apprentices; more important, the rents and taxes which had paid for them could no longer be collected or paid. The war-lords could compel a self-sufficient agriculture to maintain their men and horses but not to rebuild the past. They maintained their power throughout Gildas' lifetime; but soon after his death the English rebelled again and between 570 and 600 permanently subdued most of what is now England.

But Gildas did not write in vain. On the contrary, few books have had a more immediate and far-reaching impact than his. He uttered what tens of thousands felt. His readers did not reform political society. They opted out. They had a precedent. Two hundred years earlier, in the eastern Mediterranean lands, immense numbers had dropped out of a corrupt society to seek solitary communion with God in the deserts; but their sheer numbers forced them to form communities. Their Western imitators had hitherto aroused little response;[20] apart from the clergy of some cathedrals and a few high-powered seminaries, Latin monasticism was 'torpid' by A.D. 500,[21] and had inspired only a few pioneers in the British Isles when Gildas wrote. But within ten years monasticism had become a mass-movement, in South Wales, Ireland and northern Gaul. Its extensive literature reveres Gildas as its founding father, named more often than any other individual.[22]

Most of this literature is a sickly stew of half-truths, distorted by the ignorance and bias of medieval pietism. But there is first-hand evidence that reforming monks were many and popular in South Wales, Ireland and Brittany before the mid-sixth-century plague, rapidly increasing in numbers thereafter, and that Gildas was respected. In the seventh century the movement spread from Ireland through Northumbria to much of England, and also to eastern France; in the eighth century, English and Irish missionaries brought Christianity and monasticism to Germany.

In time, many of these houses adopted a version of the Rule of Benedict of Nursia and became the nucleus of the later Benedictine Order.

A few notices outline Gildas' life. He was born a northerner, in the kingdom of the Clyde,[23] but is said to have been schooled in South Wales,[24] where he clearly wrote, since it is only the rulers of Wales and the South-west whom he denounced by name.[25] He is said to have migrated in later years to St.-Gildas de Rhuys, in Morbihan in southern Brittany. The Welsh Annals enter his death at 570 and report a visit to Ireland in 565.[26] It was in these maturer years that the Letters were written.[27] There is contemporary evidence that some concerned Ireland,[28] and others intervene in the dispute between ascetic extremists and milder monks which sharpened in the 560s.[29] The 'Penitential' ascribed to him deals with the same problems, and may indeed be his.[30]

Gildas' reputation stood high among the early monks, but he has been less esteemed by later and modern writers. Historians who have quarried his early chapters are understandably irritated that he did not provide a clear narrative with names and dates; and the extraordinary latinity of his main invective seems tiresome, its purpose irrelevant to other ages.

The narrative is unclear because it was written from oral memory. The experience of our own age or any other defines the limits of oral memory. Most men over 60 today have learnt something from their fathers of the late 19th century; some listened in childhood to men who were born and schooled before Wellington died, and have heard of Waterloo. But, by word of mouth alone, they can have no understanding or time-scale beyond their fathers' youth; they cannot know whether a Martello Tower is older or younger than a romanesque church. So it was with Gildas. In youth he knew older men who had lived through the wars, but few who were adult before they began. All he understood of the Roman past was that it was orderly; although he knew two northern walls, he knew nothing of when or why they were built.[31] Oral memory took him back to the wars and a dateless Vortigern, but no further. But for all its obscurity his narrative remains our chief guide to the history of Britain between the Romans and the English. That period shaped the peculiarities of our future. The mid-fourth-century Roman frontier is still the border between England and Scotland; but, behind it, Britain was the only Western province where the newcomers met prolonged resistance. The conflict ended in permanent division. There was no fusion between German and Roman; Roman institutions and language disappeared; the Welsh and the English both perpetuate the languages which their ancestors had spoken in and before the Roman centuries. The present-day consequences of these divisions are better understood when their origin is known.

Gildas' strange idiom served its purpose. He aimed to move men's emotions, and he succeeded. Where political society was vicious and insecure, their imagination was as ready to be fired as a drought-stricken heath. Gildas' manifesto provided the spark, for, although many had pioneered monastic ideals before him, on the Continent as in Britain and Ireland, none had inspired a mass-movement. That movement flared suddenly and swiftly immediately after he wrote, and it spread far beyond Britain. But the idiom which moved Gildas' contemporaries is hard for later ages to comprehend, so that he is more often quoted than read.

NOTES

* John Morris's contribution to *Gildas*, ed. and trans. Michael Winterbottom (Arthurian Period Sources 7, 1978), pp. 1-4, 148-55, here reset with reorganised notes; the whole has been lightly revised.

1. *De excidio Britanniae*: the very idea of writing a Latin account of a section of (what had been) the Empire was a novel one. After some preliminaries (chs 1-2), Gildas offered a description of the island of Britain (ch. 3); he was presumably quoting from a late Roman geographer, comparable with Marcianus of Heraclea, who totted up the headlands, estuaries, cities, etc., which Ptolemy named. Nennius and perhaps Orosius used the same source. Ptolemy named 58 'cities' in Britain, 38 of them south of Hadrian's Wall. The *xxviii* reproduced by Gildas and Nennius is perhaps a scribal error for *xxxviii*.
2. *De excidio Britanniae*, ch. 26.1.
3. Gildas had no written history as a source for fifth-century Britain (ch. 4.4). He did, however, have access to various chronicles and histories which dealt with imperial Rome. He knew of Boudica (Boadicea) who rebelled against the Romans in A.D. 60/61 (the lioness of ch. 6.1). At the other end of Roman history, he knew from (among others) the works of Prosper and Orosius about the rebellion of Magnus Maximus in Britain (ch. 13.1-2) and his career on the Continent 383-388 until his death at Aquileia.
4. *Agitius*, named in ch. 20.1, was Aetius, consul for the third time in 446, the fourth time in 453, the first consul III, other than an emperor, for more than 300 years. The manuscripts have 'g' for the 'y' sound of the diphthong, as later in Fredegarius, in Old English and other Germanic dialects, but Bede, quoting Gildas, used the normal spelling, Aëtius. The letter provides the only date, 446 × 452, in Gildas' narrative. But he misplaced it; at that date, the barbarian enemy was the English (see below, nn. 11-12). The letter should have been inserted at the end of ch. 24, but Gildas had no means of learning the point at which he should insert it into his otherwise timeless narrative. The mistake misled Bede, who did not know the evidence which corrects Gildas. In his Chronicle, in 725, he entered the letter among the events of the 430s, since Gildas had placed it after the end of the Roman rule of Britain, but long before the coming of the English. By the time he wrote his History, in 731, Bede had discovered Aëtius' date (*Hist. eccl.*, 1.13) but had to retain its place in the narrative, condensing Gildas' next few chapters into a few years. Bede's Chronicle was also corrected, and all surviving manuscripts have the date 446 against the entry which is placed in the 430s.
5. *Nennius*, ed. and trans. John Morris (Arthurian Period Sources 8, 1980).
6. 'Scot' was not used in relation to northern Britain as a whole before the tenth century.
7. Nevertheless, Gildas had some knowledge of their political, administrative and military terminology. Rector (chs 1.14, 6.1, 14.1) is the late Roman technical term for governor. He employed *rex* ('king') for a Roman emperor (ch. 5.1), as often in the usage of late Roman writers. He knew that a *tyrannus* was a usurper of legitimate authority—and he used it freely: Britain was an island 'fertile of tyrants' (ch. 4.3), a quotation from St Jerome (*Ep.* 133.9) attributed by Gildas to Porphyry (a third-century anti-Christian writer). He could use *dux, rex, tyrannus* of the same person. For his use of other late Roman technical terminology, see below, n. 10.
8. *De excidio Britanniae*, ch. 23.1. Various calculations (see Nennius, ch. 66) place his accession in 425; for his death, see below, n. 13. For other examples of word-play on the names of British rulers, see below, n. 25.
9. The 'peoples of the north', as Gildas called them (ch. 23.1), the 'old enemies', were Picts (*Picti*, 'painted' or 'tattooed' peoples), who lived north of the Firth of Forth, and Irish; these were 'overseas nations' (ch. 14.1) who came by sea, with 'oars' and 'sails' (ch. 16.1); this time they threatened not raiding but settlement (ch. 22.1). The siting of the earliest known English settlements protected the Humber, Wash, Thames and perhaps the Southampton area.
10. *De excidio Britanniae*, ch. 23. Gildas used the late Roman technical terms *annonae, epimenia, hospites*, in relation to the billeting of federate allies. In ch. 92.3, *Absque ullo foedere ... foederati* suggests technical terms. Later emperors on the Continent often employed Ger-

manic *foederati* against other Germans or native rivals; and many were criticised for so doing. In ch. 92.3 Gildas seems to mean that we should have no pagan anti-Christian *foederati*, but that our proper allies should be Christian rulers who are defenders of the faith. The context is unclear but seems to rebuke the bishops who favour anti-Christian *foederati*. The districts where the first pagan English burials appear to date from the earlier sixth century are few; it is possible that some of them derived from the employment of English *foederati* by British rulers. Gildas said that the first group arrived in three ships. Bede (*Hist. eccl.*, 1.15) and Nennius (ch. 31) both named Hengest as the leader. Nennius named Thanet as their settlement. It is quite possible that the first invitation was limited to this number, and to Thanet. The calculations of Nennius (ch. 66) give A.D. 428 for their arrival; the archaeological evidence does not admit a significantly later date (see further below, n. 12).

11. The name *Saxones* was used by Roman writers as a general term for barbarians beyond the Franks. In Britain they preferred the term *Engle*; although some districts and a few writers adopted Roman usage as a collective term, no individual settled or born in Britain is known to have called himself a 'Saxon'. Gildas took some interest in their language and customs, as of the Irish who raided and settled in Britain: for example, *curuca*, 'coracle' (ch. 19.1), and *cyula*, 'keel' (ch. 23.3), accurately distinguish the native British and English words for their ships. *Cyula* here is probably the earliest surviving word of written English.

12. A contemporary in northern Gaul (MGH AA ix = *Chronica Minora*, i, ed. T. Mommsen, pp. 652 ff.) wrote in 452 that ten years before, in 441/2, 'Britain passed under the control of the Saxons (*in dicionem Saxonum*)'. The event, which seemed to him as decisive as the control of the Goths, Burgundians and others in Gaul, cannot have been other than the initial success of the revolt which Gildas described. He could not know that in the future the British would fight back. Gildas and Nennius agree that further contingents followed the first over a period of years before the revolt; the first settlement was therefore some time before 441; see above, nn. 8-11.

13. Gildas' account telescopes prolonged fighting (Nennius, chs 43 ff.), to which the Anglo-Saxon Chronicle allots twelve years, ending with the expulsion of the English from Thanet, followed by their subsequent return, further fighting, and a peace-conference where Hengest treacherously assassinated 'all King Vortigern's three hundred Elders', by definition the leading aristocracy. Similar tales are told in legend, but also in Xenophon's *Anabasis* and by Ammianus Marcellinus in the fourth century A.D.

14. The migration is located, in northern and central Gaul, and dated by Sidonius, *Ep.* 3.9; Jordanes, *Getica*, ch. 45; Gregory of Tours, *Historia*, 2,18. The signature of Mansuetus, 'bishop of the British', among many territorial bishops, in 461 (Mansi, 7, 941), suggests that the migration was then recent, not yet absorbed into normal dioceses. The British were said to number 12,000 fighting men, implying a total population of around 50,000. The likeliest occasion is after the massacre of the aristocracy. Since the emigrants took with them whatever books survived (Gildas, ch. 4.4), they are likely to have included a large proportion of the literate and well-to-do survivors.

15. He is the only fifth-century person named by Gildas (ch. 25.3), presumably in order to spotlight the inferiority of his living descendants. His parents (*parentes*) are described by Gildas as having 'worn the purple'. *Purpuram sumere* is the late Empire's technical term for 'to become emperor'; *induere* carries a slight suggestion of 'assume without adequate qualification'. Ambrosius, who is said to have opposed Vortigern in the 430s (Nennius, ch. 31; cf. ch. 66), was probably too old to be the same man but might have been his imperial father.

16. Traditions dating back to the sixth century name Arthur as the victor of Badon, and the Welsh Annals credit him with twenty years' life thereafter. Gildas did not name him, or any other of his time, but held that orderly government endured for about a generation after Badon.

17. *De excidio Britanniae*, ch. 2.1.

18. *Badonicus mons* (ch. 26.1) means a hill near a place called Badon. (The name is normal Celtic: cf. Vaubadon, near Bayeux; *Vallis Badonis* in the eleventh century, Domesday Book, Herts. 1.13; *Val Badon*, Kent and Northants.; and *Dictionnaire Topographique du Calvados*,

292, in A.D. 1180.) It was in the west, since the Welsh Annals record a second battle of Badon in 665. The earliest speeling of Bath in the Anglo-Saxon Chronicle, at 577, in an entry whose other proper names survive in one manuscript in the spelling of the late sixth century, is *Badan*. This spelling was not then English, but it persists beside the normal English, *et Hatum Bathum*. The contents-table (ch. 68) prefixed to a manuscript of *Historia Brittonum*, without reference to the battle, places the Hot Baths in the lower Severn region at *Badon*. There is no other record of the British name of Bath. Any or all of the numerous English places named Badbury or the like might linguistically derive from a Celtic *Badon*; but, since several are in regions where no other comparable Welsh names survive, they more probably derive from the personal name Bada, common in English place-names; but there is no need to suppose a 'folk-hero'. The battle was fought in the year of Gildas' birth, about 43 years before he wrote. He wrote before the death of Maelgwn, in the mid-sixth-century Justinianic plague, in or before 550 (see below, n. 25); and before monasticism became a mass-movement, in the 540s (see below, n. 22). The date should therefore be in the 490s. The Welsh Annals date Badon to 516 and Camlann to 537; but these are the only British entries in the first century of their record, inserted into a framework of extracts from Irish Annals, with nothing to suggest that the annalist had any guidance as to where they should be inserted. As with the other early Annals entries, the interval between events is likely to rest on an older tradition than the absolute dates.

19. Located by the sixth-century graves and villages of the pagan English, in four large but separated regions, Surrey, Kent and the Tilbury district; Norfolk and its borders; Lincolnshire and its borders, east of the Trent; and the East Riding; with several much smaller districts about Dunstable and Abingdon, and in Hampshire and East Sussex. (See also above, n. 10.) The English areas did not include either Verulamium or Caerleon, named by Gildas (ch. 10.2). The saints of Caerleon, Aaron and Iulius, are otherwise remembered only in local tradition. His account of Alban's passion shows that Gildas clearly did not know the district, as he described Verulamium as by the River Thames. Gildas asserted that his fellow-citizens were separated from Verulamium and Caerleon by the 'unhappy partition with the barbarians'.

20. However, ascetic movements in the West had sometimes been associated with heresy. The instance which affected Britain was Pelagianism, since Pelagius was a Briton. In ch. 38.2 Gildas quoted from *de Virginitate* 6 (*Patrologia Latina*, ed. J.-P. Migne, 30, 162 = 18, 77 = 20, 273 = 103, 671). The author was a Pelagian, contemporary and sympathiser of the early fifth-century Sicilian Briton (see above, pp. 17-51), and may have been British himself, the obvious interpretation of 'one of us'. The work evidently still circulated in Britain a hundred years after publication. Like other British and Irish writers from the fifth to the eighth centuries, Gildas was not a 'Pelagian heretic'; his writing shows no sign that he was aware of the views of Augustine, of his controversy with Pelagius, or even of his existence.

21. In the West as in the East, monasticism had by the end of the fifth century 'fallen into torpor and sterility' (C. de Montalembert, *Les Moines d'Occident*, 1, 288 = English translation 1, 514). In Gildas' lifetime, Benedict of Nursia founded a dozen houses besides Monte Cassino in Italy, and there were also a few new foundations in Gaul; but no vigorous large-scale movement developed on the Continent until the next century, except in Brittany and on its borders (see below, n. 22). Gildas wrote admiringly of what seems to be monasticism: ch. 26.4. His references to 'saints' in chs 34.2 and 65.2 are to be taken thus, a regular nomenclature for monks. In referring to 'my order' (ch. 65.1) he probably meant monks. He reported that the mighty King Maglocunus had undergone a 'conversion' to monasticism (ch. 34.5).

22. The medieval literature, chiefly in the form of Saints' Lives, is immense, much of it preserved only in late and grossly corrupt versions. The essence of its story is however confirmed in a number of contemporary and near-contemporary writings, notably the works of Columbanus of Luxeuil (ed. and trans. G.S.M. Walker, Scriptores Latini Hiberniae 2, 1957; also MGH *Epp.* 3) and his Life by Jonas (MGH SRM 4,1); Adomnán's Life of St Columba of Iona; and the earliest Life of St Samson, written about 600, a generation after his death. Several of the ninth-century Lives of Breton saints also reproduce extracts

from sixth-century texts, recognisable from the spellings of proper names. These texts by themselves amply attest a sudden large-scale growth before the plague-years of the later 540s, and a rapid acceleration thereafter, simultaneously in South Wales, Ireland, Cornwall and Brittany, where very many hundreds of new monasteries entailed a massive shift of population; the impact was noticeable but less in North Wales and northern Britain, and in northern Gaul, from Normandy to Belgium. The impetus of the reforming monks was brought to Burgundy in the 590s by Columbanus and there erupted into an extensive movement in the 640s. In the 630s the Irish brought monasticism to the Northumbrians, then dominant over most of the English, and thenceforth increasing numbers of English and Irish monks founded or inspired monasteries in northern and central Europe, culminating in the conversion of most of the Germans and some Slavs in the eighth century. The early texts give not only facts and dates but also express the singleminded sincerity whose appeal gave the movement its strength, size and endurance.

23. Gildas accurately described the two northern walls (ch. 15.3; see also ch. 18.2) and probably saw them, for he was *Arecluta . . . regione oriundus, patre Cauuo*, 'a native of the Clydeside region, son of Cauuos' (Rhuys Life of Gildas, 1: Mommsen, *Chronica Minora*, iii, p. 91; Williams, *Gildas*, p. 322, misreading *Cauno*). The spellings of the proper names 'clearly belong to the sixth century' and 'can only come from contemporary manuscripts' (K.H. Jackson, *Language and History in Early Britain*, 1953, 42; cf. 306-7).

24. Gildas referred to King Maelgwn's teacher as 'the refined master of almost all Britain' (ch. 36.1). He perhaps meant Illtud of Llanilltud Fawr (Llantwit Major) in Glamorgan, where also Gildas, Samson and Paul Aurelian are said to have been schooled.

25. These were five in number (chs 28-36): in chs 28-29 Constantine of Damnonia (evidently a pun on Dumnonia: Devon, Cornwall and part of Somerset); in ch. 30 Aurelius Caninus (evidently a pun on the Welsh name Cynan); in ch. 31 Uortipor, *tyrannus* of the Demetae (the people of Dyfed, south-west Wales), 'bad son of a good king' (the latter named *Aircol Lauhir*, Agricola Longhand, in Welsh genealogies) and probably identical with 'Uoteporix Protector' whose memorial stone (now in Carmarthen Museum: V. Nash-Williams, *The Early Christian Monuments of Wales*, 1950, 138) is inscribed in Latin and Irish; in ch. 32 Cuneglasus (called 'in Latin "red butcher"' by Gildas, but 'blue [or grey] dog' is the literal translation of the name) of 'the Bear's stronghold', and in Welsh genealogies a cousin of Maelgwn; in chs 33-36 Maglocunus (Maelgwn), 'dragon of the island', who achieved power by killing 'the king your uncle' (who, in Welsh genealogy, is Eugen, father of Cuneglasus). Of Aurelius Caninus we may say that, since the other kings are listed in geographical order, south to north, he may have ruled in the Gloucester region. Cuneglasus is located by reference to his 'stronghold': Gildas' Latin literally translates Din Eirth; of several strongholds so named, the best known is Dinarth near Llandudno, three miles from Deganwy, traditionally Maelgwn's fortress. If this place were meant, Cuneglasus at one time mastered much of Maelgwn's land. Maglocunus is known universally as Maelgwn of Gwynedd (north-west Wales): in Welsh genealogy he is great-grandson of Cunedda, founder of the kingdom, who was held to have reduced the Irish colonists in most of Wales in the earlier fifth century. Later tradition regarded Maelgwn and his son Rhun as the most powerful rulers of mid-sixth-century Britain. The Welsh Annals, at 547, give an Irish record of plague-deaths, at about 550, substituting Maelgwn for the Irish names.

26. *Nennius*, ed. and trans. Morris, 45, 85.

27. *Gildas*, ed. and trans. Winterbottom, 80-2, 143-5. This material is preserved in Irish texts. The Letters were probably written during or after Gildas' visit to Ireland in 565.

28. No. 4 is perhaps the letter cited by Columbanus of Luxeuil, in a letter written to Pope Gregory the Great in the late 590s (MGH. *Epp.* 3, 156 ff.), *quid faciendum est de monachis illis, qui . . . vitae perfectioris desiderio accensi primae conversionis loca relinquunt . . . invitis abbatibus . . . Uennianus auctor Giltam de his interrogavit, et elegantissime ille rescripsit*. ('What is to be done about those monks who are inspired by a desire for a more perfect life, and leave the monastery where they were first converted, against their abbots' will? The eminent Finnian asked Gildas about them; and Gildas wrote him a most judicious reply'.) Finnian was perhaps the abbot of Moville, Co. Down (Irish national grid J 57), who died about 580. Ch. 67.3 was perhaps the passage cited by Columbanus to Gregory: *Simoniacos et Giltas*

auctor pestes scripsit ('the eminent Gildas also wrote that Simoniacs are pests'); but Gildas may have dealt with Simoniacs more largely in a lost letter.

29. In Letters 2-4 the ironic reference to *meliores*, 'the better ones', is to stricter monks. The austere rule condemned by Gildas may be found summarised in the Life of St David by Ricemarchus (Rhygyfarch): A.W. Wade-Evans, *Vitae Sanctorum Britanniae et Genealogiae*, 1944, 150ff. David's rule was termed the 'Life of Water' (*aquatica vita*) because it eschewed meat and wine, and confined the diet to fish (which lives in water), with bread, vegetables and water (ch. 2: VSBG 150). The Rule (chs 21-31: VSBG 157-8) forbids the use of animals, even for pulling the plough; condemns all property and wealth, including the 'gifts of the wicked' to monasteries; and categorically bans all personal possessions by monks, even prescribing penance for the use of the words 'my book'. Ricemarchus' citation from the Rule, *iugum ponunt in humeris; suffossoria vangasque invicto brachio terrae defigunt* is close to Gildas' *aratra trahentes et suffosoria figentes terrae*. The similarity suggests that both drew on a common source, the Rule of David, as published in his lifetime; it is not probable that Ricemarchus knew or recognised Gildas' strictures on David, or turned Gildas' disapproval to praise of his own hero, David.

30. *Gildas*, ed. and trans. Winterbottom, 83-6, 146-7. See also *The Irish Penitentials*, ed. and trans. L. Bieler, Scriptores Latini Hiberniae 5, 1963, pp. 60-5.

31. *De excidio Britanniae*, chs 15-19: all his 'information' is wrong.